D1629734

Seventy Rolling Years

SEVENTY ROLLING YEARS

SYDNEY O. NEVILE

FABER AND FABER
24 Russell Square
London

First published in mcmlviii
by Faber and Faber Limited
24 *Russell Square London WC*1
Printed in Great Britain by
Ebenezer Baylis and Son Limited
The Trinity Press, Worcester, and London

SEVENTY ROLLING YEARS

SYDNEY O. NEVILE

FABER AND FABER
24 Russell Square
London

First published in mcmlviii
by Faber and Faber Limited
24 *Russell Square London WC*1
Printed in Great Britain by
Ebenezer Baylis and Son Limited
The Trinity Press, Worcester, and London

TO MY WIFE

WHO DURING THE WRITING

OF THIS BOOK

HAS LEARNT

MORE ABOUT ME

THAN SHE EVER KNEW BEFORE

TO MY WIFE

WHO DURING THE WRITING

OF THIS BOOK

HAS LEARNT

MORE ABOUT ME

THAN SHE EVER KNEW BEFORE

Contents

Illustrations

ACKNOWLEDGMENT

The author would like to make acknowledgment to the following for permission to reproduce their photographs: Tom Blau, Camera Press (frontispiece); Anthony Buckley, plate 6; Fox Photos, plate 26; Douglas Glass, plate 30; Keystone Press Agency, plate 20; Lafayette, plate 11; London News Agency Photos, plate 29; *Radio Times Hulton Picture Library*, plates 8 & 11; J. Russell & Sons, plate 11; Sky Photos, plate 16; Sport & General Press Agency, plate 8; Hay Wrightson, plate 31, and A. C. K. Ware, plates 17, 32 & 33.

Foreword

In this book I have recorded some of my recollections of what I have done, things that have happened and men I have met during the seventy rolling years of my life from the year 1888, when I became a pupil in a brewery, until the present day. Though it may appear something of a pilgrim's progress in serious business, it also contains many excursions into lighter topics and memories of people whose lives and aspirations have differed widely from my own.

Some tell me that this may be termed a success story. I hope they are right; anyway, if it is so, I have had longer than most of my contemporaries for making a contribution to the events of my time.

It has been said that there is no such thing as luck, but as I look back through the kaleidoscope of years, I see that this is certainly not true in my case, for I remember many instances of good fortune coming to my aid on critical occasions. It was a stroke of good luck that when I was seeking my first job, my youth was regarded as a special asset. The early death of my chief was another accident (and here I of course imply 'luck' in its sense of 'fortuitous circumstance') which offered me the chance of greater responsibility. Then, again, the very misfortunes of my industry during the early years of the century provided opportunities I might not otherwise have enjoyed.

There must be few today who realize the manifold trials and tribulations of the brewers of those days; the continual political attacks, and the absurd prejudices of licensing authorities, to say nothing of the reckless purchase of public houses at high prices and cut-throat competition for the trade of free houses at prices below the cost of production; a combination of disasters and ineptitude which led to many large concerns in the metropolis and elsewhere being unable to pay dividends on their shares, and in some cases interest on their debentures.

Though harassing at the time, these alarms and excursions brought no ill-fortune to myself; indeed, the contrary. They led me first to the conclusion that the then prevalence of drunkenness allied with the low standard of most public houses formed the root of our difficulties, and then to my advocacy of a constructive policy of improvement which brought me more and more into contact with men who mattered.

Perhaps my greatest opportunity came during the First World War, when the democratic instinct of Lloyd George led him to consider the interests of the smaller concerns as well as those of the great businesses. As a result, I was consulted by Ministers and their Departments and invited to serve on Government Committees, including the notorious Central Control Board. The influence I was able to exert during that period of national crisis brought me into the inner cabinet of trade politics and enabled me to co-operate with the group of influential men who planned the constructive policy of 1919, based on the needs and interests of the people. This laid the foundation of a prosperity which has continued for nearly forty years; it also secured to brewers the respect and friendship in high places which enabled them to survive with credit and dignity the even greater economic and practical difficulties of the Second World War.

While I owe much to all these adventitious factors, I regard as one element in any success I may have achieved the family tradition early instilled into me by some of my older relatives; that the pursuit of riches and power should not be the sole objective of a man's life, and that when the time comes to look back on one's life-work an awareness of public service conscientiously performed is more rewarding than the attainment of material wealth.

Landmarks and Milestones

A friend who knows my story and its ramifications suggests that I should begin my book with a dated list of memorable occasions, pointing out that the arrangement of many of my chapters is not chronological, since they are expansions of themes and policies rather than autobiographical surveys of neatly and logically interlocking periods. Accepting this suggestion, I have drawn up two lists of 'things done and roles fulfilled', hoping that the generous reader will agree with my insistent friend. However, who is to account for any man's 'memorabilia', apart from his inevitable recollection of the highlights in his personal life and his career? So if some of the matters I choose to list seem less momentous to others than to myself, I must plead for a man's right to idiosyncrasy and recall attention to William Allingham's 'four ducks on a pond'.

To begin with a résumé of my years of office, on committees and collective organizations, and a chronologically arranged list of happenings which meant much to me:

Brewing Industry

1907–58. Council of Institute of Brewing: President 1919–21.
1917–58. Council of the Brewers' Society: Chairman 1938–40.
1919–58. National Trade Development Association: Chairman 1946–48.
1920–58. Court of the Brewers' Company: Master 1929–30.
1922–58. Council of the Federation of British Industries: Vice-President 1958.

Home Office

1917–21. Central Control Board (Liquor Traffic).
1921–55. Council of State Management Districts.
1942–44. Morris Committee.

Ministry of Agriculture

1917–23. Hop Control Committee.

Ministry of Food

1940–46. Chairman, Advisory Committee to Ministry on Brewing Industry.

* * *

1873. Born under the sign of Cancer. See footnote, page 21.
1877. Death of my father and move to Brighton.
1888. Entered the brewing industry as an articled pupil at Brighton.
1890. First post at the Putney Brewery.
1896. Became a head brewer and interested myself in problems and policies.
1897. Rowing and sailing are my recreations, first on the Thames and later on salt water.
1908. Political alarms lead to definite ideas and my first plunge into the public press.
1912–13. The Sir John Cass Institute—and novel suggestions on technical education.
1914. A trip to Scandinavia, and early problems of First World War.
1916. My advice to authorities on war savings which, though torpedoed by prohibitionist influence, led to appointments to Government Committees, Hop Control, Central Control Board and to State Purchase proposals.
1917 onwards. I co-operate in planning a constructive trade policy and the drafting of the Private Member's Bill nicknamed 'Brewers' Litany Bill'.
1919. I join Whitbread's.
1920. I commit a technical crime by damning a Government Bill in a letter to *The Times*.

1921. I help to draft another Private Member's Bill which leads to a conference at Downing Street and the Government Act of that year.

1922 and onwards. I continue as adviser to the Home Office and to promote active policy of 'Sobriety plus good service' and better public houses.

1929. An excursion to Australia.

1930. I give evidence before Royal Commission on Licensing as an independent witness.

1933. Collective advertisement of beer as a beverage.

1938–40. Chairmanship of Brewers' Society.

1939–45. Second World War—advertising space given to the Government. Carrying on under incendiary raids. Whitbread's survives—in a desert of destruction.

1945. I receive honour of knighthood after twenty-eight years' honorary service to the Home Office.

1946. My marriage to an old friend.

1948. Unexpected recovery from operation. Am reputed a good patient, and return to currency.

1955. A less good patient in Baden Baden.

1958. Am still in partial harness and am persuaded to write these memoirs.

I

Origin and early days—Father Tooth—My entry as Pupil to learn the 'mystery and art' of brewing—Dislike of office work—Outline of brewing process—End of pupilage and search for post

Sometimes when I have told people that by January 19th, 1958, I had been at work for seventy years, and have talked of this and that, what I have done and haven't done, the mistakes I have made, the mixed company I have kept, the kindness and help of friends (many of whom are no longer with us), which have enabled me to achieve so many of my ambitions, I have been told that my reminiscences would make a readable story. I hope they are right, and trust that these friends will find the written word as acceptable as the spoken. Anyway, I like to think that a record of my experiences may serve as encouragement to some of the many young people who, like myself, must embark on a career with no great resources behind them and with none of those commercial contacts which smooth the path for the more fortunately endowed.

Somewhere I had read that Coleridge wrote, 'I could inform the dullest author how he might write an interesting book. Let him relate the events of his own life with honesty, not disguising the feelings that accompanied them'. Well, I may be a dull enough author, but I have tried to follow this formula, respecting events, scorning disguises, and hoping that the honesty shines through.

Autobiographies usually begin with a note on the subject's fore-bears, and to this convention I bow. One of William the

Conqueror's captains was a Nevile, and the name appears on the Roll of Battle Abbey, together with the Nevile arms. No doubt this captain was the ancestor of all the family in Britain. Several branches have found their place in English history, but I can find singularly few personalities to boast of in recent generations of my own branch of the family. My father was Christopher Nevile of Thorney, a poorish property of some five thousand acres in the topmost corner of Nottinghamshire where it juts into Lincolnshire. My family bought Thorney in 1567, according to Thoroton's *History of Nottinghamshire.* My grandfather, Commander Nevile, inherited the property in 1809 on the death of his brother, Nevile George, who died a bachelor and seems to have been a sad rake. Commander Nevile had served with distinction in the Navy with H.M.S. *Orion* in the action off Ushant in 1794, known as 'the glorious First of June', when Lord Howe defeated the French. He was a scrupulous old gentleman who was so shocked by the discreditable conduct of his brother George that he decided to take no chances with his own sons, and had them trained for the Church. Thus my father became rector of Wickenby, one of the livings in the gift of the family, and succeeded to the property on his father's death.

My father lacked commercial sense but was reputed to be a good speaker. He had contacts with quite a few men in high places; one such was W. E. Gladstone, who was not at all popular with our young family. Once, when the great man was lunching at Thorney, my sister Blanche was forbidden to go to a party, as my father felt that she should forgo it and stay at home to meet the statesman. It was clear to all of us that there was no joy for her in the encounter, for she said, on being asked her impression of him, 'I've often heard of wickedness, but until I met him I didn't know what wickedness looked like'—an unusually concise expression of the prejudice against Gladstone harboured by many Tory enthusiasts much older than my sister.

I was the thirteenth of my father's fifteen children by his three wives. He had first married Gertrude Hotham, by whom he had seven children. She was a daughter of Lieutenant-Colonel George Hotham of Beverley, another of whose daughters married Sir John

Lubbock the banker, whose son, the first Baron Avebury, sponsored many important public measures, including the Bank Holidays Act of 1871. By this marriage my half-brothers and sisters were first cousins to the Lubbock children, and in later years, when Edgar Lubbock was a director of Whitbread's, I saw something of him, and it was thanks to him that I first visited Whitbread's brewery in 1892. He was succeeded in that role by his nephew Cecil Lubbock, with whom I had much to do thirty years later, as these pages will show.

My mother, who was my father's third wife, was the daughter of Robert Tooth of Swift's Park, Cranbrook. Robert Tooth had interests in hop-growing and brewing, and to a lesser extent in banking. Three of his sons built up the great Australian brewery of Tooth & Company, Sydney, but he himself was eventually ruined by the failure, in 1866, of the banking house of Overend & Gurney. Like my father, he had a large family, nine sons followed by six daughters; my mother, Mary Anne, was the oldest of the six. I have been told that it was his custom to give each of his sons five thousand pounds on his twenty-first birthday, telling him to go out into the world with it and see what he could do. If he prospered, well and good; if he came back having spent or lost the money, then his father pronounced him unfit for business and advised him to go into the Church. But no such story lay behind my Uncle Arthur's entry into the Church, for Father Tooth had a sense of vocation; when I first knew him he was already well-known as one of the group, including the then Lord Halifax, who were promoting Anglo-Catholicism in the Church of England.

So far as I know he is distinguished by being the only member of my family who ever saw the inside of a gaol, so I include a special reference to him. Arthur Tooth was born in 1839, was educated at Tonbridge and Trinity, Cambridge, took his degree in 1861, and was ordained priest in 1864. In 1868 he was preferred to St. James's Church, Hatcham, a living then in the gift of the family. Father Tooth introduced Anglo-Catholic ritual into the services at a time when strong evangelical forces within the Church were working to make these illegal, and Hatcham became a storm centre. Much of the organized opposition was directed from outside the parish and caused serious disturbances in church. My uncle caught one of the men responsible and learned from him that the demonstrators were being paid two shillings a time to interrupt.

In 1874 the Public Worship Regulation Act was passed, under which the Church Association brought charges against Father Tooth for wearing illegal vestments and for other ritualistic actions. Since the Act was a secular measure, he wrote to his bishop and offered to discontinue the practice if he would pronounce it against the ecclesiastical law. The bishop declined to intervene, so Father Tooth refused to attend the secular court on a matter which he considered to be a spiritual one. In his absence the special court under Lord Penzance admonished and inhibited him for three months. Father Tooth defied the court, public interest was aroused, and great crowds flocked into Hatcham. On one occasion it was said that three hundred police were called in. A few days later Arthur Tooth was arrested and lodged in Horsemonger Lane Gaol, the first clergyman to suffer imprisonment under the Act. The incident figured in the Spy cartoon in *Vanity Fair*, with a sympathetic article.

His imprisonment was adjudged illegal because of a technical irregularity, and he was released. He returned to Hatcham to find the church door locked against him, but obtained entry and refused admittance to the young clergyman appointed to conduct the services, whose name was Randall Davidson (later Archbishop of Canterbury). My uncle was compelled by ill health to resign the living in 1878, and on recovery devoted himself to an orphanage and institution he had founded. In this way he passed the rest of his life. Half a century later there was a meeting in Caxton Hall to celebrate the fiftieth anniversary of his release from prison. Two of my sisters went. Though they arrived early they found the hall crowded and the doors closed, and obtained admission by explaining that they would be the only relatives present. They were found places on the platform and heard Lord Halifax and others pay tribute to my uncle's work of long ago. When he died in 1931 at the age of ninety-two I was among the large congregation at his funeral, when his courage and faith were remembered. At his old church of St. James's, Hatcham, the vicar, though a strong evangelist, paid a moving tribute to the old fighter's memory.

But to return to my own story. By the time I came on the scene on July 12th, 1873,[1] the family's finances were in poor shape. The expenses of my father's large family, the agricultural depression, the rebuilding of the parish church at his own expense and an unfortunate investment in the then Manchester, Sheffield and Lincolnshire Railway, had sadly depleted our resources. When my father died at the age of seventy, I being four years old, my mother was left with seven young children and an income which even in those days was regarded as very modest. My elder brothers had been sent, in accordance with family tradition, to Eton where the eldest, George, won the school sculls in 1850, at the age of fifteen, I believe a record. His success may have been due to his being a poor mixer, so that he spent all his free time on the river. But when it came to my turn Eton, and indeed any other of the great public schools, was out of the question.

I have naturally few recollections of Thorney. My clearest one was that on my fourth birthday, when I achieved my first pair of knickerbockers, I gave an early indication that aquatic sports would be my chosen recreation. Somehow or other I got myself afloat on a garden seat on the lake, and had to be rescued by my brother Richard.

Most children have their ambitions, or at least used to, though nowadays they do not seem to look so far ahead. My first was to keep an 'eating shop', then I wanted to be an engine driver, then the Navy attracted me; I ended up by becoming a brewer, and since I have given a good deal of attention to encouraging catering in public houses, perhaps I have not got so far from my original ambition. I seem almost to have turned full circle.

On my father's death in 1877 my mother, who had a brother at Brighton, took a house there. She moved a year or two later to

[1] I have been amused, while writing this, to find in the Whitbread 1957 calendar an account of the signs of the Zodiac, in which under the sign of Cancer (for July) are these words: "If you were born under Cancer you have a natural affinity with the sea, and indeed with all forms of liquid. . . Whatever you do you feel an underlying need to serve the public. . ." Well: perhaps there is something in astrology after all, for I have loved yachting, beer is a liquid, and I have devoted much time to public service!

Bognor, then a small Victorian resort very different from Brighton. My eldest half-sister, Gertrude, was forty years older than myself and lived at Whitby. She offered to take charge of me for a time so as to help the family finances. For four years I received my first education under her care, returning to my family at Bognor when she moved to London. Then I was sent to a small preparatory school for boys conducted by a Mr. Travers. There were about twenty small boys and one girl, his daughter.

Those days were recalled to my mind a year or two ago. I was spending a few days at a small hotel on the South Coast and I found among the guests a charming old lady who turned out to be the Connie Travers who had shared my lessons. It was strange to be talking about the events of days over seventy years ago, when I was an unpromising schoolboy, very slow in the uptake. We laughed over one instance of my simple-mindedness. I had arrived a little late one spring morning, and Mr. Travers asked me to oblige him by running along to the nearby chemist's to ask for a box of 'round squares' for his throat, as he was a little hoarse. Unaware that the date was April the First, I was of course only too glad to trot off on this errand, but as the exact description of Mr. Travers's requirements eluded me, I merely asked for some 'squares' for him, as his throat was sore. Somewhat puzzled, the chemist made up the package of tablets and back I ran to school with it, to be greeted by a burst of laughter which seemed pretty pointless to me. Still completely innocent of the joke, I solemnly laid the packet on the master's desk, and was startled by an even louder burst of laughter from the boys, who quite wrongly gave me credit for having thought up this neat reprisal and landed Mr. Travers in unwelcome expense. Though such wiliness was quite beyond me I willingly basked in the glory of it, and have often had the feeling in later life that a similar lucky accident has contributed to a reputation for subtlety quite foreign to my nature.

When I was about fourteen my mother left Bognor and returned to Brighton. She took a house in Kemp Town, not far from Brighton College, where it was intended that I should go as a day boy. But my mother's income was so small that she had to decide whether she should spend what money was available on school bills, or on a premium enabling me to begin at that early age to follow some calling. Since her brothers had been successful in Australia, and in the hope that they might help me in my career, she decided that this calling should be brewing. This was something of a shock to my half-sister, Gertrude, who took an affectionate interest in me. Hers was the philosophy of the old Victorian county families: she divided her world between 'gentlemen' who entered the Services, the Church, the Law, or other professions, which meant putting service before money, and those engaged in trade whom she regarded as a lower form of life, as they supposedly put accumulation of wealth before service.

While her philosophy is much out of date today, at least I owe much to it. I have a vein of perversity in my character, and I determined to prove that she was wrong in thinking that I should find no opportunity for public service in the brewing industry. My half-sister never, of course, foresaw the possibility of my enjoying contacts and friendships with some of the great men of the brewing world, like the Whitbreads, the Barclays and the Buxtons, who, whilst deriving wealth from their businesses, were more widely known as leaders in social service and philanthropic enterprise.

My mother's hope that I should go to her brothers' large business in Australia was never realized, but I have enjoyed my life in the brewing industry and have never regretted her decision. So it came to pass that in January 1888 she and I took a cab from our Kemp Town house to Waterloo Street in Hove where the firm of E. Robins and Son had their brewery. The only point of the interview I remember was Mr. Robins' opinion that, though I was unusually young, it would be a good thing to get experience early. On the 19th of January, 1888, I was duly articled as a pupil at the brewery where, in exchange for a premium of £100 a year, it was agreed that I would be taught the 'mystery and art of brewing'. Nowadays things have changed; brewing has become a science, and a qualified brewer is expected to have a diploma in his hand. In those days a pupilage for two or three years, usually followed by a few months' work in a consulting chemist's laboratory, was considered a sufficient training to secure a post as an assistant brewer.

All the same, I am not sorry to have learned my business when it was still a 'mystery'; nor am I sorry that I started so early. I had five or six years' start on most men entering the industry, and probably gained a more thorough knowledge of detail. Nowdays many industrialists prefer a more comprehensive general education, and my early start had its drawbacks from this point of view. Without a public school and university background I made none of those friendships and formed none of those contacts which make life so much easier and so much more agreeable in after years. I have sometimes wondered if this circumstance was not the cause of that sense of inadequacy which from time to time has beset me, and my occasional lack of self-confidence.

At Robins' I was articled to the brewer, T. K. Amos, a man of twenty-six who had served his pupilage in the same brewery. He was a sportsman, and a charming and lovable personality, whose tragic circumstances in later life were a grief to all who knew him. Soon afterwards I was joined by W. B. Thorpe, a cousin of Amos. Thorpe was two years older than myself and far more mature; but after his pupilage closed he failed to get a berth in brewing and eventually entered the Bank of England; in his own words, 'At least, a gentleman's life'.

My pupilage preceded the era of the great combines, although even then there were some quite large concerns in London, other big cities, and Burton-on-Trent. For the most part trade was in the hands of local breweries, such as Robins of Brighton, so 'local' indeed that they shared the trade of the town with many others; in Robins' case with twenty other Brighton breweries. As Robins' brewery owned about thirty public houses and several off-licences, it was a good training-ground for a keen youngster anxious to get more than a glimpse of every side of the business. Besides the brewery proper it comprised a bottling factory, a wine and spirits department, a bonded warehouse, and the houses already mentioned. The business was owned by one Ebenezer Robins, but managed by his brother Thomas ('Mr. Tom'), who was not content to take my hundred pounds a year and leave me to pick up what I could. He saw to it that I contributed my full share, and during my two years I learned something of the working of each department, though I was not uniformly successful. In particular, I loathed book-keeping, for which I had no aptitude, and this led to my first rebuke. It was 'Mr. Tom's' habit to call each Saturday for a list of defaulting customers and other malefactors; being a devout Churchman, he was suspected of praying for the reformation of bad payers on Sunday! At the end of my first week in the office he called for a sight of the book it was my duty to keep. After one glance at its pages he silently added my name to his list of people to be prayed for.

I never succeeded in overcoming my dislike of routine penmanship, and took every opportunity to delegate it to others. Thirty years later, when I was discussing with the partners at Whitbread's the proposal that I should join the board, they asked me to promise never to carbonate their bottled beers. To this I agreed, stipulating that they, for their part, should never ask me to write in a book. These undertakings were faithfully observed by both sides, but I often wonder whether the secretarial staffs at Chiswell Street have been sufficiently aware of the boon thus conferred on them.

We saw Ebenezer Robins infrequently, but usually when there was trouble. I remember on one occasion, when trade had been slow and profits unsatisfactory, he came down in a fury and told his brother to cut all salaries and wages by a quarter. 'Yours too, Tom!' he stormed. It says much for the staff's knowledge of the difference between the old man's bark and his bite, that no murmur arose, and he quickly relented, not only restoring the cuts but giving every man a book of his own choosing. I was not really affected, as at the time I was paying to be there rather than being paid, but I shared in the book-distribution and chose Faulkner's book on brewing, then a standard textbook.

I enjoyed the practical work at the little Waterloo Street brewery, which I used to reach at five-thirty in the morning for 'mashing'—that preliminary process essential to the rest of the day's work; this done, we would in summer go off for a swim from the West Pier, acquiring a mighty appetite for breakfast which followed the ritual of 'setting the taps'.

Mashing? Setting taps? For the benefit of my lay readers I will give an outline of the brewing process. Brewing is one of the fermentation industries, that is to say an industry that utilizes micro-organisms in the service of man. Beer is a fermented beverage; all fermented beverages are the results of the fermentation of some form of sugar, each differing in character according to the source of its fermentable extract and method of production. Thus wine is the product of the sugar obtained from grapes; cider of sugar from apples; mead of sugar from honey; in beer the extract is obtained from cereals, principally barley.

Before a fermentable extract can be obtained from barley the grain must be turned into malt. To do this, it is first steeped in water and allowed to germinate for some eight or ten days before being dried off in a kiln. During the process the starch is modified into a form which is convertible on infusion with hot water into a sugar extract which will ferment. This process is conducted in 'maltings', usually in country districts within easy reach of the markets where barley is sold. Nowadays this malt extract is frequently supplemented by sugars from other sources. In brewing, the malt is first ground, then infused with hot water (or liquor, as water is termed in a brewery) and digested for a time in a vessel called a 'mash'-tun which is fitted with a false bottom or strainer. This is the process of 'mashing'. After a digestive period of generally two hours the 'taps are set', the extract, called wort, is drained off, passed to the brewing coppers, and boiled with hops, which supply both flavour and preservative qualities. The remains of the malt left in the mash-tun are sold for cattle-food under the name of 'brewers' grains'. After boiling, the hops are strained off and the wort is cooled before passing to fermenting vessels, where yeast from a previous brewing is added, and fermentation begins. At this stage account is taken of the quantity and density, or 'gravity', of the wort by the Customs and Excise Authorities, in order to estimate the duty chargeable.

As fermentation proceeds the yeast, which consists of multitudes of small cells, works on the extract of malt, converting the sugar it contains into alcohol and carbon dioxide gas. Some of the gas is retained in solution in the beer and gives it that sparkle termed 'condition'. During fermentation the yeast multiplies itself some four or five times and in the case of English beers rises to the surface, where it is skimmed off; some is retained for future brewings, and the rest is variously disposed of. At one time brewers' yeast was used in the baking of bread; but that trade has now passed almost completely to the distillers, who manufacture bakers' yeast by a special process. The utilization of surplus yeast has been a major problem to brewers for many years, for it is of high intrinsic food value which should not be allowed to go to waste. Much is now used in the making of vegetable extracts such as 'Marmite', which though of vegetable origin are claimed to possess the food value of meat extracts.

The English method of brewing takes about six days in the fermentation stage, after which the beer is transferred to storage—or 'racked', as the term is, into casks. The fermentation of English beers is controlled at temperatures from 60 to 70 degrees Fahrenheit, and the yeast rises to the top. This is the main difference between English and Continental or lager type beers. Lager beers are fermented at lower temperatures, during which the yeast sinks to the bottom. Thus the English process is known as 'top fermentation' and the Continental as 'bottom fermentation'. After fermentation, lagers are stored in cold cellars, and are eventually drunk at temperatures round about forty degrees Fahrenheit, whereas English beers are best drunk at about fifty-five or sixty degrees.

Most brewers produce several kinds of beer; and these differ from brewery to brewery, and from district to district. Originally, individual breweries brewed the types of beer for which their particular methods, the materials most readily available, and especially their water supply proved most suitable. Thus Burton brewers concentrated on pale ales and strong beers, London on stout and sweet mild ale, and Scotland, Yorkshire and the West Country each produced distinctive types to meet the tastes of their respective consumers, as created by local conditions.

In London it was customary for public houses to stock stout and mild brewed in London, and pale ale from Burton; some London firms owned breweries in Burton to supply their customers. But as technical knowledge and skill developed, it became possible to treat local waters to resemble the characteristic Burton supply which had made the beers from that town world-famous, and thus enabled Burton-type beers to be brewed elsewhere; so that in time almost all breweries, wherever they were, could supply all the varieties their customers required. But, though producing these different kinds of beer, each brewery aimed at brewing a distinctive quality which found favour with its own customers; and was careful to secure uniformity, because the beer drinker is curiously conservative. Once he has become accustomed to one 'palate' or flavour, he resents any change. This is evident when smaller breweries amalgamate with a large combine and their houses are supplied from the new parent brewery. There is almost always criticism before the 'regulars' settle down to the new beer. In times of national crisis it has sometimes been necessary, to save transport, for brewers to supply each other's houses in districts where the one brewery is distant and the other is on the spot. Complaint or criticism at once comes from the consumer, not always because the beer is inferior, but because it is different.

Nevertheless the British Public likes to have a choice and any monopoly in a district by a single concern is to be deprecated. Even after thirty years, the complaint is still heard in Carlisle that there is no choice. I shall refer later to the Government monopoly in Carlisle, my connection with which I number among my most interesting experiences. One thing is certain: once a beer of a particular character has found its market, it is important that the uniform standard be maintained; and it was no doubt with this in mind that an old and wise craftsman is said to have given one last piece of advice to his pupils. He said to them, 'If when you take up a new job you find a rat in the mash-tun, leave it there. The customers may like the flavour!' Few of us would take that advice too seriously and yet it is not without its glimmer of wisdom.

During my pupilage at Robins', I passed through all departments in succession, turning a hand to every process learning to become a practical brewer. Now it was in the brewery itself, now the small bottling factory, now the wine and spirit department. This department included the bonded store, that is to say the warehouse in which spirits could be kept to mature before duty must be paid. I went also, but briefly, into the hated office, where I made a poor show, and was happy to switch my interest to the public houses, where I collected moneys due and looked at accounts. I did not have an opportunity of practising malting, as Robins' did not make their own. I even tried my hand at making a cask, but found this entirely beyond my powers. During the second year I attended at the Brighton Technical College to get a smattering of analysis. Anyway, by the time my two years' pupilage was over, I had gained a knowledge of the outline of the brewing industry. The firm offered to retain me for a time, at a salary, but I needed other experience and better ultimate prospects, so I looked farther afield.

2

My first post—Comparison between 1890 *and* 1957*—Trade depression in London—I become head brewer—Growth of responsibilities—Visit to America—Principal national organizations of the Industry—Setback in profits and study of brewery economics*

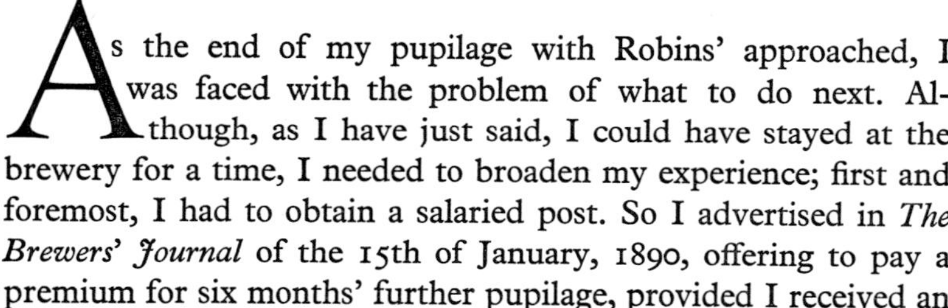

As the end of my pupilage with Robins' approached, I was faced with the problem of what to do next. Although, as I have just said, I could have stayed at the brewery for a time, I needed to broaden my experience; first and foremost, I had to obtain a salaried post. So I advertised in *The Brewers' Journal* of the 15th of January, 1890, offering to pay a premium for six months' further pupilage, provided I received an appointment as under-brewer at the end of the period.

In those days the position of brewer in a good country brewery had plenty of attractive features. While as a brewer he was responsible for smooth running and high-class production, and all the administrative details were left to him, he still had considerable latitude in arranging his working hours. There was usually a house attached to the brewery for his use, and he could often keep a horse in the stables. He was encouraged in the interests of the business to make friends in the neighbourhood and so he often got a day's shooting here and there. His salary was moderate, but he was generally allowed to take one or more pupils whose fees added to his income, to whom he was able to delegate part of his work as they grew in knowledge and experience. There had been a noticeable swing in favour of brewing as a career, especially among young men who shared my dislike of office work; so there were scores of applicants for every position. So I was lucky to receive a letter from Mr. Arthur J. Brandon, of the Putney Brewery, asking me to go along for an interview.

The Putney Brewery offered just what I was seeking: the business was small but expanding rapidly, and a position there promised opportunities not so readily available in the country: London was not only a centre of brewing but also the home of the various trade organizations in which I was destined to take much interest in the years to come. Yet Putney in those days was very different from the busy London suburb of today. When I left the station to walk to the brewery, down what is now the crowded High Street, I had some difficulty in discovering 'Gardener's Lane', the address given me. But I found the brewery, and was soon facing Mr. Brandon in his office for this vital interview. I was desperately anxious not to miss what seemed to be a good opportunity.

I was to find in later years that under a kindly and rather hesitant manner Arthur Brandon concealed a vision and enterprise, combined with a judgement of men and a shrewd appreciation of values, that I have never known surpassed: qualities which, together with the respect and affection he inspired, resulted in the growth of the business from small beginnings to the substantial concern it became under the name of Brandon's Putney Brewery Limited. Two memories connected with that interview are still with me. When the question of my age arose, I asked to be excused from answering, on the grounds that my youth was 'my only disadvantage'! To this Brandon replied dryly that if he appointed me, this was a failing he would 'expect me to grow out of'. I remember also that he asked me when I could start, as he needed someone at once. My answer , 'Let me start tomorrow', seemed to please him, although my eagerness was startling; however, he came to Brighton the next day, a Thursday, heard what Tom Robins had to say about me, and arranged for me to go to town on Monday and start work on Wednesday, the 29th of January, 1890.

I have always believed that it was actually my lack of years that secured me the appointment, because the head brewer was anxious to have an assistant whom, in his own words, 'he could train in his own ways'—a process which in practice I found bristling with drawbacks, yet had to make the best of; and perhaps one learns more under a chief with a critical temperament than under one more tolerant. Looking back, I am inclined now to think that my most valid complaint against him was that he made me do the lion's share of the work. He himself had had to work hard for months single-handed before I arrived, and he took the chance of my advent to slacken off. But it was all good experience for me.

Six months later, on the 31st July, 1890, I was formally appointed assistant brewer and thus obtained my first executive post in the calling in which I hoped to find not only a livelihood but an opportunity to make my mark in public service, and incidentally to show my sister Gertrude how wrong she was. I was already deeply interested in some of the unsolved problems of the Trade and studied them diligently in the two Trade papers, *The Brewers' Journal* and *The Brewing Trade Review*. Still, I think I realized, impatient as I was, that older heads than mine could safely be left to ponder these matters for the time being, and as my first move, obviously, was to establish myself, I settled down to my task as second brewer, working as deputy to my chief and taking charge in his absence. For this post of responsibility I was paid the magnificent salary of a hundred pounds for the first year, but all the time I was learning.

* * *

At that time Brandon's trade was expanding rapidly and overtaxing the capacity of the brewery, which was old and cramped. Plans for rebuilding were under way but in the meantime we worked day and night, and the number of hours I was expected to put in would certainly not be tolerated today. I never thought of complaining, but determined to make the most of any opportunities that arose, cramming thus into a very few years a detailed experience of the business far more comprehensive than I could have gained under the easier conditions of today. Yet no young man is ever the worse at the beginning of his career (given normal

I. THE AUTHOR AND HIS MOTHER

At 6
I want to keep an Eating Shop

At 16
I start my career at Brandon's

My Mother

At 46
I join Whitbread's Board

At 76
I retire from Managing Directorship

2. Thorney

The family home and scene of my first aquatic adventure

3. Thorney Church, rebuilt by my father

health) for a few years of hard work—even though I attributed my prematurely grey hair to lack of sleep during those early years; even this greying had its advantage, giving, as it did, a somewhat spurious impression of age and wisdom.

It may be as well at this point to outline the general features of the Trade as I found it on entering Brandon's Brewery in 1890. The succeeding half century was to see many changes, in some of which I was to play a part. To begin with, there is an astonishing contrast in the numbers of breweries in 1890 and in 1957. In 1890 there were 11,364 licensed 'brewers for sale'; in 1957 there were less than 450. In addition to those 'brewers for sale' there were many who brewed exclusively for their own consumption. In my younger days many large country houses and farms brewed for their own use and for servants and employees. Even cottagers whose assessments were under £8 per annum could brew without licence and free of duty. If the assessment was between £10 and £15, a licence was required but no duty was payable. Above this limit, ordinary beer duty was chargeable.

The great decrease in 'brewers for sale' between 1890 and 1957 has not been caused by a proportionate diminution in the consumption of beer, but principally by amalgamations and by the acquisition of smaller breweries by expanding concerns; also by the virtual disappearance of the practice of home brewing in public houses. At one time there were thousands of publican brewers up and down the country, and today there are still a few survivals mostly to be found in the north and Midlands, around Walsall and Kidderminster. It seems certain that this form of home brewing must disappear. Although an interesting survival, beers brewed under public house conditions, with varying materials, unskilled control and imperfect cleanliness, cannot secure the consistent quality the consumer demands. The number of customers who like differing flavours is small, though some, like the lady who enjoyed the oysters sold in a particular restaurant in Soho because 'no two tasted quite the same', may like to take chances. But in 1890 standards were lower, there were something like ten thousand of these home brewers, and there were perhaps fourteen hundred wholesale concerns doing sufficient business to employ one or more trained technical brewers. The great businesses of Burton, London and other large centres employed many more.

Beer remains the national drink, though not consumed as universally as in those days. That gallant old scientist, Professor Edward Armstrong, used to declare that 'beer was the only safe drink all the world over'. History has shown that all great civilizations have needed some form of alcohol, and both social and medical experts have concluded that it is best consumed in diluted rather than in concentrated form. Beer appears to fill this need so long as it contains sufficient alcohol, say from three to five per cent to maintain its character.

Beer is not now drunk as generally, and is no longer supplied as a matter of course. In the 'nineties, for example, many big shops employed assistants who lived in, and to whom beer was supplied as part of basic, routine rations. Schoolboys drank beer; and in most private houses a cask was kept on tap for the servants and casual callers. It was to supply their requirements that many smaller breweries existed—breweries which owned few or no public houses but sold most of their output to private consumers and called themselves 'family' brewers. A handful exist today; for though the private customer with a cask on tap at home has almost vanished, there is still a market made up of clubs and free buyers who prefer a cheap rather than a well-known brand.

In those days beer was stronger than it is today. I find, on referring to that invaluable compendium of information, the *Brewers' Almanack*, that the average original gravity in 1890 was approximately 1055°, which after fermentation represents a content of about 5 per cent of alcohol. The national output then was about thirty-one million barrels, producing £9,500,000 in revenue. Brewing seemed to have reached its peak in 1914 when the output reached thirty-seven million barrels: a startling contrast to 1949, when close on sixteen-and-a-half million standard (that is, calculated in terms of 1055° gravity) barrels were brewed, representing twenty-seven million bulk barrels (that is, liquid barrels of 36 gallons) of approximately 3 per cent average alcohol content—but producing more than £294,000,000 of revenue.

This reduction in the volume and strength of beer is the result of increased prices generally and the many restrictions brought into being by the two world wars. In both, the shortage of grain necessitated the maximum output of beer from the minimum amount of material, and the enormous increase in taxation has been the main cause of today's higher prices and lighter beers. The duty in 1890 was 6s. 3d. per standard barrel, say one farthing a pint; beer brewed at the same gravity today would incur a charge of not less than 321s. per barrel, or more than 1s. 1d. a pint—a fifty-two-fold rise. There is also the increase in cost of materials, labour and other working expenses.

The principal market open to the large wholesale brewers was the licensed house, the family trade being somewhat *infra dignitatem.* There were, in those days, 103,808 on-licences spread over England and Wales (in which beer could be sold for consumption on the premises) and 13,722 off-licences (sometimes termed 'grocers' licences)—originated by Mr. Gladstone as a measure of social reform, to encourage consumption in private houses rather than in the apparently less virtuous atmosphere of the public house. It was easier to obtain off-licences in those days, but their competition was much resented by every licensed victualler '(the fully licensed man)' who regarded them as 'vermin'. Accordingly, the larger brewers concentrated their attention on the on-licensed trade, leaving the sale to off-licences and private houses to smaller competitors such as Brandon's.

In 1890 the ownership of public houses by brewers was growing rapidly and was developing in two directions. On the one hand, as public houses came into the market they were bought up by brewers to secure a regular output for their beers. On the other hand, in many parts of the country (notably in the Midlands and Lancashire), prosperous publicans who had acquired a number of houses purchased a brewery in order to supply their needs, continuing to conduct their retail business through managers. It is incorrect to designate such concerns as 'tied houses'—they are no more 'tied' than are the distributive branches of such multiple firms as Boots, the chemists, or Montague Burton, the tailors.

But the financial position of the Trade was not uniformly

favourable. In 1892 I attended my first annual general meeting of a large company which had fallen on evil days. One of my relations had made a small investment in Samuel Allsopp and Sons Limited, and gave me her proxy; she thought the experience would be instructive. The Company had been registered a year after the success of the flotation of Guinness in 1886 had proved something of a sensation. I have always understood that, whereas Guinness had been careful to let their customers have the advantage of early subscription, those responsible for Allsopp's had retained most of the shareholding for their financier friends. These benefited largely by unloading when, as expected, the shares rose to a premium on the Stock Exchange in the Guinness boom. One of the points made by Allsopp's in their prospectus had been that they had few tied houses and were, therefore, much in the position of Guinness. But, as it turned out, they had not the same commercial acumen. Since other brewers were then busy buying houses, Allsopp's first found their free customers being lost to other concerns, so they cut their prices, and then plunged wildly into the market at the time when the prices of licensed houses had reached a maximum. The combined result of loss of trade, the sale of beer on unremunerative terms, and the purchase of public houses at extravagant prices had reduced their profits to a point where they were unable to meet the interest even on their debentures.

In the ordinary way, few shareholders take the trouble to attend the annual general meeting of companies in which their money is invested; but when they cease to receive their dividends they are apt to attend in full force. On this occasion, the hall of the Cannon Street Hotel was packed to the doors. The meeting was under the chairmanship of Lord Hindlip. The board were roundly attacked, especially by one shareholder who ended his remarks by asking, 'How much are you going to give us back?' In a very few minutes the meeting was chanting, 'Yes, how much are you going to give us back?' Presently Lord Hindlip, a commanding figure, rose to his feet, the noise subsided, and everyone waited to hear the defence. His speech was short; 'Not a damn penny!' he said, then opened the door behind the platform and retired from the meeting, which resolved that a committee of inspection should be appointed. Allsopp's troubles were followed by many similar ones elsewhere during the early years of the century.

To return again to my own history. After six years as second brewer my responsibilities had increased, though eased by the appointment of a third brewer as assistant to myself. Then the company lost my chief, R. H. Smith, who died from typhoid fever at a comparatively early age. As joint managing director with the commercial manager, A. H. Palmer, he ran the concern during Brandon's absences abroad. His sudden death caused me anxiety as well as regret; for at my age I felt I could hardly hope to succeed him. However, the unexpected happened: Brandon decided to give me my opportunity, and at the early age of twenty-two I found myself head brewer, probably the youngest in England, with two assistants even younger than myself.

My ambition to play an active part in shaping the industry led me now to take a more lively interest in the concerns of our Trade bodies. In later years I was to have much to do with all three, and indeed became chairman of each one in turn, so this is perhaps the moment for describing the three principal organizations of the brewing Trade: the Institute of Brewing, the Brewers' Society, and the National Trade Defence Association—following the order in which I came to play a part in their proceedings. The Institute of Brewing originated from a dining club which first met in 1886 and was inspired by Dr. E. R. Moritz, a well-known brewing consultant, who will reappear several times in these pages. In 1890 this society of technical brewers and scientific advisers was constituted as the Institute of Brewing of London. Similar bodies were established in other centres of brewing and in 1904 these provincial bodies were amalgamated with the original London Institute, as the Institute of Brewing. The united body set itself to the task of applying scientific methods to the technical problems of brewing. The amalgamation was brought about largely by the efforts of Edward M. Strouts, at that time a member of the brewing staff of Reid and Company, which later joined forces with Watney's, when he became head brewer to Watney Combe Reid. Those were early days, and when I first joined the Institute its activities had little of today's complexity. But it gave me the opportunity of meeting progressive spirits, though when I joined it, introduced by Strouts himself, I hardly expected that twenty years or so later I should become President. I regularly attended the meetings, and though our discussions were technical they were not entirely unconvivial. I treasure a postcard from Strouts which led to a good deal of speculation in my family circle, for it followed closely on one such meeting, and its message was:

'When we parted last night, did you ask me to dinner? If so, when and where, and did I say yes or no?'!

* * *

The Brewers' Society represents the commercial and political interests of the Trade. Originally there were many local Associations, the most powerful being in Burton and London. All these bodies were amalgamated on a national basis in 1904, but it was not until 1917 that I was elected to the committee of this august organization.

The third important body is the National Trade Development Association, formed in 1888 under the name of the National Trade Defence Association to protect the interest of the whole trade, whether wholesale or retail. Its function was and is to maintain friendly relations between all sections and to represent the whole industry when occasion demands. In these three principal national organizations I have taken a wellnigh lifelong interest, and to their various *démarches* shall inevitably revert.

A year or two earlier, when Arthur Brandon found it impossible to exercise constant personal control, the business at Putney had been registered as a private company; and in July 1896 it was floated as a public company by the issue of debentures, Brandon still retaining control by holding the ordinary shares. This brought in extra capital with which in the next few years we were able to complete the rebuilding of our own Putney brewery, and also to absorb the Star Brewery at Walton-on-Thames (which we closed as a brewery and retained as a store) and the brewery of Burrows and Cole at Twickenham, which became our bottling factory. We also acquired a malting at Fulham.

These new Brandon enterprises came under my direction, one

and all, so it is obvious that my hands were pretty full. For years I never went to bed until I had visited the brewery, however exacting the day's work had been elsewhere, and I never failed to walk round on Sundays, both morning and evening. But nevertheless I still found time to spend a few hours weekly at John Heron's laboratory in the City, learning all I could about the new methods of scientific control. Today most breweries have their own well-equipped laboratories as a matter of course; but at that time the scientists had not come into their own and many old stagers still relied on tradition and craftsmanship, and often produced uncommonly good beer.

I used to arrive at Heron's laboratory about twice a week in the early afternoon. I would work with two or three other enthusiasts until nine, when we retired to a chop house for an evening meal. Among the friends of those days were two I kept up with for a long time. One was P. C. Loftus, a rather wild Irishman who bought a small brewery on the East Coast, from which he derived a satisfactory income for many years. Though a keen brewer he was also an enthusiastic politician, and entered Parliament for Lowestoft. He never held office but he became recognized as an authority on finance and a rather eccentric power in political diplomacy.

The other was that delightful and explosive character 'Bob' Chichester, who became an expert maltster. A younger son of the well-known Devon family, he had originally been destined for the priesthood. According to his account, when passing a brewery one day after leaving Eton, he was so attracted by the smell that he decided to become a brewer instead of going to the University. Known to me and his friends as 'John Barleycorn' (a very apt pseudonym) he remains one of my few surviving friends of those early days. He now lives in retirement at Hove and we often meet and talk about our experiences. He was also an enthusiastic campanologist, and had rung 'Grandsire triplets' in many churches.

London was a happier place to live in in the earlier part of the century than it is today. The week-end habit had not arrived; as a general rule, when engaged in business in London one lived there permanently with brief holidays at the seaside or in the country. Most country families of means kept a house in London to which they came during the season early in May, staying until the middle of July, Goodwood being regarded as the end of the season.

Although the top hat was becoming less universal, it was worn by those working in banks, finance houses and especially the Stock Exchange. Frock coats and top hats were the uniform for social occasions. Instead of writing letters of thanks, it was customary either to call or to leave cards on one's hostesses. Hard as I had to work during the week, my Sundays were usually free, apart from the visits of inspection I have already mentioned. During the London season I used to attend morning service in a West End church, then stroll in Hyde Park, where I hoped to meet any of my relations or friends who might be up from the country, and then go to lunch at the house of one of those families who were kind enough to invite me.

While I could not afford to hunt, shoot or fish, I met with much kindness from family friends who did their best to keep my head above water in the social world: particularly Mrs. Harry Cholmondeley, whose husband was a half-brother of Sir Charles Strickland (who had married my half-sister, Annie). One of our favourite stories was of how Sir Charles had saved from suffocation an unfortunate footman who had managed to get himself locked in the strong-room. No workman could be found, on a Saturday night, to come and release him, so Strickland contrived to bore a hole in the wall. They lived at 95 Piccadilly, which on their death became the first home of the R.A.C.

Then there were Colonel and Mrs. Clayhill who lived in Chester Square. He was very much a man-about-town. As a very young subaltern, he had taken part in the Charge of the Six Hundred at Balaclava and by some miracle had survived. Mrs. Clayhill used to encourage me by prophesying great things for me. She would refer to her husband's brother, whom she regarded as inferior in intellect, yet who for all that had done well in brewing. She thus betrayed her society woman's estimate of the difference between social distinction and commercial ability.

It was usual to retire to one's club for a spell after Sunday luncheon, then at half-past three issue forth either to drop cards or call on the various ladies to whom one was indebted for hospitality. In those days most ladies made a point of being at home on Sunday, the day when men were free and able to call.

Another acquaintance of these days was J. H. Torr, a supporter of the Public House Trust Movement, a body with which I should later have much to do, and a man with quite a prejudice against brewers. As he knew my family he overlooked my business, and asked me to luncheon occasionally. I was already an enthusiast for public house improvement and was constantly advocating the advantage of sobriety to the brewing industry. This was a novel idea, for brewers were alleged to thrive mainly on the mis-spent money of drunkards, and Torr considered me as some kind of crank. He could not conceive how a brewer, whose business it was to sell beer, could speak of his business and social welfare in the same breath. Our conversations were fruitful, for he made it clear to me that if my idea was ever to carry conviction—my idea that sobriety was in the best interests of the Trade, and that there was no real conflict between the brewing industry's interests and the public's well-being—I should have to concentrate on the economic aspects of the drink problem.

I have another reason for remembering his hospitality, for on my first visit to his house I met his daughter Rosita; just a schoolgirl like any other, I thought, a pleasant fourteen-year-old. Then I chanced to say something about a member of my family which aroused her interest, and she gave me a look which suggested that there was more in her than met the eye. I was right, for she became Rosita Forbes, writer and explorer.

But these were diversions; most of my life centred on Brandon's. Much of our business was with off-licences, and the demand for bottled beer was now increasing rapidly. Therefore we decided to start a bottling department, bought premises at Wandsworth, and appointed a manager. Bottling was then regarded as a separate business, somewhat beneath the dignity of a wholesale brewer. There was the keenest competition for this new trade, so that prices fell far below costs of production. Many brewers lost money, Brandon's among them. We had to cut our losses by closing down the Wandsworth factory, and I volunteered to restart bottling on a smaller scale at the Twickenham brewery.

I was troubled by the expense, inconvenience and waste of space involved in sending beer from the brewery to the bottling stores in cask, so I conceived the idea of delivering it in bulk—in tank wagons—and I put on the road what I believe to be the first such wagon ever used for beer, or indeed for any food product. As cases of bottles had to be brought back on the empty wagon, the vehicle was more handy than handsome, of the 'Heath Robinson' school, for we had to surmount the cylindrical tank with racks for the crates. However strange it looked, it was efficient, and the forerunner of the tanker now in general use.

I was so pleased with the results that I turned my mind to the possibility of applying tank delivery to public houses; with this end in view I took out certain patents and dreamed of great developments. But I had difficulty in finding suitable tanks for the public house cellars. The glass-lined tanks then available could not be easily cleaned by retailers, so I tried glazed earthenware vessels, but they would not stand pressure. A maker of enamelled ware assured me he could provide vessels to my design, and I got some for experiment, but found that the enamel contained an element of lead which would contaminate the beer. After this setback I felt that my role in life was administration rather than invention, and I abandoned the idea of tank delivery to retailers. One of my early imitators, who omitted to consult me, got into sad trouble through lead contamination by using inferior enamelled vessels in some houses without testing them. Some years later, brewers revived the idea, but only to a limited extent.

Although I had learnt something of the bottling business during my pupilage, when I took charge of bottling, I found I was rusty, so for the one and only time in the first twenty years of my working life I took a five weeks' holiday and devoted it to a hasty trip to the United States, where I spent three hectic weeks studying American bottling methods, at that time much in advance of those in England.

The consumption of beer in the States was rising rapidly, but so many breweries had been put into production that the supply was in excess of even a rising demand. Competition was keen and only the most efficient concerns could trade at a profit. Our prospective output at Brandon's being on a small scale, I was not interested in visiting the large breweries of Chicago and Milwaukee; I confined my inquiries to the many smaller plants in the Eastern States, which originally brewed ale similar to the strong beer imported from England, until, faced with the competition of German-type beers, they had evolved a process of chilling and filtering top fermentation ale and thus produced an article free from sediment, something like the bottom-fermentation lagers. This method, then successfully adopted by most American brewers, was being suggested to English brewers for both draught and bottled beers. By a curious coincidence I was able to learn much of this new process both on my voyage out and on the journey home, for unknown to me Worthington's of Burton-on-Trent had decided to adopt the system in England. On board ship I met experts concerned with the process and from them I learned much I might not have come by otherwise. On the outward journey I travelled in one of the smaller White Star liners, the *Germanic*, and met the engineer who had supervised the erection of the new plant at Burton. On the return journey in the *Oceanic*, thanks to a similar stroke of luck, I met the American 'master brewer' who had been engaged by Worthington's to install and work the process. Both were enthusiasts, and my conversations with them during the leisurely voyages, coupled with what I saw in America, gave me an insight into the process I could not have secured in any other way.

As it happened, the experiment by Worthington for draught beer proved to be in advance of its time, although the process became common practice for bottled beers, and was later adopted by some large brewers for draught beer as well.

I was received everywhere with true American hospitality. I called on one small firm which hoped to sell machinery to English brewers, and found the principal about to set off on his travels; he said, 'I'm off tomorrow for ten days to call on a round of my brewer customers; why not come with me, and I'll introduce you? Some won't let anyone into their bottlery, but others will be tickled to meet a Britisher and will be glad to show you what they wouldn't let their immediate competitors see.' I accepted this promising offer, and we departed next morning to make the round. I was amused to see how 'light' an American business man could travel. My friend managed to carry all he needed, including his business papers, in a bag hardly big enough to contain the minimal toothbrush. Each day we made an early start, our first call being to buy cigars of two qualities, which my friend placed in different pockets. The cheaper brand was offered to the underling in the customer's reception office, and the better one to the customer himself as a preliminary to talking business. I remember his annoyance when, having presented one of his best to a man he mistook for a prospective customer, he discovered he was actually the 'drummer' of a competitor. I learnt much during this trip, especially in the smaller concerns working roughly on the same scale as Brandon's. I found that the factory where the greatest secrecy was kept was usually the worst equipped. I have often noticed that the concern which welcomes visitors is likely to be the most advanced.

But I have recollections of America beyond those concerned with brewing. I was paying my own expenses during the trip, and accordingly avoided the costlier hotels and unnecessary frivolities. I had been warned against the danger of fire in American hotels and on my first night, when I stayed at an establishment called the 'Saint Denis' (long since demolished), I was careful to ask if I could have a room near the fire escape. The reception clerk said, 'I guess I can fix you up', and I was taken along a passage with notices at intervals—'This way to the Fire Escape'—until we reached a case on the wall in which were fire axes and other tools. Next to this was a door with the notice 'In case of fire, break down this door'. This was the door of my room, so I felt safe!

Before using my introductions in New York, I decided on my arrival to get on a streetcar and ride the full length of the city in order to get the 'feel' of the place. It was a slack time of day, so I was able to chat with the conductor. When I told him I was from London, he said, 'Oh, then you will know my cousin, Pat Daly!' I pointed out that London was even bigger than New York, but he went on: 'You must have met him, he's a fighting man'; and then, oddly enough, I remembered that a few days before I left on this voyage I was taken to the National Sporting Club by that jovial old sportsman, Arthur Wolton, the well-known hop merchant so popular in those days in the brewing trade. While we were in the anteroom there, my host had said to a man, 'How are you, Daly? I wish you luck.' This example of the smallness of the world delighted my conductor friend.

Soon after my return to England the Trade was faced with a local misfortune which caused anxiety to all brewers. There had been an outbreak of illness among beer drinkers in Lancashire which was attributed to a form of arsenic poisoning. On investigation some of the beer sold in the district was found to be contaminated with arsenic in sufficient quantity to be dangerous. The brewers concerned had been using glucose supplied by a firm of sugar manufacturers. Glucose, which has recently, in certain of its forms, become popular with dietitians, is a form of sugar derived from starch obtained from cereals such as rice, by treatment with an acid which is afterwards removed. This particular glucose had been manufactured with an acid produced by a new process involving the use of iron pyrites which contains arsenic, a fact that neither the sugar manufacturers nor the brewers had suspected.

There was something like panic in the brewing trade, although the original trouble was confined to a small area. Throughout the country every brewer hastened to have his beers analysed to make certain there was no contamination. Now arsenic is widely distributed, and occurs to some small extent in many varieties of coal and coke. Many brewers found that although contamination in their beers was negligible they yet contained a trace. It was discovered that materials dried in kilns by direct heat—and these included both malt and hops—were liable to contain slight quantities, and it was then learned that many other foods were affected to some extent. Therefore, a Royal Commission was appointed to investigate the possible degree of contamination in foods generally. Although no legal limit was laid down to control the permissible traces of arsenic in various foods, a recommendation was made that no material containing more than a specified minute quantity should be used as an ingredient, in the manufacture of any food product. Such a recommendation, in fact, assumes the force of law since an excess would be regarded as rendering the food unfit for consumption. Nowadays, with higher standards of laboratory control, there is no danger. Even then the risk was remote, as a story current at the time testifies. A brewer's traveller and a meat salesman were lunching together in a grill room. The butcher pulled the brewer's leg on the vexed subject of arsenic, so the brewer bet his companion five pounds that there was more arsenic in his grilled steak than in the pint of beer. Accordingly the steak and the beer were sent to be analysed. No arsenic was found in the beer, but the steak, having been grilled over an open coke fire, yielded appreciable traces. So the amazed butcher paid up.

I have always felt that the low price at which beer was then being sold, and the pressure to secure economy of production by using the cheapest materials, were responsible for this misfortune. It helped to confirm my conviction that quality and not cheapness is the foundation of success.

In 1899 the prosperity of Brandon's was interrupted. The new brewery had been built to allow for expansion and was capable of brewing more than three times the capacity of the old plant. We found that the cost of brewing the beer was higher than in the old brewery, in which we had been brewing day and night to full capacity, even buying beer at peak periods. Also, the interest on the capital involved in the building of the brewery and the new businesses we had acquired was a heavy charge to be subtracted before the new enterprises began to earn profits. On top of this we were faced with teething troubles, as it were, of the beer itself. However carefully a brewery may be planned, there is always a period of uncertainty. We were forced to reduce our dividend in 1900 from 7½ to 5 per cent. This was a most serious reverse, although we were better off than many of the larger breweries which were passing through a bad time and paying no dividend at all. Energetic action was needed.

So we called in Reginald Mason, of the well-known firm of accountants, Mason and Son. In those days few breweries had any real system of costing and by the end of our investigation I had learnt much about the expenses of running a brewery. One of the factors contributing to loss was our excessive outlay on fuel. My study of this helped me in later years, when I was called upon to advise on national coal economies during the war.

When we had finished the brewery with our own labour, we had retained a considerable number of men on the assumption that they could be usefully employed, but we found that we were wrong; this prejudiced me against works departments. We also realized that the maintenance of sufficient transport to cope with our highest peak periods meant waste during the slack periods of the year. So we cut down both departments, keeping available only sufficient for our normal needs and hiring transport for all peak periods. The stopping of these and other leakages resulted in an economy in production unusual at that time.

In order to surmount our brewing difficulties we called in that doyen of brewing consultants, Dr. Horace R. Brown, F.R.S., who combined high scientific attainments with many years of practical experience. I must have had a weakness for new ideas at that time, for I remember getting Horace Brown to give me an introduction to one of his most successful clients, and before seeing him, I asked Brown what new methods I might expect to find at the brewery. Brown answered, 'My dear Nevile, that brewer never did anything new in his life. That's why you have much to learn from him!' His hint, that originality does not always pay, and that it is usually wise to follow well-established principles, was not lost on me.

In the long run this temporary reverse turned out to be a stroke of that good luck which has consistently attended me. Though harassing at the time, the surmounting of our difficulties resulted in a grasp of economic management and a knowledge of technical brewing which served me well in later years. My study of the fuel problems, for instance, led me to choose 'Fuel Economy' as my theme when, not long after these events, I was asked to read a paper at a meeting of the Institute of Brewing. This was my first appearance there, and as a result of choosing this topic as the 'practical subject' left to my discretion, I found that I had come overnight to be regarded as an expert on fuel problems in the industry.

* * *

Although unable to indulge in those traditional sports of hunting, shooting and fishing which call for abundant leisure and plenty of money, I found time for quite a bit of recreation in other directions. As a boy I tried both cricket and tennis, but my near sight, only partially corrected by glasses, not only prevented my keeping my eye on the ball but often precluded me from seeing it at all. I also took up golf and had lessons from that great master J. H. Taylor of Mid-Surrey; but though I belonged to various clubs for over forty years, I never succeeded in overcoming my hatred of the game. No one can say I didn't give it a fair trial. I subscribed, too, to the Surbiton Beagles, and for a few winters hunted with them; but my real instincts were, as I proved at the age of four, aquatic, and swimming, rowing and sailing attracted me, each in its turn.

Putney was, in a sense, the metropolis of rowing, so I joined the London Rowing Club in 1896 and for ten years or so was a diligent and enthusiastic rowing member, though I achieved no marked success. I rowed for the club at most of the regattas up and down the river, including once or twice at Henley. They told me I was a promising oar, but I did not train well, invariably losing staying power before reaching the condition coaches considered necessary. I often think this was due to 'the family heart' sometimes referred to by doctors when subjecting me to a thorough examination, though in practice that organ has served me well.

In 1904 my cousin Leonard Lucas Tooth (afterwards Sir Leonard) interested me in sailing, and I joined the Tamesis Club at Teddington. The club had no first-class racing craft at that time, so with one Spooner, a New Zealander then secretary of the club, and in partnership with that well-known boat designer Linton Hope, we formed a syndicate and built an 'A'-class boat, *Kia Ora*, to enter in first-class events on the Thames. This was before the days of the Marconi rig, but Linton Hope was advocating the sliding gunter as opposed to the balance lug favoured by the old school, who sailed mostly from the Thames Sailing Club at Surbiton, a couple of miles further up the river. A practical advantage of the gunter was that it permitted of reefing to adjust the sail area to the existing conditions; whereas the balance lug neces-

4. Father Tooth

5. The famous cartoon entitled *The Christian Martyr* by 'Spy'; published in *Vanity Fair* in 1877

6. BRANDON'S BOARD

Arthur J. Brandon
You are very young, I shall expect you to grow out of that

Sydney Foulsham
We must sell cheaply

Chester Foulsham
You know everything. I know one thing, you are wrong.

sitated three different sizes of lugsail which had to be changed to suit the particular day.

Spooner took immense trouble over his design, and boasted valiantly, but his confidence was sadly misplaced as we had a really bad year which we initiated by capsizing in the first race while rounding the distance buoy. The experts hold that success lies first in the efficiency of the crew, next in the set of the canvas; the design of the hull comes third only in importance. Trusting that they were right, we applied ourselves to perfecting our handling, had a fresh set of sails, and re-arranged our rigging, with the result that 1906 proved a really good year, as we won the Queen's Cup at Bourne End Regatta, the great event of the year, in record time, and were in fact the champion boat of the season. We were fortunate in having a reaching wind at Bourne End which suited our design. Years after, I came across an article in the *Yachting Monthly* in which our time was quoted as an instance of specially fast travelling for a small boat; but our performance is long out of date now as the 14-foot National Dinghies succeed in planing under suitable conditions, and would leave us far behind. At the end of that year we sold *Kia Ora* and built another boat, *Moana*, with which, although not as successful as with *Kia Ora*, we had quite a good season, being second at Bourne End.

Our rivals were a wonderful lot of good fellows; one I remember particularly was the eminent artist Sir Arthur Cope, who at that time was painting a portrait of King Edward the Seventh. Troubled to find that a sitting was arranged for the same day as the Queen's Cup Race, he was bold enough to ask if the date could be changed, so that he could compete for the prize given by His Majesty's mother, Queen Victoria. He was informed that 'His Majesty also was a busy man', and the appointment must stand. So Cope had to find a substitute, who was a lesser helmsman.

At the end of the season I felt I needed salt water, and Tooth had acquired other interests, so we broke up the syndicate and I next bought a small four-tonner on the Crouch and found great relaxation in singlehanded cruising with an occasional friend. All this was before the days of the auxiliary engine, which to my mind has sadly impaired the charm and skill of sailing up to one's mooring. Nowadays, engines being general, moorings are laid so close together that sails are lowered and the mooring picked up under power.

For forty years I was never without a craft of some kind, all small, which I handled myself; with the exception of the 40-tonner Dutch Boeier *Maaslust* bought in 1932 which I kept for three years and for which I needed a crew of two . . . Gooding, an old bargee, and his son. Gooding's wife was a fine-looking woman who had been the victim of a wretched, and now notorious, miscarriage of justice: a real tragedy, as she never recovered from it. Living at Littlehampton, she was charged with being responsible for a series of 'poison-pen' postcards, and sentenced to a short term of imprisonment. Soon after her release the offence was repeated by someone and she received a longer sentence. There was yet another repetition, but this time before her release, which led to a more complete investigation, as a result of which the card-writing was found to be the work of an enemy. She received the Royal Pardon and a substantial sum as compensation, but the experience left an indelible mark on her. At least, Gooding attributed her trying temper to her unfortunate experience.

I had five berths on *Maaslust* as well as good accommodation for the crew, and several times entertained guests and took *Maaslust* to her home in Holland, covering much of that country. There is a lot to be said for canal cruising as one need not worry about one's guests' seasickness or about reaching any particular port, as one can tie up wherever one happens to be. As many Dutch speak English there is little trouble over victualling, and I recall only one difficulty of this kind.

I had reached the outskirts of Rotterdam and had nothing for dinner, so I decided to go into town by taxi and buy a chicken. The taxi driver seemed unable to understand my pronunciation of any of the words for 'fowl' or 'chicken' I found in my dictionary, so I tried gesticulation, flapping my arms and saying 'Chuck-chuck'. This did the trick, he indicated understanding, and off we went, stopping before a private house. This did not surprise me, as poulterers' shops are not common in Holland; cockerels are kept alive in a backyard and the buyer points out the one he would rather see dead. However, I was to find that 'chicken' or 'fowl' has an international meaning not then suspected by me. As soon as I had explained my need for a chicken in the best Dutch I could command, the lady who answered the door promptly replied in English, 'Oh yes, I have plenty very nice young ladies!' She was disappointed to learn that I needed only something for dinner, but agreed to come with me to a more appropriate establishment, and made a good selection for me, so that I arrived back on board with a pair of excellent birds of the edible variety.

3

Licensing Laws and Temperance Agitation—Local Option Bill, 1892 *—Refusal of Licences by Justices,* 1901*—Act of* 1904*—Licensing Bill of* 1907*—Budget of* 1908

My first ten or fifteen years in the Trade were employed by me in learning my job and establishing my position. When I touched upon the composition and functions of the principal Trade bodies some pages back, I hinted that almost throughout my working life I should be much concerned with all three of them, but before I enlarge on Trade politics, at this epoch intensely lively, I feel I should paint in their background in even clearer colours. During these closing years of the nineteenth century the temperance party was extremely active; and drunkenness, for a variety of social causes, was depressingly prevalent. Perhaps no business or commercial undertaking has ever been quite as severely hedged about by restrictive legislation as ours has been, so constantly faced with propaganda directed towards its extinction.

Anything like a full résumé of English licensing laws would be inappropriate here; not only would it take up too much room, it would also be too technical to be generally interesting. Nevertheless, it is important to realize that public-house legislation has more than four hundred years of complicated history. Broadly speaking, we may say that the control and administration of public houses, the principal outlet for the brewers' products, dates from the Act of 1828, which operated with few important modifications until the war of 1914–18. But to say this is not to imply that no further legislation was suggested during those ninety odd years. Hardly a parliamentary session passed without some Bill being introduced to affect (and usually to attack) either the brewers or the public house. The efforts of the temperance bodies were unremitting, some reflecting moderate shades of opinion which envisaged such reforms as any reasonable person would support, some echoing the fanatical prohibitionist whose state of mind is summed up in a line from a poem by A. P. Herbert: 'Let's stop somebody from doing something!' There were, of course, people with temperance views on both sides of the House; but in the main hostile legislation was supported by the Liberal Party—the so-called Party of reform—while the brewers' interests were suspected to be the affair of the Conservative Party. So the Trade was concerned in a fight for life and adopted the negative policy of defence rather than such development of its service to the community as would put it beyond reproach. This defensive attitude was contrary to my ideas. My own principal interest has always been to foster the constructive policy of improvement and good service, which in the long run is the only sound basis of commercial success.

The first weeks of my pupilage as a brewer saw the beginnings of a legal test case which, when decided by the House of Lords, affected the status and prospects of all licensed property and eventuated in legislation and stormy political struggles during the early years of the twentieth century. This was the celebrated case of Sharpe *v.* Wakefield, and it arose from the refusal of the local magistrates, in the autumn of 1887, to renew the licence of one small wayside inn. For many years it had been assumed that a licence, once granted, would be renewed each year subject to good conduct. Values had been based, and many millions of capital had been invested, on that assumption. This case was to decide whether the Justices could refuse to renew the licence of a well-conducted house. If the Justices could refuse licences at their discretion a local bench might destroy much of a brewer's business by a stroke of the pen, and bring ruin on those whose living depended on the continuity of the business; or it could even go so far as to establish local prohibition.

It might appear that the danger of this was remote, but in fact it did not seem so to those immediately threatened. The licensing benches are composed of Justices of the Peace. No one connected with the Trade is allowed to sit at licensing sessions, but there is nothing to stop the most bigoted prohibitionist from acting and exercising his influence, with the result that many benches allowed prejudice against the Trade to outweigh their judicial impartiality. The effect of a decision confirming justices' right to do so would therefore place a new and effective weapon in their armoury, for previously they had been uncertain of the full extent of their powers. The case went from court to court and eventually reached the House of Lords, on 30th January, 1891, before the Lord Chancellor (Lord Halsbury) and four learned Lords. Judgement was delivered on the 20th of March, and the appeal was dismissed. It was decided that the justices had absolute discretion to refuse licences as they thought fit.

There was much alarm in the Trade at this result and great delight among prohibitionists and the temperance movement in general, though in fact justices did not make any substantial exercise of their power of refusal until the end of the century. The year 1892 saw Gladstone victorious in a general election—the last victory of that long career—and a year later the Liberals introduced the hard-fought Intoxicating Liquor Traffic (Local Control) Bill, which came to be known as the 'Veto Bill'. The Bill gave powers under which, if ten persons in a licensing area so demanded, a poll of residents could be taken to determine whether it was the wish of the majority that the sale of drink should be totally prohibited within their particular licensing area. This came to be known as 'local option'.

Local option was not a new idea in the early 'nineties, for Sir Wilfrid Lawson and other of his more fanatical temperance supporters had been agitating for it since the 'seventies. In 1880 a resolution in favour had been passed in the House of Commons. The principle of local option has always been supported by the ardent militant temperance party, as a stage towards total prohibition. It could be advocated as an apparently democratic measure enabling the inhabitants in each district to decide for themselves whether they wanted public houses or not. But there was a more subtle ground for support. The insecurity created by local option, by which all licensed houses in a neighbourhood might be swept out of business by the chance of a local vote, would on the one hand effectively discourage the investment of capital in public houses, and on the other prevent the entry into the Trade of satisfactory tenants and employees. Who would take up a career with so uncertain a future? The phrase 'the best public house is the worst public house' became common at temperance meetings. A great church dignitary at one temperance convention frankly stated that their object was to 'throw such odium on the Trade that no respectable man would willingly enter it'.

There was one popular objection to local option: that only those districts would 'go dry' in which a majority of voters had their own private cellars (and private cellars were far more numerous then than today). This led to the popular use of the old cry 'One law for the rich and another for the poor'. The opposition to the Bill was so great among the general public that it was quietly dropped from the Government programme, although its sponsors and supporters did not renounce its principles.

The law itself was a complex one, and its administration was further complicated by conflicting opinion among the Trade, the public, and organized temperance. Accordingly, the Government of Lord Salisbury and Mr. Balfour appointed a Royal Commission in 1896, under these comprehensive terms of reference: 'To inquire into the operation and administration of the laws relating to the sale of intoxicating liquor, and to examine and report upon the proposals that may be made for amending the aforesaid laws in the public interest, due regard being had to the rights of individuals'. The Commission consisted of twenty-four members, representing equally the interests of the Trade, the temperance movement, and 'the public'—the last being the open-minded section between two apparent irreconcilables. The Commission sat for a hundred and twenty-three days, spread over rather more than two years, and heard evidence from more than two hundred and fifty witnesses. In 1899 it issued its report or, rather, two: a majority report and a minority (signed by the chairman, Lord Peel), came at a time when the Government were preoccupied with the Boer War, so nothing happened.

In 1901 the justices began to act decisively on the powers given them by the Sharpe *v.* Wakefield judgement and to refuse the renewal of many licences throughout the country. As a result, a deputation from the Trade had talks with Mr. Balfour which led to the Act of 1904.

This Act recognized that there were in many places more licensed houses than were needed: but that a sporadic or wholesale reduction would cause a sense of insecurity amongst owners and licensees which would end in lower standards of service. Accordingly, the Act introduced the principle that renewal of existing well-conducted licences should not be refused without compensation. Where the number of licences was regarded as excessive by the justices, the owners and tenants of those selected for extinction should be compensated from a fund levied by the justices on all the licensed houses in the district. When a new licence was granted, the holder should pay a sum, termed 'monopoly value', which would be agreed between the justices and the Inland Revenue. These new licences did not contribute to the compensation levy, and were not entitled to compensation in the event of a subsequent refusal.

Although in fact the cost of compensation fell on the owners and occupiers of licensed premises, the Trade's opponents, who had hoped to secure a wholesale refusal of licences, were infuriated by the Act, which they called the 'Brewers' Endowment Bill'. On the other hand, the retailers who resented having to contribute towards compensation dubbed it the 'Mutual Burial Fund'.

The 1904 Act was no unmixed blessing to the brewers, nevertheless it was heartily condemned by the Liberal opposition, who resented what they insisted was the creation of a vested interest in the right of renewal. They gave notice that they would take their revenge as soon as they returned to power, as they did in 1906 by a large majority which owed nothing to their licensing policy. Within a year they had tabled the Licensing Bill of 1907 which, with various minor provisions, limited the right of renewal of licences to a period of fourteen years and provided for local option

"HITTING THE HAPPY MEAN."

Licensing Bill. "OH! MY FRIENDS! MY FRIENDS! DON'T HIT ME! I COME BETWEEN YOU AS A PEACEMAKER!"

at the end of that period. If this had passed into law it would have been nothing less than an act of confiscation, as public houses had been valued on the assumption that their licences would, subject to good conduct, be for all practical purposes permanent. The Bill would have destroyed the security on which many millions of public money stood invested. Moreover the prospect of local option after fourteen years would have precluded improvement, and would have ensured a deterioration in the standard of service. So naturally, strong opposition was to be expected from the Trade, but the Bill also aroused powerful resentment in other quarters. The financial world recognized this as a first instalment of confiscation on a large scale, likely to threaten the security of many industries in which public money was invested.

But the most startling opposition came from the general public and was expressed in agitation up and down the country, agitation which took dozens of unmistakable forms. There was a great outcry in the press, letters streamed in from all corners of the land to Members of Parliament, protest meetings were held; posters and speeches and resolutions added in their various ways to the strong chorus of condemnation of this bad bill. It became abundantly apparent that the people of this country were not willing to submit to the threat of prohibition, and the Government must have been astonished at the turmoil that resulted. As for the Trade, a monster rally was organized in Hyde Park, and special trains were run to London from all over the country on the 27th of September, 1908. My own share in the rally was a small one, but I look back on it with pleasure, for the occasion was an historic one. I led a contingent of about two hundred and fifty of our own staff and workpeople from the Putney brewery, including some of our publicans and local traders. We were soon swallowed up among more than half a million people in Hyde Park that day: I believe the greatest number ever assembled there.

One immediate result was the decision—based on the probability of bankruptcy—that all possible expenditure should be curtailed until the effects of the Bill (provided the Bill were passed) were known. 'All possible expenditure' quite obviously included the subscriptions customarily made by brewers to charitable bodies. Most directors suspended these on the ground that they had no right to give away money which did not belong to them. When the Archbishop of Canterbury reproved us for this in the House of Lords, I wrote my first letter to *The Times* and reproved him!

A friend of mine, a partner in a neighbouring brewery at Battersea, persuaded me to join him in writing a pamphlet on the improvement of public houses and the evils of local option. Soon *A Bow at a Venture* by Fred G. Thorne and Sydney O. Nevile appeared on the bookstalls and, although hardly a 'best-seller', the little pamphlet aroused enough public interest to achieve a sale of several thousand copies. As a local brewer known to be active in opposing the Bill, I was persuaded to appear at protest meetings in the South-West of London. I also went to meetings organized by the Liberals in support of the Bill. At one of these I contradicted the speaker, the Hon. Geoffrey Howard (who was not a teetotaller himself, but who supported the Bill as a good Liberal), and was invited on to the platform to speak, in the hope that my presence there might save his supporters from attack by the hostile audience.

I doubt if any Bill has been met with such a fury of opposition. During the Bill's progress through the House there were several by-elections, all of which the Government lost by crushing majorities. There was an exciting one at Peckham, where the seat was taken from the Government by a majority of several thousand. The successful candidate went to Manchester to support another triumphant fight against the Government. Here the Government candidate was no other than Winston Churchill.

In the general election Winston Churchill had been elected as a Liberal, having left the Conservative party only a few months before, and he had then defeated William Joynson-Hicks, later Lord Brentford, by a handsome majority. (It is a measure of the seriousness of the Tory landslide of 1906 that, whereas all six Manchester seats had been Tory strongholds, in this election the whole lot were lost to the Liberals.) But the by-election of 1908 saw a very different state of affairs. By this time the Liberals had antagonized the whole country by their Licensing Bill and by other measures (including a highly controversial Education measure). The promotion of Churchill to Cabinet rank (he was appointed President of the Board of Trade in the Cabinet re-shuffle following the resignation of the Prime Minister, Sir Henry Campbell-Bannerman) made it necessary, as the law then stood, for him to offer himself for re-election. On such occasions it had been common for no opposition to be offered, but the mood of the people was such that they welcomed the chance to get another Liberal out. Joynson-Hicks was not the man to disappoint them; he too had political scores to settle. And so the teetotal 'Jix' was found in opposition to the teetotal Bill, as represented by Churchill, who found himself defeated by a substantial majority. When the Bill went to the Lords it was thrown out. The public disapproval of this Bill was so marked that the Government abandoned it, but they did not abandon their antagonism to the Trade, an antagonism which was increased under the smart of this defeat, while the rage of the prohibitionists was comparable to that of wild beasts deprived of their kill.

So far as the Trade was concerned the opposition was organized by Frank Whitbread, Chairman of the National Trade Defence Association, and William Waters Butler, then Chairman of the Brewers' Society. Butler was a member of the great Birmingham firm of Mitchells and Butlers; he afterwards received a baronetcy for public services in that city and in the country generally. I was much associated with both these public-spirited men in later years and I shall have something more to say of them.

The Government, who blamed the Trade, was determined to get its revenge. In the Budget of 1908 a crushing increase in licence duties was imposed, designed to cripple both licensees and brewers. Up to that time the maximum was £60 for the largest houses, but under the new scheme each house must pay duty representing one half of its assessment. This amounted in many cases to several hundreds of pounds.

The London brewers were particularly hard hit. Not only were their houses situated in valuable positions, where assessments were high, but they were selling beer of a higher gravity and at a lower average price than elsewhere. Accordingly, their profits were small, and indeed many of them were not paying any ordinary dividend at all in those lean years. In this emergency the London brewers agreed on what then appeared to be the desperate expedient of raising the price of beer from fourpence to fivepence a quart! To meet the traditional demand for a drink for one penny, five glasses at a penny a glass were to be served from each quart, instead of the customary four. It was this novel proposal that led me to enter a wider sphere of Trade politics.

Brandon's lay just outside the London area most affected by the increase in licence duties. We owned many off-licences which were not thus affected, our on-licensed houses were mostly in country districts on the outskirts, and we had only a few highly assessed houses in London. Nevertheless, we decided to support our larger London friends. Then three days before the new prices were to come into effect, I discovered that our next-door brewery company at Kingston had no intention of joining the movement, and hoped to benefit by underselling its neighbours. This raised a difficulty, for our houses were cheek-by-jowl with theirs over a large area of Surrey and Middlesex. We felt we could not join in a battle of prices, and I had to tell the London brewers that we could only co-operate where the increase in price was general. We agreed that we would maintain the price where there was no competitive undercutting. As a result, I was asked to join the organizing committee, which brought me into contact with the 'big noises'.

The brewery that refused to co-operate was a smallish concern at Kingston. It happened that a Croydon brewery also had interests in the area. The Croydon brewers disagreed with me and declared that they were not going to be intimidated by the brewery at Kingston. In the event, prices were maintained in the area I had agreed; but the Croydon brewers found their tenants in the area so dissatisfied with the competition from Kingston that they quickly surrendered and withdrew from the scheme altogether. On the whole, I felt that at Brandon's we had come out of the affair with credit; we had kept faith with our friends in the Trade, and at the same time, by supplying an article of high quality, we had served the public well—and reaped the reward which this merited.

More than one piquant incident of these days is still remembered by old-timers. The brewers' proposal to arrange with the publicans to meet the cost of increased licensed duties by raising the price of beer from fourpence to fivepence a quart resulted in quite a furore at the time: the cost had remained stable for generations and the 'fourpenny' was indeed an established and important element in the pattern of life among the industrial classes. Not unnaturally, this proposal was much canvassed as a political issue, and interpreted as an attempt by the brewers to discredit the Liberal Party; as such, it was roundly denounced by Lloyd George in his notorious Limehouse speech, in which he attacked the brewers and the landowners. This campaign was not without its interesting and even amusing happenings. There was, for example, one free publican running a large house who was buying his beer at cut prices, and who decided he would utilize the political prejudice to increase his business by underselling his neighbours. Other publicans in the neighbourhood felt that he should not get away entirely with this profit-making device, so two competing houses decided to follow his example.

The Limehouse speech, with its ample press notices, attracted wide attention, with the result that charabancs (at that time horse-drawn) were driven in from surrounding districts to the propitious neighbourhood, and carried price and destination labels which read 'Sixpence all the way to cheap beer'.

One hot June evening I went there too, and found a horde of people bivouacking in groups on some waste land, each party equipped with stone jars which a numerous staff carried back to the public house for refilling as soon as the parties emptied them. Before long, extra police had to be drafted into the neighbourhood to check the growing disorder, a disorder which increased in intensity until the problem was solved by the Lords throwing out the Budget and the price of beer returning to normal.

Another intriguing incident occurred at Shepherds Bush, where a lady also running a large house discovered a glass which had every appearance of holding half a pint although it actually held no more than a fifth of a quart. Her immediate neighbours in the Trade complained to their local Licensed Victuallers' Society and invoked the aid of the brewers owning the house, whereupon the lady brought an action for slander against several of her detractors and even subpoenaed certain members of the committee organizing the master scheme to give evidence on her behalf. This trouble too was settled by the benevolent action of the House of Lords.

The result of this punitive Budget was not exactly what the Liberals expected. As often happens when undue taxation is imposed on one section of the community, other sections suffer. In this case the local authorities found themselves faced with a serious loss of revenue from the rates. It was discovered, much to the relief of the publicans, that the increased licence duty entitled them to corresponding reductions in their assessments, since the annual value of the house would be depreciated by the increase in duty. This annoyed the radical-controlled London councils who saw not only the hated publicans escaping the full force of the attack directed against them, but also saw a considerable slice of local rates being diverted into Government coffers. When the Budget went to the Lords they threw it out, as in the case of the 1907 Bill. The result was the celebrated Parliament Act of 1909, which defined and restricted the power of the Lords over the Commons, and the Finance Bill was passed in 1909. Meanwhile the relief resulting from the lower assessment was found to be so substantial that the London brewers, who had abandoned the price increase when the Finance Bill was thrown out by the Lords, decided that it was not necessary to attempt to raise prices again.

As on other occasions this Trade difficulty had resulted in my making friendships and contacts which served me well in later years.

4

My interest in improvement of Public Houses—Pattern of Public Opinion—The Trust Movement—Individual Instances of Improvement—Westminster Gazette—Presidency of Ealing and Brentford Licensed Victuallers' Association—Instance of Bad Old-fashioned Tenant—Early Technical Education for Licensed Trade 1910 *and onwards—*Morning Advertiser *interview,* 1913

I suppose everyone who looks back on a busy life finds some things in it by which he would best like to be remembered. My own seventy years of work have brought me into close touch with almost every side of a complex industry. The recollection I find most rewarding is of the share I have taken in promoting the policy of public house improvement, with its consequent influence on sobriety, as well as on the reputation and profitability of the 'local' in particular and the brewing industry in general.

It was the Licensing Bill of 1907 which caused me furiously to think. I came to the conclusion that the political difficulties of the Trade had two main sources: one was the prevalence of drunkenness and the other the failure of public house management to move with the times. I had some sympathy with both criticisms.

My practice of visiting the brewery at Putney each night entailed my passing public houses on Saturdays at closing time (then midnight), and I became more and more concerned at the evidence of drunkenness and disorder which was too often obvious at 'turning out time', and I began to understand the depth of prejudice against the Trade which had led the social workers to propound their policy of prohibition as the only solution. I also appreciated the force of the criticism, becoming more and more general, of the low average standard of public houses in working class districts and of their failure to supply a more varied range of refreshments. My conviction grew that unless the Trade could improve the general standard of these houses, prejudice was justifiable; and that higher standards and better surroundings would of themselves encourage sobriety.

These ideas were even then not entirely new. The terms 'reform' and 'ideals' were current, but neither word seemed to be right: 'reform' was too sanctimonious and 'ideal' unattainable. So my thoughts ran in the direction of improvement, development and progress as a more practical indication of what was needed if the Trade were to surmount its difficulties. If one takes the long view, as every responsible citizen should, it is clear that the only solid foundation for the prosperity of an industry is the quality of service it can render. I like to think that the present prosperity of the brewing business during recent years is evidence of the truth of this principle.

Opinion throughout the Trade was that drunkenness was deplorable but inevitable, no practical remedy could be suggested, and one prominent member of a great brewery argued, when an approach to the Government was suggested, that it was not the business of the Trade, but of the Government, to frame proposals, which the industry could accept or contest as seemed suitable. But at that time measures brought before Parliament were purely restrictive; their aim was not to promote sobriety but to repress the Trade and deprive the public of its services. Repression does not decrease drunkenness: as we were later to learn from America's gallant Prohibition experiment.

As I revolved this problem in my mind, I came to the conclusion *that there was no conflict between the permanent commercial interest of the brewing trade and the best interests of the public.* Before I develop the principle of this assertion, let us look at the position a little more closely, as I saw it then.

The pattern of public opinion in those days was complex and not too easy to explain. Militant social reformers held that drunkenness was the greatest social evil; they had concentrated on the policy of prohibition of all forms of alcohol as the only permanent cure. But the great mass of the people were not greatly interested; they regarded alcoholic beverages as part of their diet. Even among thoughtful people there was a curious apathy. It seems to have been felt that some degree of drunkenness was a corollary of civilization, increasing and diminishing according to certain known factors, such as degree of prosperity, conditions of work, housing, etc. So the reformers concentrated on total abstinence as their objective: socially, through such bodies as the Salvation Army, the Blue Ribbonites and other smaller organizations; and politically, under the banner of such bodies as 'The United Kingdom Alliance', a militant organization formed in 1853 to 'secure the total and immediate legislative suppression of the traffic in intoxicating liquors as beverages'. In 1884 the more vigorous organizations were federated under 'The National Temperance Council', a powerful political force with much influence not only in Parliament but on licensing benches. There were more moderate advocates, but the militant bodies dominated the so-called temperance movement.

As the function of the Trade was to supply 'intoxicating liquor' (what a damnable term) to the community, it was naturally opposed to prohibition; and since the licensing law was mainly restrictive, was driven into defending itself when attacked. I argued to myself that drunkenness, apart from being an evil in itself, could not be profitable in the long run since it impaired earning power and thus impoverished the very classes upon whom the Trade depended for its prosperity. So at a meeting of brewers held to consider the unsatisfactory condition of the Trade in 1908, I bluntly declared my opinions: that brewers could make more money out of 'England sober' than 'England drunken'; that they should not leave 'temperance reform' to the prohibitionists; and that they should face the problem not merely as a matter of conscience but also on grounds of commercial interest.

This was a point of view so novel that my friends were taken aback. Most of them regarded drunkenness as regrettable and a great inconvenience to the Trade; yet how, they wondered, could sobriety, which necessarily meant a lower intake, be made to pay? I was actually contending that sobriety was commercially, as well as socially, desirable. Time has proved me right, but in those days I was looked upon as a bit of a crank. As the witty prohibitionist Sir Wilfrid Lawson used to say: 'Those who advocate reforms are first called mad, then bad, and then . . . everybody knew it before!'

The average industrial public house of 1907 was notably inferior to its counterpart today. There were exceptions, but in the main, since it was licensed to sell exciseable drinks, little interest was taken in other refreshments. Its customers were almost all men. The relatively few women who used it were written off as *déclassées*. But there was a growing opinion that the public houses ought to cater for the supply of other refreshments beside beer and spirits, and should be suitable for women and perhaps children, too, much as in France. However, the extreme temperance party vigorously and usually successfully opposed any attempt to improve the standards of service; they were still alleging that 'The best public house is the worst public house'. Their aim was the total discrediting of the public house, which they even sometimes referred to as 'the citadel of Satan'.

I had seen something of the influence of women as a moderating factor. I was then wine secretary to my rowing club (where I was known as 'Bung'), and I had noticed that behaviour was much better at those functions to which ladies were admitted after a regatta, than when there were only men. I believed that something similar would apply in public houses. Though efforts to supply solid meals in ordinary pubs had not been very successful, partly owing to licensing restrictions, some progressive traders were doing well with light refreshments. This was a potential source of income which might far outweigh any decrease in takings resulting from a decline in drunkenness. By improving our houses and our services we stood to attract new customers and broaden the basis of our trade. I was convinced that the brewers needed a *constructive* instead of a defensive policy; that it was foolish and indeed wrong to wait for attack and never put forward alternative proposals.

The 'Trust' Movement

The 'Trust' movement, originated by moderate temperance opinion, interested me. It had been suggested as a compromise: envisaging not prohibition, but houses catering in enlightened fashion for the genuine needs of the public. It was particularly opposed to the tied house. Its promoters considered that the 'profit motive' was the main obstacle to the temperance movement, and thus regarded the ownership of public houses by brewers, then rapidly increasing, as fundamentally opposed to social reform; and they refused to co-operate with brewers or to lease houses from them. They supported what they termed 'disinterested management', that is to say, the principle that those concerned with the control or management of houses should have no interest in the sale of alcohol. The movement was established on the basis that the dividends for those who provided the capital should be limited to five per cent, and that the houses should be conducted by managers who should receive commission on food and soft drinks and none on intoxicants. The promoters also hoped to obtain from the licensing benches concessions usually denied to the Trade, if they showed themselves to be independent of brewers. A great deal was made of the fact that their houses supplied tea and refreshments, in the hope that licensing benches would be more ready to give permission for alterations and improvements to them than to ordinary traders.

Perhaps the earliest example of a Trust was the People's Refreshment House Association, founded in 1896 under the inspiration of the Bishop of Chester 'to manage licensed houses on reformed lines'. This Association is still very much alive and now controls a hundred and fifty-nine houses in Britain. At the beginning of the century Lord Grey initiated a series of public meetings and other activities to promote the 'Public House Trust' system, which was to be organized by counties. Each county association was to acquire and manage houses within its own area on a non-profit making basis (except for the five per cent interest on the capital invested), and the main profits were to be devoted to improving the premises. In order to demonstrate their sincerity they refused to accept tenancies of brewery-owned houses and would sometimes even refuse to sell the local brewer's beers, preferring to obtain supplies from a distance. Despite this rather hostile attitude, the Trusts did not meet with antagonism from most brewers; it was often far otherwise. Indeed, it is said that one Hertfordshire brewer regularly supplied two barrels of water to 'The Wagon and Horses' at Ridge Hill, Hertfordshire, when that inn ran short during a time of drought.

In 1919 the Hertfordshire Trust broke away from the official Trust movement and became Trust Houses Limited. They decided to rent houses from brewers and run them on the same lines as the free houses they had secured. Although they bought beer from brewer-owners, they refused to enter into a formal tie—a principle they maintain to this day. Later, when faced with commercial difficulties and realizing the need for efficient as well as philanthropic control, they went further and secured the services of two prominent members of the Trade, Thomas Skurray, later chairman of the Brewers' Society, a distinguished man of the highest principles, and a well-known London publican, William Coxen (later Sir William Coxen, Lord Mayor of London). Under their direction the company re-established its finances and consolidated its position; it now controls more than two hundred hotels and public houses. It is now perhaps the largest and best-known group of modest hotels in the country. Although originally founded merely to operate public houses on improved lines, Trust Houses have given much attention of late years to many old and historic inns which had been allowed through neglect to fall into disrepair. They have displayed great ability—almost genius—in restoring and equipping with period furniture many famous old inns which might otherwise have disappeared.

Having adopted the constructive policy of improvement as a principle, I discovered several men in the Trade whose thoughts were moving in the same direction; they included such men as Edwyn Barclay, Frank Whitbread, Cecil Lubbock and Frank Mason of Charrington's. Several breweries were making tentative experiments on their own, but we were all hampered by the restrictive policies of licensing benches, and no concrete move was possible. Whitbread's had formed a company to establish a co-operative kitchen to supply many of their houses with cooked food;

but they found it impossible to secure permission from the licensing authorities to provide the necessary facilities, and had to abandon the venture after losing some £50,000.

Some smaller concerns like my own were rebuilding their houses on improved lines when opportunity occurred. Fuller, Smith and Turner of Chiswick, another family concern, built the well-known 'Clarendon' at Hammersmith, which is still a large catering establishment. The Brentford Brewery had established friendly relations with a broad-minded bench and were steadily rebuilding their small village houses; they issued a pamphlet under the title 'Drink your beer in better houses'. The celebrated Birmingham scheme of 'fewer and better' was also under way. Thanks to co-operation and understanding between the brewers' association (led by William Waters Butler), and the licensing authorities, a new system of redistribution of licences was evolved. Old and unneeded licences in the city were surrendered in exchange for new licences in the outer ring of new housing estates, often in the ratio of two or three to one.

I was especially interested in an experiment made by Charrington's in the south-east of London. They had persuaded the justices to allow them to enlarge one of their properties, by way of experiment. The new house was divided into two parts, each approximately the size of the property replaced; one half was a large lounge with ordinary bars according to customary practice; the other was devoted to the sale of soft drinks and refreshments only, with a door connecting with the ordinary bars. Thus a man could take his family into the refreshment half, then walk through into the bars and either meet his friends or bring his drink back and sit with his family. Like other experiments, it proved somewhat before its time and had to be modified, but it was a striking contribution to the movement. A small point intrigued me—and I hope it will prove my point that 'improvement' involved several unexpected considerations—for I noticed that the chairs were of rather Spartan model, and asked if something more relaxing would not be preferable. The reply was that in a house of that size supervision was difficult; the usual procedure was for one of a group to come up to the bar and carry back drinks to the rest; it would not be easy to judge the condition of a customer if he were lounging on a sofa.

There were in fact quite a number of us doing what we could to promote improvement. In spite of the conservatism of the Trade on the one hand and the obstructive attitude of most licensing authorities on the other, we battled on, and the Press was sometimes sympathetic. In 1906 I wrote a letter to the *Daily Telegraph* which touched off a little burst of controversy showing, if nothing else, that people were beginning to take an interest. My letter was enlarged upon by the editor of the serious newspaper of those days, *The Westminster Gazette*: I was interviewed and then the paper published an article under big headlines, 'Beer Plus "A.B.C.".' This article was really a symposium, for it covered interviews with brewers, licensed victuallers, temperance workers and so on, wherein each ventilated his own opinion and ignored my original suggestion. One temperance man said, 'This is an excuse to get more people into public houses and to make it easier for them to drink'; another, 'Many people would go in for beer under the pretence of going in for tea and cake'; and another, 'We were expecting the move, and know how to meet it'. The magistrates interviewed said that this was an old dodge to get a poor and inconvenient house rebuilt and thus increased in value; the undertaking to serve refreshments would be soon forgotten, and the result would merely be a large increase in the sales of beer. The brewers, for their part, complained that they were prevented by the magistrates from improving facilities. Every party to the argument found one or several other parties blameworthy. Still, the letter and even the 'follow-up' article had done good by leading to exchange of ideas (as well as of recriminations) and, not least, to clarification of my own.

In 1908 I accepted the Presidency of the Ealing and Brentford Licensed Victuallers' Association, which covered a large area in the South-west of London. I decided to strike a constructive note in my speech at their annual dinner, as a change from the usual sustained lamentation. I reminded my hearers that goodwill was the foundation of good business, and that the best defence against aggression was good service. I suggested that the Trade should exert itself to win favourable public opinion and not limit itself to complaining of injustice. I concluded in a rather florid after-dinner style by declaiming that a policy directed to improved service 'would bring the friendship and respect of our fellow countrymen, the security of our business, and the prosperity of our Trade'. This was my first public advocacy of a constructive policy; it was widely quoted in Trade circles and, I believe, helped to dissipate some of the current lethargy.

I remember among the incidents of that night that the lusty Tory Sir William Bull, M.P., replying to the toast for Parliament, gave us his own considered reply to the topical enquiry: 'To what good object would you apply the £400 per annum recently voted by Parliament to its members?' His sturdy answer was 'To William Bull, the best object I know!'—a statement symptomatic of his hearty 'Britishism'. I recollect, too, that my subscription list on this occasion showed a sum falling short by a few pounds of the record amount collected by my predecessor, Henry Pullman of the Isleworth Brewery. This being so, I asked if anyone would give me another tenner and enable me to establish a new record . . . upon which Henry Pullman brought down the house by shouting 'I'll give it myself'. Altogether it was voted a good evening, and I was satisfied with my first public appearance which I had approached with so much trepidation.[1]

I further examined the economic aspect. Would sobriety reduce profits? If so, however much we might lessen general prejudice, we could not expect wholehearted support from those responsible to the Trade's shareholders. I have already explained that drunkenness, apart from being a social evil and consequently the source of our political difficulties, was to my mind a commercial misfortune, and I once again put this novel notion before a meeting of brewers in which we were considering some particular difficulties which had arisen. Some of my conscientious friends now felt that I was over-emphasizing the commercial aspect, but I was often to find myself an object of suspicion; accused now of hypocrisy, now of insincerity, now of being a crank. As a matter of honesty and a

[1] While correcting these proofs I have received an invitation to attend the Annual Dinner of the Ealing and Brentford Society and thus celebrate the 50th anniversary of my chairmanship.

means of self-protection I had frequently to insist that my opinions were partly a matter of conscience and partly a declaration of sound policy in the interests of shareholders in brewery companies and of brewers themselves. Reduced to its simplest form, my conclusion was this: Sobriety is socially desirable and therefore in our country's interests; sobriety will pay, and is therefore in the interests of the Trade—thus there is no conflict.

However, critics were numerous and vociferous. The prohibitionists attacked me openly, and so did the more conservative types in the Trade and among the customers. They argued that the pub corresponded to just the bar, the bar only, in hotels, where there was no demand or need for general refreshment; that the industrial classes, like the animal kingdom, had their evening meal and later needed their drink; that it was the brewers' function to supply beer, not to interfere with the retail trade by telling them how to run their business, and so on.

Again, there was the opinion of one of our most experienced political members: he held that it was 'not the function of an industry to suggest to Parliament how it should be governed, but to await proposed legislation, to support it if good and oppose it if bad; for the Trade to initiate legislation was merely to invite trouble by admitting shortcomings'. This was all very well, but since the only legislation ever proposed was inspired by its opponents, the Trade found itself constantly on the defensive. Nevertheless, our small group was always ready to support 'what was good', favouring various Bills designed to ease and encourage public house development. Throughout these difficult years I seized every opportunity for advocating the idea that such improvement was sound business, a worthwhile investment, not merely propaganda.

A major consideration in those days was the comparatively low standard of the workers engaged in the public houses, which were open from 5.30 a.m. right through to 12.30 a.m. Employment was uncertain, most of the work was casual, unskilled and ill-paid.

Yet another difficulty was attributable to the general scarcity of skilled tenants. When applications for licences were being considered by the justices, the most scrupulous attention was paid to personal character and reputation, but none whatsoever was directed to fitness for the job based on training or even aptitude. Such matters seemed to be quite beyond the concern of either legislation or licensing authorities. How, in the face of such indifference, could a start be made towards establishing the principle that the retail trader should regard his work as a calling demanding training, study and skill: in a word, a lifelong career; and not, as so many saw it, an unexacting, light occupation for a man's retirement with the opportunity to pass on the 'real work' to a band of casual, unskilled cellarmen and barmen?

I had a gruesome experience which illustrates how far from my ideal were some aspirants for posts of responsibility. We had built a large and expensive house to replace a worn-out building, and it was important to us to install a tenant with sufficient capital and experience to run a large business. A broker brought us a client, a member of a well-known retailer's family, who, we were assured, knew the business inside and out and could boast a long and unblemished record. We soon had reason to be dissatisfied: we did not like his methods. He became unable to meet his obligations, his account fell much in arrears, and he pressed for better terms. I had a heart-to-heart talk with him and we quickly found ourselves at cross purposes. He wound up the conversation with the remark that no man knew the trade better or could work harder than he. 'I drink,' he said, 'between fifty and sixty whiskies every day, and no man can do more than that, I don't care who he is!' We agreed to part company, and secured a tenant with vastly different ideas of conducting the business and whose methods were more in accordance with our principles. Both he and his wife had good experience and were keen on catering, treated their staff with consideration, almost as members of their family, and above all made it a rule never to drink with a customer or to lend money. We soon had reason to be gratified with our selection; the business rapidly improved both in volume and character, and our tenant met his obligations to us and indeed paid a better rent than his predecessor. He was so successful that he saved sufficient money to be able to retire after a few years, but not before he had introduced as his successor a friend who continued the business with equal success. This worthy tenant reinforced my faith in the future of constructive ideas. I learnt much from him and used to consult him in matters to do with the retail trade.

It was obviously useless to improve premises, with the idea of better service, if the licensee and his helpers were not prepared to march with the times. In the old days it used to be said that anybody could keep a public house, but the business of a licensed victualler nowadays is in many ways highly technical. He must have a wide variety of complicated restrictions clear in his mind; he must have technical skill in handling beers and wines; he must know all about storing and serving food and drink. One of the brewers' chief problems, for example, is to ensure that his beer reaches the customer in good condition. And so it came to pass that I initiated a discussion at the Institute of Brewing (it was in 1911, I remember, the year in which I became chairman of the London section) with the rather formidable title: 'On the Desirability of Applying Greater Technical Knowledge to the Cellar Management and Retailing of Beer'. I seemed to have struck oil—indeed, midnight oil: as the discussion looked like going on all night. The practical brewers deplored the inexpert handling of their products, which could never be made fool-proof; and the commercial managers present, although admitting that much was wrong could not suggest practicable remedies. When the Institute's Journal reprinted this discussion, it occupied almost a record number of pages—sufficient evidence that I had hit upon an important and so far neglected subject. This success encouraged me to go on with a project which had been forming in my mind for some time. We should, I argued, organize a proper training scheme for the staff in the retail licensed trade.

At first sight the obvious course would seem to be a collective scheme organized by one of the Trade bodies, but the proposal was at that time too revolutionary to be acceptable. Those who were most concerned were the technical brewers, who were troubled if the commodity they had taken so much trouble to produce was mishandled in the retailer's cellar. But the control of the public house was not in their hands, being the responsibility of the commercial management (and, as with so many other industries, there was not cheerful co-operation between production and selling departments).

If the brewers pressed for better conditions and more highly-skilled work in cellars, the outside management, having no technical knowledge, too often considered that the brewer should just produce good beer and leave its distribution to them; they also feared the resentment of old-fashioned retailers who would take amiss any criticism of established customs.

There were other points to bear in mind. I was convinced of the need for extending the trading of the licensed house beyond the mere sale of excisable drinks. Consequently, any scheme of training should be more comprehensive than would be likely if it were organized by the brewing interests. Although some of my friends agreed with me, it was not possible at that time to secure whole-hearted support for a collective scheme, so I turned my attention to the possibility of interesting the Sir John Cass Technical Institute, which I was at the time advising on scientific courses in connection with the fermentation industries, and suggested the possibility of their breaking new ground in technical education by initiating courses for workers in public houses. This led to results about which I shall shortly have more to say.

By 1913, my ideas and activities seem to have attracted attention. In that year I was asked by the *Morning Advertiser*, the old-established daily newspaper owned by one of the retail organizations, if I would grant them an interview to be one of a series given by 'prominent personalities'. Soon afterwards a column appeared in which I communicated my ideas on improvement, higher standards, provision of more general refreshment, and possible methods of curbing excess. Needless to say, I was roundly criticized by some of the old school, who resented any attack on existing standards and believed in fighting enemies rather than cultivating friends. However, I was also complimented by some of the wiser heads and, on balance, felt the publicity to have been worth while.

5

Visit to Denmark—Start of First World War—Early days of War—Substantial increase of Duty—Hop Growers' Problems—Personal War-time activities—Restrictions of Materials 1917—Report of the Government Committee on Food Supply—Easy Money over Barley Deal—Friendship with Hugh Paul—War Savings campaign—First meeting with Lord D'Abernon—Central Control Board (Liquor Traffic)—Hop Control Scheme—Colonel Serocold—First appearance at Committee of Brewers' Society

Early in July 1914 I went to Hamburg to see the manufacturer of some German bottling machinery, unobtainable in England, which we had bought for the brewery. There was tension in the air, but nobody at that time really expected war. I remember looking out of the window and watching a Zeppelin which kept pace with the train. In the carriage with me was a German who spoke perfect English and talked freely about airships and other developments of German science. He said he had been in England to watch the tennis at Wimbledon, but I have wondered since if his visit had been so innocent.

When I had finished my business in Hamburg, I went on to Copenhagen, to visit the Danish breweries of Carlsberg and Tuborg. The Carlsberg Brewery has an unusual and romantic history. It was founded in 1847, when technical brewing in Denmark was at a low ebb, by J. C. Jacobsen, who quickly achieved success and made a large fortune. In 1876 he established the Carlsberg Foundation, to which he made over his business. His son had meanwhile established a brewery of his own and, having in his turn made a fortune, also made over his business to the Foundation, the combined concern being known all over the world as the United Carlsberg Breweries. The profits from this enterprise are devoted to the famous Carlsberg Research Laboratory, the Carlsberg Institute of Biology, the Ny Carlsberg Glyptothek Art Gallery in Copenhagen, and the Museum of National History at Frederiksborg Castle, a mediaeval structure. I am told that the Research Laboratory has one overriding rule, a truly liberal one, which is that all of its findings shall be made available to the whole world.

The Carlsberg Research scheme has, I believe, but one counterpart in the world. This is the Wellcome Foundation (established in 1924 by the late senior partner of Burroughs & Wellcome Ltd., the well-known firm of manufacturing druggists) conducted under the inspiring leadership of Sir Henry Dale, O.M., G.B.E., past President of the Royal Society. On the 4th of April 1955 the Wellcome Foundation decided to entertain members of their Danish sister organization at a dinner in London to which I had the honour of being invited by one of my 'in-laws', Dudley Robinson, a managing-director of Burroughs & Wellcome.

The occasion stands out in my memory as assembling the greatest galaxy of scientific stars it has ever been my privilege to meet, and it was a special delight to me to renew my acquaintance with Sir Henry Dale, who in the First World War had been one of my colleagues on the Central Control Board.

The other great Danish brewery, the Tuborg, is, on the other hand, a commercial concern established later than the Carlsberg breweries, but on friendly terms with them. It was then, and still is, regarded as one of the best-designed, most economical and most efficient breweries in the world. I was impressed with the spirit of loyalty to their organizations and the sense of patriotic citizenship which animated everyone connected with both concerns, not only then but on subsequent visits when I have taken parties of my own staff to visit Copenhagen. I spent a delightful fortnight in an hotel overlooking the Sound and was all the time impressed to see the happiness and contentment of the Danes. Every evening of those warm summer days they bicycled out in their hundreds from Copenhagen to drink coffee and beer in the gardens opposite the hotel, and to bathe in the Sound. But in the outside world, international tension was increasing and the prospect of war became daily more menacing, so I decided to return without delay. There was a great exodus of tourists from the Continent, and I had difficulty in finding a berth for the return journey. I arrived back at Brandon's a few days before the outbreak of war.

Immediately after the declaration of war on the 4th of August we encountered the first of the problems the next few years were to bring. An order was made closing the banks for some days, and in the meantime we were faced with the necessity of paying wages. Happily the same difficulty prevented our customers from banking their takings, so they brought them to the brewery in gold sovereigns and we were more than able to meet our outgoings.

The war soon brought graver trials. Many members of our staff, including Brandon's only son, Chester, were already in the Territorials, and went at once into the Army. They included my senior under-brewer, A. W. Kibble, eight of our staff, and many operatives whose departure left a big gap in the manning of our small business. As these were the days before conscription, we thought it right to encourage our men to enlist, and so undertook to pay half wages to the dependants of those who joined up, and to make up army pay to the equivalent of full salaries if half pay were insufficient. This well-meant offer did not always result in domestic harmony since a number of our men's wives found their first instalment more than they had expected, and realized that their husbands had not been taking home all they earned.

But if there was a serio-comic situation in a few homes, there were others—many others, as the war progressed—to which came only tragedy. I remember, for instance, that we had engaged a retired Sergeant-Major, a magnificent fellow, through the Corps of Commissionaires, to supervise our transport. We told him he was free to rejoin if he wished, but he replied, reasonably enough, that he had served twenty years with the Colours and felt he had 'done his bit'. But the next day the Guards marched through Putney on an enlistment campaign with the regimental band playing, and within five minutes he was in my office saying he could not stand it, and he must 'be with the boys again'. Poor fellow, he never came back.

Before long the strain on our labour force drove me to what seemed at the time to be the desperate expedient of employing women. As rolling barrels and washing casks were heavy jobs, I turned to the type of labour then employed in laundries and for similar work. Though surprisingly efficient, these women caused an unexpected difficulty. A contingent of my cellarmen formed the backbone of the choir of their parish church, and a deputation came to me with the complaint that they could not stand the language the ladies used!

The next problem in those early months was transport, because not only our men, but also many of our vehicles were called up. There had been a scheme whereby the Government had paid a small subsidy on certain vehicles to ensure their being available in the event of war. This scheme we had supported for part of our transport, and these wagons went at once.

The military authorities were feverishly anxious to secure as many vehicles as possible of all types. Despite the Government's intention to ensure the continuance of ordinary business, individual officers requisitioned so many vehicles that I had difficulty in retaining sufficient drays for our needs. I had recently been approached by an American manufacturer of electric wagons which they were anxious to export to England; and although I had little confidence in their suitability I decided, in the emergency, to pursue the matter. They seemed to be too slow—ten or twelve miles an hour—as against the twenty miles an hour of petrol lorries: this would limit their mileage to about thirty miles a day. However, the American representative demonstrated that thirty miles a day would enable the average vehicle to make three deliveries within a ten-mile radius. He lent me a vehicle and went out in it himself for a week's work, showing me his log at the end of it. This revealed that in practice only 15 per cent of the wagon's time was spent in travelling, whereas 85 per cent was passed either in loading at the brewery or in unloading and delivering at the different houses (in those days a leisurely business); also, much

7. TANK WAGONS

The very first tank wagon—holding 360 gallons

An early electric wagon, 1920

A modern tank—contents 2,880 gallons

At Marble Arch

On the Embankment

8. Demonstration against the Licensing Bill of 1907

travelling time was spent standing still in traffic blocks. He argued reasonably enough that his wagon would go as fast as a petrol vehicle when standing in a traffic block or outside a public house. So I took a risk and bought some of the first consignment of electric wagons ever to be sold in this country, and certainly the first ordered by a brewery company. I managed to secure the necessary charging plant, and had no occasion to regret my venture.

In November 1914, the brewers received the first major shock of the war—there were plenty to follow—when the Chancellor of the Exchequer, Lloyd George, proposed an increase in duty which would put up the price of industrial beer from twopence to threepence a pint. It was assumed at that time that people had a fixed amount to spend on beer, and that this increased cost would result in a corresponding decrease in beer consumption of about one third; thus the consumption of raw materials would be effectively reduced. Whatever the brewers might have felt, there was one allied trade which faced the lessened demand with great alarm —the concerns growing and selling hops. As all but a very small quantity of the hops grown were used by brewers, the expected reduction in brewing, it was estimated, would result in great loss to the hop growers, ultimately, if not at first. The difficulties of the hop growers had no immediate impact on myself, but within a year or so I found myself intimately concerned. In the meantime, my outlook was that of the brewer, and I was interested to learn something of the workings of the Chancellor's mind from my friend Cecil Lubbock.

I was in close touch with Lubbock then in connection with my public house policy. His reputation had secured him the confidence of Lloyd George, who often asked for his advice in matters to do with the Trade: at present he wished to learn by how much, in the brewers' estimation, duty could be increased without this increase defeating its own purpose. Lubbock's reply was incisive: he said that in his opinion the new duty would mean a reduction in sales. If one were to estimate a possible decrease in output of 20 per cent, then an increase in duty of 15s. 3d. per 'standard' barrel, making 23s. in all, would leave the Trade roughly in the same position as before. L.G. accepted this figure and adopted it. By this time political antipathies had been forgotten in the national emergency and the Chancellor commended the new duty to Parliament, pointing out that every time a man drank a pint of beer he would be contributing to the cost of the war. The Trade, owing to the absence of troops abroad, expected a considerably diminished output, but war is a thirsty business, and as there was soon full employment and rising wages throughout the country, these fears were not wholly realized.

I began to associate myself with local movements, and enrolled, like many other middle-aged business men, in the volunteer movement, and attended drills under the command of an elderly member of the H.A.C. For many years I had been responsible for other people, and I found drilling a restful experience—it was a relief to find oneself acting under the orders of someone else. We learned to march, to dig trenches, and to charge, in the belief that sooner or later we should have to repel an invasion. We were particularly instructed to howl when practising charging the enemy, an accomplishment which I was told I could perform with considerable skill. We threw dignity to the winds. It was decided that when we had learnt to march with reasonable efficiency, we should parade the district in the hope of attracting recruits. We were promised a regimental band, but when the time arrived, this was not available. There was difficulty in finding a substitute, but at last a boy's drum and fife band was secured. When it arrived we discovered that, though filled with youthful enthusiasm, the only march they could play was 'Onward Christian Soldiers'. Thus I found myself, together with many substantial business men, marching through the streets of Putney to the martial strains of that celebrated hymn. So far as I can recollect, we did not gain many recruits.

I took an interest in the Derby scheme. The army was still on a voluntary basis, but everything pointed to conscription, for which public opinion was not yet ripe. Under the Derby scheme everybody who was or might soon be of military age was invited to register his willingness to join the army when needed. When registered, they could apply for temporary or permanent exemption if and when their turn came. I joined a committee to help work the scheme. Our duty was to interview those who applied for exemption, whether total or temporary. I remember interviewing a man who expressed his willingness to join, but asked for three months' grace in which to wind up his business. I found that he had a yard filled with a vast variety of old and apparently unsaleable iron railings and fences, much of it worthless, but some old and interesting. He told me that his business consisted of collecting old railings, which he got for practically nothing as 'old iron', and assembling them into a form suitable for surrounding graves; these 'surrounds' he exported to America, for there was a demand among American 'morticians' for these antique railings from the old country. This was a new kind of business to me.

My experiences were varied and often interesting. There was one young man who applied for permanent exemption on the ground that he was the 'sole support of his widowed mother'. When I called to see him he was out, and I was asked to wait by a dear old lady who was sure he would not be long. She sat down and began to tell me what a terrible thing this war was. Her son was on the Stock Exchange and had been doing so well; but since the war started, things had gone badly and he was nothing but a 'sad expense' to her! I also came across instances of extreme poignancy. There was a young man, himself in poor health, who with great difficulty was making a home for three invalid sisters, one of whom was blind. There was little difficulty in his case—his health was such that no medical officer would have passed him fit for any form of service, quite apart from his family responsibility.

I also served on an agricultural committee, whose duties were to check the numbers of livestock in the district which might sooner or later be required for food. One might have thought that in Putney there would be few such animals worth recording. Yet there was, for example, a pig-farm of considerable size attached to a large mental hospital, and pig-populations, as we all know, are anything but stable. Since the forms and records we dealt in arrived at intervals of three months, there was no small difficulty in keeping them up to date.

The increasing menace of the intensified submarine warfare reached its peak in 1917, when the loss of allied shipping was enormous and the consequent loss of food and raw materials almost brought the nation to its knees. It was stated that at one time there was no more than three weeks' supply of grain in the country, so naturally more and more stringent regulations were enforced to restrict its use in brewing. The Customs and Excise, as advised by the Ministry of Food, limited the number of 'standard' barrels each brewer could produce to a quota based on his pre-war output. At the same time, the authorities were urging the Trade to brew the largest possible amount of beer from the available material, so the beer grew weaker and weaker.

When pressure on food supplies became acute the Government appointed an expert committee to examine and report on the national diet. Their report was broadly to the effect that grain used for bread provided the greatest amount of food; but they also added the rather unexpected opinion that, in terms of calories, barley used in brewing produced a greater food value than the same amount of grain fed to livestock. My old friend, Dr. Beavan, a Fellow of the Royal Society, and himself a member of the committee, showed me his original draft of this section of the report, which ran: 'Examined in terms of calories, a pound of barley given to a brewer results in a greater food value than the same amount given to a pig, *owing to the uneconomical arrangements of the latter animal*' (my italics). These particular words were, of course, far too concise for a Government report, which devoted two or three pages to expressing the same conclusion.

Although the amount of grain allowed for brewing was so severely limited, the teetotal party had not been idle; they had been clamouring for prohibition in order to 'stop this destruction of food material'. The publication of the report was a sad setback to them, and for a time there was less talk about brewers destroying food. But one immediate and inevitable result of the grain shortage was a sharp rise in prices, and those engaged in the barley market profited hugely. I had a particular instance of this. One day a merchant told me that he had a cargo loading in New York which his firm had instructed him to sell on terms ex-ship at a London port; he pressed me to take part of the cargo. It happened that we had decided at Brandon's not to add to our stocks, in view of the diminution of the rate of brewing and the possibility that it might be brought to a complete standstill. Although I mentioned this, the merchant persevered, saying that the parcel would be a good bargain; and in the end I booked the consignment on the basis that, if my Board decided not to add the parcel to our stocks, I would take the risk myself. A few days later my friend advised me to increase the insurance cover because the market value had risen. This he did several times while the ship was in the Atlantic, and when the ship was in the Channel, almost home, she was torpedoed off the Isle of Wight. We received from the insurance company a cheque for over £4,000, although we had done nothing but pay the premium—an excellent example of how money could be made in wartime with a minimum of effort. Still, I had long since decided not to make personal profit out of the war and I allowed several other opportunities that came my way to pass unheeded. I like to think that in some small way I thus won some of the confidence and influence I have enjoyed.

Quite early on I had another trading experience which was to bring me a rich dividend—not in money but in friendship. Just before the war I had bought two thousand quarters of barley from Paul and Company of Ipswich, 'ex-ship Ipswich', and was expecting its arrival. I later learned that the barley was in a German ship when war broke out, and the vessel had taken refuge in a small port in South America, and lain there doggo. After a while I learned that Paul's had managed to get the barley transferred to a neutral ship which duly arrived at Ipswich. By that time the value had risen considerably, and I put in my claim for it, offering to pay the extra cost of transfer from ship to ship in the South American port. But that very good fellow, Hugh Paul, then a young man, with whom I had transacted the original business, felt bound to contest the claim that the barley was still due to me. I felt I was right, and I took Counsel's opinion, with the result that I was advised that more could be said for Hugh Paul's contention than for mine. I thought it well to surrender the point, and in doing so I sent the opinion to Hugh Paul in case he found it of value. In this way I lost for Brandon's a parcel of cheap barley; but it was not all loss, and indeed it was mostly gain. It was the beginning of a long friendship with Hugh Paul which proved valuable in the First

World War and still more so in the Second, when he occupied a high position in the Ministry of Food.

In those war years wages were rising, and in 1916 the Government launched its campaign to raise money by means of War Savings Certificates. It occurred to me that the Trade could be a great help to the Government if the interest of innumerable slate clubs, loan clubs, Christmas clubs and sick clubs operated in licensed houses could be enlisted. The number and variety of these clubs is bewildering, but their general principle is the same: the customer pays in his weekly shilling or so, and the licensee collects it and acts as the club treasurer. The money is usually deposited with his brewer for safe keeping and is shared out at Christmas. This distribution at Christmas has been attacked by critics on the ground that it leads to excess drinking; but this is not true. Winter is the time when extra money is needed in every household for clothing and fuel as well as for Christmas festivities. It has often been assumed that, when the money is distributed, it is spent in the pub; and that this is the sole object the publican has in view. This also is not the case. If all the money distributed in licensed houses during the period when the funds are divided were spent in the house, the takings would be more than doubled. As a matter of fact, the actual increase in takings for the weeks immediately before Christmas is seldom more than five per cent; and that would be accounted for by the natural increase in business as Christmas approaches, even if there were no club share-out.

I found that among them three breweries alone were holding £70,000 for distribution at Christmas. Up and down the country the amount thus held must even then have run into millions. (The popularity of these clubs has much increased since those days. The figure held by Whitbread's alone in this way for the year 1957 exceeded half a million pounds). It seemed to me that the licensed houses and the breweries between them had the organization, the resources and the machinery to play an effective part in the new War Savings movement. I foresaw a great sum of money being put at the Government's disposal through savings groups in the pubs, with a minimum of labour or effort on the part of the authorities. Full of this idea, I called on Sir Robert Kindersley (afterwards

Lord Kindersley) President of the Savings Committee, with my suggestion, only to come up against a formidable snag. What Kindersley told me in effect, was that while the idea was interesting, he could not act upon it because the temperance people would be up in arms. It appeared that much of the organization of the Savings movement throughout the country was being undertaken by social workers who were (as he put it) 'unfriendly to the licensed trade, so that their opposition would make it impolitic to register a war savings association in a public house'.

This decision seemed to me a misfortune—there were the people in the public houses with good money in their pockets and little to spend it on. The publicans had time on their hands and were willing to undertake work so important to the well-being of us all. At about this time I happened to be asked to read a paper before the Institute of Brewing, and in accordance with our practice of sometimes admitting a paper more general than technical, I gave an account of the War Savings Movement as it affected the Trade. At Brandon's we had formed a savings group in the brewery—indeed, I think we were one of the first to do so. Eighty-five per cent of our staff had joined, and in December 1916 we in our small business held nearly 3,000 certificates. I did not quote these figures to boast about our share in them—but to demonstrate that if the staff of a comparatively small brewery could do so well in a few short months, the customers of tens of thousands of public houses north, south, east and west might well, given the opportunity, have invested enormous sums in the same way, and with no direct strain on official staffs or organizations.

My paper was mainly a description of the different ways of running savings groups within concerns employing labour, but I naturally told my hearers of my failure to interest the authorities in savings collected through pubs. It was this, rather than the rest of my talk, which aroused the most lively exchanges afterwards. I had in my audience a representative of the National War Savings Committee, also Lord d'Abernon, at that time chairman of the Central (Liquor) Control Board. Mr. Foa, the representative of the national committee, said he would take back to his colleagues the feeling of the meeting: that use should be made of the slate club organizations in national savings: he did not admit that prejudice prevented this, in spite of what I had told the meeting. Lord d'Abernon urged that this opportunity should not be missed. He was much concerned with increasing the usefulness and raising the standard of public houses, and asked me afterwards for more details of my rebuff at the hands of the savings authorities. His next move was to arrange a further meeting with the heads of the savings movement; but without avail. Thus, at a critical time in the war, when the Government needed every penny it could raise, prohibitionist obstructiveness deprived the war effort of many millions of pounds. Later, when the financial position had become even more acute and the influence of the prohibitionists was on the wane, the authorities withdrew their objection and large sums of money were collected through the pubs. But the golden opportunity had been thrown away. However, my association with Lord d'Abernon was not over; for he asked me to join the Central Control Board (Liquor Traffic).

My next wartime activity was to do with the hop-growing industry. Representatives of the industry had had meetings with the Board of Agriculture to evolve a scheme for saving the industry from ruin. The result was a Hop Control Committee, under the chairmanship of Mr. Foster Clark, who became Hop Controller. Mr. Foster Clark was the founder of the well-known Maidstone firm of food packers and canners, and at first sight it would seem unlikely that he should have much interest in hops. But he was Mayor of Maidstone, in the heart of the Kentish hop-fields, and knew something of the problems of the hop growers. He was a shrewd, practical business man, gained the confidence of all concerned, and filled his post with marked success during the period of control which lasted for more than six years.

The Hop Control Committee consisted of representatives of the Board of Agriculture, the hop growers, the hop merchants, and the hop factors. To these was added, to begin with, one brewery representative, Colonel O. P. Serocold of Watney's. The Committee met for the first time on the 20th August, 1917. A fortnight later I received a letter from R. E. Prothero (later Lord Ernle), President of the Board of Agriculture, asking me to join the Committee to help Colonel Serocold. I attended my first meeting on the 3rd of September. Later we were joined by two other brewers, but they lived in the country and could not attend regularly.

In the early months of the war the hop trade had not succumbed to the disaster it had foreseen when Lloyd George increased the beer duty; but since then the position had steadily worsened, and in 1917 the hop growers suffered a crippling blow. In January an order was made restricting the brewers' output to 18,200,000 standard barrels, and in March a new order reduced this still further to less than a third of the pre-war output. It was evident that the demand for hops would dwindle to almost nothing, for the brewers held unused stocks of their own. The hop trade held some 100,000 hundredweights of the 1916 crop still unsold, and a full crop was being grown for the 1917 harvest. It was evident that there would be a huge surplus, and unless something could be done the growers faced ruin. The scheme was to reduce the acreage cultivated by one-half; to take over all unsold hops at a valuation; to purchase the 1917 crop according to quality at an average price based on the cost of production plus twenty per cent profit; to raise the money required by an overdraft guaranteed by the Government; and to hold the whole stock until taken by the brewers.

When Mr. Prothero asked me to join the Committee, Colonel Serocold was ill and could not attend the first few meetings. The two other brewers appointed later were Mr. William Sykes of Yorkshire and Mr. C. Reid of Hatfield, but in the all-important early days of the control it fell to me to carry the responsibility of representing the brewers' interests single-handed.

The system of marketing hops has traditional features of its own. The growers market their hops through factors, who act as their agents on a commission basis. The factor provides warehouse room, samples each pocket of hops, and arranges for their sale to the established hop merchants. The latter, in turn, sell them to the brewers, many of whom wish to secure the growths of particular growers from year to year, in order to ensure a uniform flavour in their beers. So it is a custom of the trade to give the first offer of individual growths to the purchaser who bought them the previous year; English brewers prefer to buy individual growths rather than select on the strength of grade samples as most foreign brewers do. The hop merchants in those days naturally bought the hops as cheaply as they could, doubtless using the argument that brewers bought at the lowest competitive price, which was true enough. On joining the committee, I found much prejudice among the growers against the brewers, they thought my sole object was to beat down the price. After a few days I found this attitude wearisome and explained that our beer could not be brewed without hops, that I had been asked by the President of the Board of Agriculture to help further the scheme, and that my object was to maintain the hop industry; but that if the present temper of 'pull devil pull baker' were to be continued, I should ask the President to find another devil, as this devil was not going to play. This seemed to put things in a new light to the growers and a better atmosphere prevailed.

Each grower was invited to send in particulars of his costs of production in order that an average cost could be estimated. There was a lively discussion about what should be charged to meet the expenses of the Control, which would include the cost of the executive, the interest on the overdraft, and warehouse rent. Generous expenses were also allowed to certain grower members for travelling either to the board meetings or to consultations with their fellow growers. It was thought that the whole crop could not be absorbed by the brewers for a long time, and so the interest on the Government-guaranteed overdraft, and cost of warehousing, could not be estimated. At first, the growers pressed for a high figure as the cost of running the Hop Control—larger than I thought reasonable, although I was prepared to agree to whatever was really necessary. After much discussion, I brought the matter to a close by agreeing on behalf of the brewers to accept any figure the Controller might think appropriate, provided that proper economy were exercised and that any balance should belong to the brewers to be disposed of as they might decide. This was agreed, and the Controller fixed the figure for the control expenses at five shillings a hundredweight, to be increased if necessary. An average price was fixed by the Controller and the representatives of the Board of Agriculture—among whom was W. W. Berry (afterwards

Sir Walter Berry), himself a large grower of hops. To this price was added a figure representing the rent of the land, a 20 per cent profit, and interest at 5 per cent on the working capital employed by the grower in cultivation. For the first year this average price was £8 10s. 0d. per hundredweight, on the assumption that the crop would average eleven hundredweights per acre. A valuation committee then valued each growth according to the differing qualities above and below the average. Thus the various growths were priced according to quality, and so adjusted as to bring the average to the figure fixed by the Controller.

Our next business was to get the hops into the hands of the brewers with the least possible delay, so as to lessen the overhead costs of the Control by way of interest, rent, insurance and so on; also because the risk of destruction by enemy action was appreciable, although raids then were a much smaller hazard than in the war of twenty years later. When our discussion had reached this point I undertook to explain and commend the scheme to the Brewers' Society. I was not then a member of the Committee of the Brewers' Society, but I was asked to meet them. I explained the general lines of the Control and urged its acceptance—we must keep the hop-growing industry alive, and sooner or later hops would be urgently needed; indeed the time might come when the supply would be short (as indeed it became later). The committee thanked me and undertook to 'recommend to brewers such arrangements as Mr. Nevile and his brewing colleagues might find it necessary to support in order to maintain and help the hop-growing industry'.

I was well satisfied with my first appearance before the Society. The merchants were anxious to distribute the crop, and the brewers rose nobly to the occasion. Although it had been expected that many of the hops would lie in the Control's hands for months, possibly years, the whole crop was taken off the market into the breweries within a week or two. The expenses proved much less than five shillings a hundredweight, and a large sum accumulated in the hands of the Control to the credit of the brewers. When at last the Control was discontinued, several years after the end of the war, this money was employed in research and in other directions for the benefit of the Trade as a whole. My visit to the Brewers' Society resulted in the authorities concluding that I was altogether too active to be allowed to run about uncontrolled, and I was invited to join the Council, on which I have sat continuously from that day to this, a period of more than forty years. I believe that this is a record; certainly I am now by several years the 'father' of the Council.

The second year Serocold and I had a curious experience. Foster Clark had satisfied himself that we were fair and so asked us to suggest a price based on the costs as returned by every grower. These varied greatly. Serocold thought that we could hardly question them; so we accepted them as they stood and based our suggestion on the average as returned. When we reported our figure to Foster Clark and Berry (who acted as vice-chairman) they seemed startled and asked us for our basis. They then told us that they had disregarded many of the returns as being inflated, and had only considered those they regarded as trustworthy. So they consulted the leading hop growers on the Committee and fixed the price at thirty shillings below our figure.

Serocold and I were agreed that the circumstances and hazards of the hop growers justified generous arrangements; but we little anticipated they would form a precedent for the present Hop Marketing Board and would in fact endow hop growing land with the truly large capital value which has proved to be the case.

* * *

These, then, were not years of spectacular achievement in the Trade; in common with other enterprises, particularly those depending on food substances and fuels, we were happy in being able to keep alive. These years were valuable to me personally, however, for they brought me into contact with notable administrators and organizers, thus giving me insights which would prove most useful in the strenuous years to come.

It has always been my policy (and those who know me best have recommended that I try to make no secret of it) to sweeten negotiations, if possible, over a well-spread table. Many of my 'affairs of State' were discussed at dinner—often the dinner was a very late one—and usually at Oddenino's in Regent Street, then controlled by 'Oddy' himself, a truly great restaurateur. When I first met him he was head waiter of the East Room of the Criterion. He subsequently took charge of the Café Royal, whose affairs at that time were at a somewhat low ebb. His terms there were a small salary, with a handsome commission on increased profit, terms which, owing to his genius and popularity, returned him so large an income that when his agreement ran out the proprietors suggested a renewal on a lower scale. This did not suit him, so he acquired the next-door restaurant, which he re-christened with his own name.

When I was dining one evening with Owen Wightman, 'Oddy' told us the story of how, owing to war conditions, he had found himself without lager beer, and a customer, a noted K.C., had offered to help, and secured him his appropriate ration. As the K.C. refused to accept any fee for his help, 'Oddy' told him that on any Monday evening he cared to choose he must dine *ad lib.* on the house. 'And,' said 'Oddy', 'he has hardly missed a Monday night ever since then; he is over there now'! So his friend had not done so badly. But, as 'Oddy' philosophically remarked, 'it's not cost me so much after all, as most of it comes out of Excess Profits Tax I should otherwise have to pay'.

But Oddy's luck did not continue. Although a superlative caterer, he was somewhat lacking in commercial acumen. The costs of two expensive lawsuits, some bad investments in Italian enterprises, together with a period of bad health, impaired his fortunes, so that he sold the restaurant and I fear was not too prosperous in his declining years.

Yes, indeed, I candidly admit that I owe much to the good services of 'Oddy' and countless other fine hosts whose hospitality has both cheered and softened the hearts of those I have taken out to lunch or dine. The well-known prescription for a soothing and civilizing medicine—'a large, cold bottle and a small hot bird' has stood me in good stead.

Brewing and the side-issues and ramifications of brewing have of course been my chief concern, but I have also tried my tongue on themes other than these, and even dabbled in politics for a time.

Unlike my father, who possessed an unusual ability to speak at length and to hold an audience without previous preparation, I was intensely nervous. I found great difficulty in expressing myself when on my feet facing a meeting. I early realized the necessity of overcoming this deficiency if I were ever to cut any ice, so I early joined a small debating society and later the Conservative 'United Club', a body consisting mostly of young barristers with political ambitions, which held meetings and discussions and also offered young speakers opportunities for displaying their ability at small political meetings. I was never a fervent party politician, and was not much of a success at indoor meetings of sympathizers; though, rather to my surprise, I was happier and more successful when persuaded to try my skill at street corners in tough districts, faced with hecklers and, occasionally, missiles.

There was not much to be said for the organizing ability of the Tory Party at that time, especially when they failed consistently to train good working-class speakers and to brief their election workers sensibly. I remember being struck by the reply of a lady canvasser who, when asked if she had arranged for a distant voter to be returned to his residence at Ealing, replied, 'Oh no, what was the good—he'd voted'! I have often thought the gentler sex to be the more practical one, though sometimes short-sighted in matters of long-term policy.

But my political ambitions did not last long. Early in the 'twenties I was startled to receive a suggestion that I should contest the seat of the Isle of Wight as an independent conservative, and was urged not to refuse without meeting a deputation who invited me to attend a small meeting on the Island to discuss the possibility. Though flattered, my visit to the Island convinced me that the enterprise was well above my weight, and I was quite satisfied that even a merely adequate performance of my duties as an M.P., in addition to meeting my responsibilities at that time, would have been out of the question. Then there was something else. I was never, as I have said, a keen political partisan and as I interested myself more and more in trade organizations, my conviction grew that it was inappropriate for representative bodies to show support to any political party. The function of a trade society is to secure conditions under which its members can individually and collectively serve the public whatever Government may be in power, and it is unwise as well as improper to do other than abstain from party politics unless issues are raised directly affecting their industry. Collective partisanship merely results in arousing the hostility of one party, while the other hesitates to risk falling under suspicion of helping its friends. So party politics were not for me.

There was another wide sphere of human interest which made slighter appeal to me than to other members of my family: the world of horses. It goes without saying that like many and many a more knowledgeable punter I have taken a brief interest in one or two especially noble-looking creatures at race-meetings, but this was a realm in which I was quite a tyro. My elder brothers, living in the country, were naturally much concerned with horses. Indeed, my brother George perpetrated a book *Horses and Riding* during a period of convalescence after breaking his leg while hunting (quite incidentally it was this accident which led to his meeting his future wife, who lived to be a centenarian). This book was, I believe, the only attempt at authorship in my family until this effort.

My brother Edward boasted of following the Blankney for seventy years without missing a season. He was also known as a breeder of Shire horses, his greatest success being a filly, Barmaid, who fetched the record price of her day, when sold by Sutton Nelthorp, who had purchased her at a moderate price from my brother.

But lack of both time and money placed hunting far out of my reach; indeed I cannot remember ever being across a horse; my nearest approach was a ride on a donkey in Egypt when I was visiting the Pyramids on my return from Australia.

A more epoch-making trip was one I made at the mature age of eight (seventy-six years ago), when I succeeded in persuading the milkman to take me with him to Goodwood in his cart; an achievement which got us both into sad trouble. I have a happier remembrance of my first substantial bet. I was spending a week-end at Brighton, and my old mentor Amos told me he had a persistent dream that a horse named Manifesto had won the National, which led me to invest what was for me an unusually large sum on that great horse. It was a red-letter day when the dream came true, for the starting price had been twenty to one.

I put that bet on with one Wilde, then a well-known bookmaker who was the subject of quite a good story a year or two later. Wilde suffered from a breakdown, which took the form of refusing to speak for many weeks—his silence eventually being broken by the talkative hairdresser whom we both patronized. The conversation ran, 'Good morning, Mr. Wilde.' No answer. 'Nice morning, Mr. Wilde.' Again no answer. 'How are you, Mr. Wilde?' No answer. 'Will you take this chair, Mr. Wilde?' No answer. 'Now, how would you like your hair cut, Mr. Wilde?' That broke the spell. 'In absolute bloody silence,' said Wilde. The incident finally found its way into *Punch*, though not for several years.

9. *Kia Ora* winning the Queen's Cup, 1906, in record time

10. On *Maaslust* in Holland

11. SOME OF MY COLLEAGUES ON THE CENTRAL CONTROL BOARD

Sir John Sykes, Secretary
How much is a 'small' or 'moderate' amount?

Sir John Pedder, Vice-chairman
A civil servant may not defend himself

Lord d'Abernon
You brewers are so British

J. H. Thomas ('Jimmy')
I won't use the war to get prohibition

Sir William Butler, Bt.
Fewer and better public houses

6

Year 1917—Central Control Board—Carlisle—Appreciation of Lord d'Abernon—Association with different Government Departments —Lord Younger and Others—Milner Committee on State Purchase —Back door attempt to secure State Purchase—Fuel Economy— Protection Committee of the Institute of Brewing—Evidence before English and Scottish Committees—State Purchase Proposals dropped —First invitation to Chair of Brewers' Society

The year 1917 was perhaps the most interesting year in my career—it was certainly the busiest. It was then that I began my connection with the Hop Control, already mentioned, and with the Central Control Board (Liquor Traffic), the State Purchase proposals and other public matters of lesser importance which, none the less, loomed large at the time.

The Central Control Board (Liquor Traffic) or 'Liquor Control' as it was usually called, had been established under the Defence of the Realm Act (No. 3) of 1915, and was empowered to make regulations governing the sale and consumption of drink wherever these were necessary to further the prosecution of the war. The chairman of the Board was Lord d'Abernon, whom I had met in connection with my War Savings paper mentioned in the last chapter. D'Abernon had been raised to the peerage in 1915, after a distinguished career in both diplomacy and Parliament. He had spent many years in Turkey and the Middle East and had represented Great Britain, Holland and Belgium on the Council of the Ottoman Public Debt, afterwards becoming Chairman of the

Council. He was also financial adviser to the Egyptian Government, and later Governor of the Imperial Ottoman Bank. As Sir Edgar Vincent he represented Exeter in Parliament for a number of years. When I first met him, he was a man of nearly sixty, and with his long experience in difficult public problems was an ideal chairman for an organization such as the Control Board. His was indeed a magnificent presence. Lady Oxford and Asquith numbered him amongst the four handsomest men she had ever met, and she was a good judge. He also held decided views on drink, and especially on the public house, which in many particulars matched my own. I knew that he had adopted the principle of the improvement of the public house, but I was not merely concerned with being associated with a man whose view, I respected and agreed with. I felt, though this was not the general feeling among brewers then, that the Trade should co-operate with Government authorities. Brandon kindly, and shrewdly, allowed me to add membership of this Board to my many other activities, so I accepted the invitation to do so and became one of what at that time was, I suppose, the most unpopular body of men in England.

In addition to d'Abernon, the members of the Board at that time included Sir John Pedder, then Assistant Secretary to the Home Office, who acted as chairman in d'Abernon's rare absences; Lord Leverhulme; Sir John Denny, a great ship builder; Sir George Newman of the Board of Education, an expert in medical science in relation to public health; Viscount Astor; the redoubtable Sir William Towle, previously hotels manager of the Midland Railway; the Rev. Henry Carter, a leading temperance advocate; Lord Snowden; R. S. Meiklejohn of the Treasury; Sir William Waters Butler, Bart., of the great Birmingham firm of Mitchells and Butlers; Sir Henry Dale and the redoubtable J. H. Thomas.

The most prominent member of the Board after Lord d'Abernon was Sir John Pedder, who was primarily responsible for the text of the various Orders. A typical Civil Servant of the highest class, he appeared at first sight a somewhat remote bureaucrat and it was some time before I came to appreciate his human qualities. He represented the Home Office on the Royal Commission on Licensing from 1929 to 1931, and on many other important and sometimes international conferences. He was an authority on licensing laws and for several years edited that annual book of reference, *Paterson's Licensing Acts*. It was during one of our tours in Scotland that his sterling merits became apparent to me, and as time went by our friendship deepened. After the abolition of the Control Board he was Chairman of the Council of the State Management District Council on which I acted in an honorary advisory capacity. At the latter end of 1931 he told me he contemplated retiring from the Home Office, but on the other hand did not wish to give up work entirely.

Since I had long considered drunkenness a serious commercial disadvantage to the Trade, and had over the years advocated the formation of a Trade Committee to study its incidence, I suggested to Sir Richard Garton, chairman of Watney's and then a leader in Trade politics, that such a committee should be formed under the chairmanship of Pedder; but Garton told me later that Pedder's services would be so valuable to Watney's that I could greatly help by sounding him as to his views about joining the Board of that company. He did actually join Watney's when he left the Home Office, and served on that Board from 1932 to 1949, retaining a lively interest in brewers' affairs until the end of his days.

Another outstanding member was the Reverend Henry Carter who later wrote a history of the work of the Board—the most prominent personality, at that time, in the temperance party. When I joined the Board he and Pedder formed the sub-committee which was generally termed 'The Star Chamber'. Their function was to ensure observation of the Board's Orders and their methods were, to my mind, the least justifiable of the Board's activities. While breaches of the Board's Orders by licensees were legal offences and could be dealt with by the ordinary processes of law, the 'Star Chamber's' method was more direct; but, in my view, indefensible. The Board had wide powers, and when information was received to the effect that one licensee or another was not conforming, they ordered the house to be closed on the thin pretext that it was hampering due prosecution of the war. This arbitrary action naturally caused intense resentment among the licensed

Trade organizations and I have always thought had much to do with the disapprobation in which the Board was held. It was rather inconvenient to me as I was often charged with undue friendship towards the Trade's enemies, this being, no doubt, one of the reasons which in 1919 occasioned objections to my becoming Chairman of the Brewers' Society.

Another member of the Board for whom I had the greatest admiration was Henry Dale, later Sir Henry Dale, who (as I describe elsewhere) became President of the Royal Society and has for some years been Director of the Wellcome Foundation. As I mentioned in the first few pages of my fifth chapter, I was the only English brewer guest at the dinner given by the Wellcome Foundation to its sister organization, the Carlsberg Research Laboratory of Denmark. It was a real pleasure to meet him again after so many years.

J. H. Thomas (Jimmy Thomas) was another interesting character. At heart a great citizen, with attributes which he concealed under far too free a flow of language, he had a commanding influence in his Labour Union. On one occasion, when trouble seemed to be boiling up at Carlisle, trouble which looked like culminating in a railway strike, and we were somewhat anxious, he told us, 'I have my eye on it; as soon as it becomes necessary I shall go and talk to them'. This talk did indeed come to pass, and the agitation died down. When I congratulated him on being appointed Secretary for the Colonies, all he said was, 'I'll take damn good care not to let the British Empire be b—— up'. His retirement from political life, owing to indiscretions arising from too free a choice of companions, was a tragedy.

The Secretary to the Board was J. C. G. (later Sir John) Sykes. Jack Sykes was a charming and lovable personality with a whimsical humour and a great capacity for analytical detail, together with a placid temperament when faced by emergencies. I remember that on one occasion, when we were on one of our periodical tours of Scotland, he showed me a telegram reading: 'CHAIRMAN DIFFICULT REFUSES TO ATTEND CABINET MEETING PLEASE RETURN AT ONCE'. When I said how sorry I was that our tour should be interrupted he showed me his reply: 'MANY THANKS INTEREST-

ING TELEGRAM MY NEXT ADDRESS WILL BE ROYAL HOTEL INVERGORDON'. I never knew what reception his lighthearted reply earned, but nothing serious came of any of it.

The business of the Control Board had been to 'make such regulations as would be necessary for the conduct of the war', in all cases where difficulties arose over the sale or consumption of drink. When I joined the Board, some twenty Orders covering the greater part of the country had already been put into operation. They followed one general pattern and included restrictions on the hours of opening and the sale of spirits, as well as the notorious 'no treating' order. In my opinion, this last regulation was very necessary when first made, as 'group' drinking was a real cause of drunkenness; but later, when general sobriety had been ensured and supplies were short, it became a mere irritant. The prejudice against it became so intense that it was abolished on the 3rd of June, 1919, before the end of the Board's life.

One purpose for which Butler and I had been invited to join the Board was to advise on the direct State Management Schemes of Carlisle, the Gretna area and the Invergordon and Cromarty districts, all of which have remained nationalized ever since. To these had been added a smaller area at Enfield, north of London, which was returned to private enterprise in 1921.

The acquisition of the breweries and licensed houses of Carlisle and parts of Scotland may, to some extent, have been an experiment in State Purchase itself; but the immediate motive was to put an end to the crisis which had arisen in those districts. The great munition factory at Gretna just across the Border was then in process of construction, and many thousands of workers of both sexes were employed, including many Irish. The nearest town was Carlisle—a sleepy cathedral city with many small public houses, mostly run by pensioners and widows quite incapable of handling the horde of tough customers which invaded the city every night. The consequent disorder necessitated more strenuous control than could be applied through ordinary channels by such Orders as operated in other munition centres, so the decision was taken to place the districts under direct State management. The Board accordingly acquired the four or five breweries which owned most of the public houses of the neighbourhood, together with a few free houses, but not the two hotels, 'The Crown and Mitre' and 'The County Hotel'. These hotels occasionally caused some competition, but otherwise made little difference to the working of the scheme. To all intents and purposes drinking in the Carlisle area was 'nationalized' and established as a Government monopoly.

The acquisition of Invergordon and Cromarty was dictated to some extent by the establishment there of a Naval Dockyard employing many thousands of new workers; but before long it became a base for the American Navy, whose crews were dry at sea but apt to be very wet on shore; so the area of control was increased from time to time as the thirsty crews travelled farther into the surrounding country.

Responsibility for the various state-owned districts rested in the hands of a sub-committee of the Control Board, called the Public House Committee, with a General Manager in each district. The General Manager at Carlisle was Edgar (later Sir Edgar) Sanders, who had been Clerk to the Justices of Liverpool. He was an expert in licensing matters, had been chairman of the Magistrates' Clerks Association, and had been appointed as Assessor to the Board before the acquisition of Carlisle. There was a separate manager for the Scottish districts, Mr. C. M. Blunt, with two local managers under him. The much smaller district of Enfield was under the part-time management of Mr. Madden, then managing director of the small Surrey Public House Trust Company, which owned a few houses in Surrey. In each district the Board appointed local advisory committees, whose opinion was asked on matters affecting the district, final decisions being made in London by the Public House Committee. Nominally these decisions were subject to the approval of the Home Secretary as advised by the Board, but in practice this approval was automatic. As a brewer member of the Board, I was naturally invited to join the Public House Committee, which at that time consisted of, among others, Butler (Chairman), Towle, Philip Snowden, and Astor, with J. S. Eagles as Secretary. Sykes also attended as secretary to the Board. The principle of direct control was to place all houses under management as they came into the Board's possession, giving a modest compensation to the outgoing tenants and retaining as managers any regarded as suitable and willing.

William Waters Butler, my brewer colleague, was a great character and will long remain one of the best-remembered Trade personalities of that period. He was born in a public house owned by his father who, having bought other licensed houses, purchased a brewery to supply them when Waters Butler was still in his teens. Butler quickly gained a knowledge of brewing, and became brewer in charge. He told me once that on his twenty-first birthday his father asked him what he ought to do for him. Young Butler's reply was, 'Well, Dad, I am your brewer, and what is more I am a good brewer, and I think I ought to be worth a thousand a year', to which his father agreed. He continued, 'But I am not only your brewer, I am your son. Don't you think I ought to have a share in the business?' to which, although somewhat startled, his father again agreed. Butler also told me that by his twenty-second birthday, in addition to his salary as head brewer, he had drawn a further three thousand pounds as his share of the profits. Later, he persuaded his father to amalgamate with an older-established firm, Mitchell's of the same city. When I first met Butler he was chairman of the combined concern, Mitchells and Butlers, one of the largest firms in the country. As their houses were mostly under management, and they thus took the retail as well as the wholesale profits, they were also one of the most prosperous.

It was said that when Butler first heard of the proposal of state purchase, his reply was 'They'll buy my brewery over my dead body'. But somehow or other an interview with Lloyd George resulted in an example of the Premier's incredible powers of persuasion: Butler left Downing Street almost fanatically convinced that state purchase of the brewing industry was a matter of vital importance to the country, a measure which all good citizens should support.

His pride in the industry, coupled with his unrivalled knowledge of both its wholesale and retail sides, had long established him among the leaders. As I have already recounted, he had been chairman of the Brewers' Society in 1907 and with Frank Whitbread, then chairman of the National Trade Defence Association, had organized the fight against the notorious Licensing Bill of 1907. The mass demonstration against the Bill in Hyde Park has already been touched upon (when I spoke of our Putney contingent). The crowd owed something to four trains bringing several thousands of customers from Birmingham itself. They marched in procession, carrying banners with such slogans as 'Thou shalt not steal' and 'There was no time limit to this'. When the Central Control Board bought up the Carlisle concern, the financial success of the scheme can be largely attributed to Butler's enthusiasm and also to his seconding several members of his staff to organize the undertaking—a most enlightened and patriotic action.

The profits of Carlisle have been uniformly high. They have often been quoted by the supporters of nationalization, but it must be borne in mind that these profits are attributable to factors which would seldom exist if the scheme were applied on a nation-wide scale. The breweries, including the public houses, were taken over at a low figure at a time, indeed, when it was possible that brewing would cease altogether. They are not charged with income tax, or profits tax, or surtax, nor indeed does the capital contribute to the national income through death duties, as is the case with private enterprise. Again, whatever the interests of the consumer may be, a monopoly ensures good profits, whether or not the customer is satisfied with the product. Lastly, although perhaps I should not say it out loud, the enterprise had from its inception the services of Butler, Towle and myself, each of us having made his way from small beginnings under highly competitive conditions. I doubt if any brewery enterprise in the country could have so strong a panel of advisers. Our usefulness was enhanced by the fact that our services were honorary, enabling us to press our advice with a force which would not have been possible had we been salaried officials hampered by the inhibitions of the Civil Service.

From time to time the members of the Board visited the various districts to keep in touch with the business and to maintain association with the local advisory committees. We used to leave London by the night train and arrive at Carlisle at about six in the morning. During the day and part of the next we would inspect properties in the area and attend a meeting of the local committee. Then we would catch a night train to Invergordon, spend the day in that district, visit the houses in the Cromarty area next morning, and catch the mid-day train back to London. I did not sleep very well in trains, and I usually reached London rather the worse for wear. All the same, I found the work full of interest. Indeed, the meetings of the local advisory committees were a delight in themselves. In each there were members representative of labour organizations, the justices, local councils, religious and temperance leaders; each approached the work with varying degrees of approval or criticism. The magistrates and the local landowners, though supporting the Board as a patriotic duty, much disliked the authority being taken out of their hands. The temperance people would have much preferred total prohibition, which they hoped to secure as a result of the war. They questioned the principle of the Board in improving the public house, on the ground that this had the effect of making the pub 'respectable'. Indeed, when a large employer of labour who was also a strong temperance advocate was shown round the scheme, his parting words were, 'Sir Edgar, do you realize you are doing the devil's work?'

The labour representatives were divided in their loyalties; some were themselves strong advocates of temperance, others objected to the restrictions put upon their constituents. Once, when a labour representative complained forcefully of the service in the Carlisle pubs as compared with that in pubs in another town under competitive enterprise, I asked him whether his comments meant that he disapproved of the scheme. His reply left no room for doubt: 'Of course it's the right thing, it's nationalization, isn't it?' —evidence to me that the merits of a national service are too often subordinated to political prejudice and conviction. As for the Scottish committees, whatever their several opinions on the drink question, they were united in their dislike of being controlled and directed from London. Their spirit of nationalism in so comparatively unimportant a matter seemed incredible to me. Our drastic methods must have caused a mild degree of obsession: as an instance, it is said that a local journalist, writing up the funeral service of a Church dignitary of the time, described the choir's rendering of Tennyson's beautiful hymn, 'CLOSING the Bar'.

As to the little district of Enfield, it was so close to London that there appeared to be no need for a separate advisory committee. But problems of a different sort arose. The munitions factory there was working day and night, and we had to provide eating and drinking facilities, especially at two sessions equivalent to 'lunch' in the middle of the night. The workers ate quickly and were apt to go to sleep afterwards; and when they were awakened to resume work, it took them some time to get back into full activity. So we conceived the idea of organizing concerts at twelve-thirty after the first night sitting and again at one-thirty after the second. It was felt to be a desirable gesture for a member of the Control to occupy the chair, and I took my turn. At first it was quite an adventure; we started off at eleven o'clock in the pitch dark in an army car, calling at one or two music halls to pick up the artists who had been engaged for the night. Then we drove through the unlit, cavernous streets, ourselves without lights, at what seemed to be breakneck speed, to cover the ten or twelve miles to the factory. I used to take the chair at both concerts and afterwards return to the manager's room with the artists, where we found a supper, generally of lobster salad and stout, awaiting us. After this, the same dark journey in reverse brought us home to bed by about 4 a.m. I found the experience interesting and amusing, but I was glad it did not happen too often, because I usually had a full day's work to get through after only a few hours' sleep. I recently met an old acquaintance who was a marshal in the air raids in those days. He reminded me that he had met me going home in the early hours of the morning during a raid and had advised me to take shelter in a nearby chapel. Too tired almost to think, I had thanked him, and refused his suggestion, on the ground that 'I am a churchman'. I was not allowed to forget this for a long time.

It is extraordinary what a man can get through if he must—or perhaps how much can be left undone without apparently mattering much. We were dreadfully short-handed at the brewery all through the war, and worked almost to the limit of endurance. In addition, the business of the Central Control Board and other public work took up at least some part of every day. But the most interesting and varied work was certainly that to do with the Board.

Many deputations came to see Lord d'Abernon on different subjects connected with the Board's work. When he received them, he liked to have a member of the Board to sit with him, to comment and advise if necessary. For preference he liked to have members unconnected with the Government departments, and thus able to take an independent view. I always attended, when invited, if I could.

I remember Lord Astor once introducing a deputation representing various temperance organizations, including many clergy of different cloth. In view of Monmouthshire's geographical position and industrial relationship with Wales, it had been decided to extend the Welsh law of Sunday closing to cover this adjacent English county. Naturally the temperance movement welcomed this decision, and the suggestion they now wished to make to the Central Control Board was that the Sunday closing regulation should be extended to the whole of the country. They urged d'Abernon and the Control Board to consider this on the ground that if industrial efficiency had increased in Monmouth, nation-wide Sunday closing would result in a similar increase in efficiency everywhere. D'Abernon promised to give the matter his full consideration, and expressed sympathy with their object. He then asked me if I had anything to say. So far as I am aware, none of the deputation, except Astor, knew who I was; they only regarded me with some respect as a member of the Board. I asked a question they had not expected. If, I said, the Board made investigations and found that other districts where public houses were open on Sundays had given evidence of greater increase in efficiency than Monmouth, would they regard that as good reason for re-opening public houses on Sundays in Monmouth and, indeed, for extending Sunday opening to Wales? This mild inquiry was given a shocked and almost venomous reception, so Astor hastily intervened to say it was a difficult question and would require careful consideration. At this point the deputation withdrew. But Lord Astor was to cross my path again, or I was to cross his.

Another deputation was prompted by a very different motive. It came to present a complaint by the Enfield workers, who believed that the beer they were receiving had been specially weakened on the advice of the Board. At that time the output of beer was reduced, and the beer itself much diluted, all over the country, and d'Abernon succeeded in convincing them that they had not been singled out for ill treatment. He also promised to do his best to get them something stronger, and sent them away satisfied. He was a man of exceptional charm, and able to make any reply he offered sound satisfactory; for, although the Board had certainly not specially watered the Enfield beer, there was little at that time that anyone could do to improve it.

I remember, too, that we had a visit from some Chief Constables from towns in the north of England, including Newcastle and Durham, who had come to tell the Control Board of a serious increase in drinking among women in their towns, which was, they emphasized, a growing evil, one non-existent before the war. D'Abernon sent for the figures of convictions for drunkenness in the towns concerned, and remarked that from the figures it did not appear that there had been any marked increase in drunkenness among women in these areas—on the contrary, there was an improvement. The Chief Constables replied that there was little actual drunkenness among women, but that their present purpose was to draw attention to the large increase in the number of women who now drank. In the old days few decent women would go into a public house at all, and now they were walking in 'bold as brass', putting down their money and calling for beer. The Chief Constables assured Lord d'Abernon that this state of affairs had been practically unheard-of in peace time; they feared that it might continue after the war. I had, of course, known that women in ordinary times used public houses much less up north than in the London district, but I was not aware until then how wide was the difference. It seemed to me strange that leading police officials should be so troubled at what in the south was a quite normal custom.

I have always regretted that it should have been regarded as proper for a man to enter a public house but unsuitable for a woman; however, that view was strongly held, particularly in the north—perhaps one reason was the low standard of public houses in the northern industrial districts—or perhaps one result!

Occasionally I used to sit in Lord d'Abernon's room while he was dictating answers to his voluminous correspondence. This in itself was an educative experience. He had an amazing facility in dealing with his various correspondents, and was able to switch his mind from one personality to another with enviable celerity, dealing with a temperance advocate, a Cabinet Minister, his trainer and jockey in connection with his racing activities, then switching to Labour leaders, all with a brevity and expressiveness which were quite a revelation to me. His first letter to myself was a graphic example: 'I am glad to hear you will join my Board. We expect much from you.'

In addition to my membership of these various committees and official bodies, I was frequently asked by Government departments, and indeed sometimes by Ministers, to advise in a personal capacity. These invitations arose from my friendship with many who had offered their services, often honorary, to the Ministry of Food, the dominant authority concerned with the output of beer. They included Walter (afterwards Sir Walter) Roffey; Hugh Paul, whom I have already mentioned, head of the firm of Paul and Company of Ipswich, one of the biggest grain importers in the country; Owen Wightman, later Sir Owen, a maltster, very prominent in the Ministry; and Dr. E. S. Beavan, F.R.S., who, though a maltster at Warminster, was far better known for his creative work in breeding more productive types of barley. It was, of course, this same learned scientist who stigmatized the pig's 'uneconomical arrangements'.

Among the people I used to meet then was Sir George Younger, later Lord Younger, the Scottish brewer and banker, known politically as the Whip of the Scottish Liberal Party, at that time a powerful group. I remember being surprised at the informality with which matters of State were sometimes handled. I happened to be with Younger one day when the telephone rang, and he said, in an aside, 'The Prime Minister'. I rose to go, but he motioned me to stay where I was, and so I could not help hearing a talk about difficulties Lloyd George was having with the Bank of England. Sir George Younger's advice was, 'Don't you stand any nonsense. Tell him if he won't agree you will take over his bloody

Bank'. As we know, this eventually happened, but not for many years to come.

These men I had known before they became associated with the Government, and so my official association with them arose naturally and in some degree inevitably. However, I was concerned in these matters more particularly because Lloyd George retained many of his democratic principles, and impressed on the powers in the Trade—such men as John Gretton, Cosmo Bonsor of Watney's, Frank Whitbread, and others—that he was anxious to know the effect various measures might have on the rank and file of the industry, as well as on the large concerns. As a director of a medium-sized brewery near London, with a reputation for having a comprehensive knowledge of the Trade, I seemed to be the answer. So I was often called upon at short notice to supply information, or to advise on how particular proposals would affect the general body of brewers, or to say what I thought would be the reaction of the public.

The possibility of State purchase of the whole brewing and licensed trade had been discussed earlier in the war: with a view, first, to giving the Government greater power for enforcing restrictions and, second, to enable them to run the Trade as a State monopoly. State purchase did not, however, come prominently into the picture until 1917, and only then as a result of the submarine menace. The threat to the nation's food supply was so great by then that it appeared that brewing might have to stop altogether—the use of grain for the production of bread provided the greatest food value, and a proportion had to be set aside for animal feeding-stuffs. Stocks of malt were not expected to last over November, after which date, unless conditions improved, no further barley would be available for malting. In these circumstances the proposal of State purchase of the industry as a State monopoly was revived, and Lloyd George asked the Brewers' Society to form a small committee, representing different interests, to discuss the system and method of purchase with Lord Milner, who would be in charge of the transaction. It was indicated that one representative from Burton, as a great brewing centre, and one from London would be appropriate, together with three (afterwards increased to five) from other parts of the country.

A meeting of the London brewers was called to decide who should be charged with the responsibility of representing the interests of the metropolitan brewers. I was startled, the day before the meeting, to hear that my name might be suggested, and I said I had my doubts as to my being acceptable. I was told that in view of my knowledge of the Trade, my contacts in Government circles, and my reputation for having a broad outlook and for not being committed to any particular one of the larger interests, I might be asked. The meeting duly took place and I was, in fact, asked to accept this responsibility. I was pleased with the handsome compliment, and explained at once that since the work would be largely confidential I could not well report to the whole committee, but would consult Cecil Lubbock, who was both Master of the Brewers' Company and Chairman of the London Brewers' Council, and known for his impartial outlook.

I regarded this responsibility seriously, if for no other reason than that the capital value of the interests I represented must have exceeded a hundred million pounds. Delegating almost all my daily work to others, and visiting Brandon's solely to advise and superintend, I made a point of calling upon each of the brewers in London, and doing my best to obtain a clear idea of each one's particular interest. I was gratified by the kindly reception I received, for I was supplied freely with confidential information and found wide divergences in the circumstances and needs of the different companies. I had always known of the variation existing in the values of properties owned by different brewers. Some had bought houses wisely, and could claim that their assets were worth twenty shillings in the pound. Others, with less foresight, had given far higher prices for houses of doubtful worth whose trade had now depreciated and whose value, therefore, was now somewhat low. Again I came across breweries the prosperity of which depended largely on free trade and this circumstance brought problems of yet another order. Altogether, I acquired an insight into the affairs of the Trade which might have enabled me to profit largely from speculation on the Stock

Exchange, when peace came. But I had at the outset decided that I should be making a poor use of the confidence reposed in me if I used to my own benefit any information supplied in these conditions. I have been told that this was altruism and shortsightedness, but I think myself that the detached attitude I took brought me both friendship and respect from many much wealthier than myself. My responsibility (for the interests represented were large and varied) seemed formidable.

Our small committee of Trade leaders deliberated several times before meeting Lord Milner, though there was not much we could do until we had had our formal interview with him. When we did meet him he gave us an outline of the Government's proposals. Our Committee consisted of Colonel Gretton, M.P., representing the breweries of Burton; Colonel J. Gaskell, Cardiff; Sir Edward Holt, Bt., Manchester; Mr. W. Sykes, Tadcaster; Sir George (later Lord) Younger; Colonel Hall Walker, M.P. (later Lord Wavertree) and myself. When we next met we decided to tell Lord Milner that the industry would not raise any political opposition, but would co-operate to its utmost, provided that the Government would undertake that there should be no interference with the conduct of individual businesses until a Bill, providing for State purchase on an agreed basis, had passed its second reading. For a time nothing seemed to happen, and then conditions improved and the proposal was shelved for the time being.

However, some of the political supporters of State purchase were not easily deterred. At the time there was a great shortage of fuel and manpower, and it occurred to these supporters that the shortages could be used to advance their aims. Greatly reduced quantities of beer were being brewed, and practically all breweries were working at less than their full capacity, so the argument was put forward that if brewing were concentrated into a smaller number of breweries, a considerable economy in fuel and manpower must result and nationalization would be plain common sense. Without waiting for authorization from the Cabinet, the Ministry of Food formed a committee under the chairmanship of Walter Roffey, prominent in that department, together with various experts and some members of the Trade, with a view to working out methods of effecting that concentration. I was asked to help with the planning, so I attended one meeting of the committee and asked, before the agenda was read, if I could have a note of the Cabinet decision. Dissatisfied with the answer that 'authority had not yet been obtained, but was expected in the near future', I consulted with the other members of the 'Milner Committee', who considered that the proposal was contrary to the agreement with Lord Milner.

In reply to a formal inquiry, the Brewers' Society learned that a committee had been set up by Lord Rhondda to study coal economies generally; and that one of the committee's findings was that the concentration of brewing would effect considerable saving. On the 11th of June there was an interview with Mr. Bonar Law, Sir Arthur Stanley, the Rt. Hon. T. R. Clynes, P.C. (Minister of Food), and Sir Walter Roffey, head of the Brewing Department. At this meeting Sir George Younger and Hall Walker made it quite clear that in their view the concentration of brewing at this stage would be in direct contravention of the understanding reached with Lord Milner. I then pressed the point that economy of fuel could be attained more quickly and without the disturbance and unrest that would be caused by concentration, if savings were competently effected by individual concerns. I offered, on behalf of the Institute of Brewing, to call a meeting of head brewers and engineers and to form a committee whose function it would be to advise brewers as to how these economies could be made. The Ministers therefore decided that although fuel economy was of vital importance the Trade should be given an opportunity to achieve it by its own efforts, setting us a reduction of twenty-five per cent to aim at. No further steps would be taken, they promised, if this reduction by one-quarter could be achieved by us. Thus settled, the matter was deferred.

I had few personal contacts with Clynes, but his modesty and sincerity of purpose were apparent. It was not easy to visualize him as the leader of a great labour union. I have often since reflected on the sadness of his descent to comparative, indeed real, poverty, in his later years, after having achieved such eminence.

The next task was to implement our promise. I called a general meeting of the Institute—I believe the largest ever held by that body—and supported by Dr. E. R. Moritz, whom we have already met in these pages, I explained the position and our new commitment. A fuel committee of the Institute was appointed, which drew up and issued to all members advice on methods of economizing. Fuel advisers were elected to serve in each district and give help to brewers. The necessary cut in consumption was made, in many cases at the cost of interference with individual brewers' methods, which robbed their products of their particular character. The great majority rose to the occasion and when necessary abandoned methods which they treasured. When the Government fuel committee was suspended in April 1919 we were pleased to receive a letter from the Controller of Coal Mines, thanking the Institute of Brewing for their efforts which were described as 'highly satisfactory'.

When the Government had deferred, for the time being, its plan for State purchase, Lloyd George set up committees for England and Wales, for Scotland and also Ireland, to recommend terms of acquisition if and when the need arose. Lord Sumner was appointed chairman of the English committee, Lord Shaw of Dunfermline of the Scottish, and Mr. Justice Gordon of the Irish. All three committees examined witnesses without delay, and all presented reports during the next six or eight months, although these were not published until May of 1918.

Now, as I have said, one of the recommendations of the advocates of State purchase was the closing of a large proportion of breweries and the concentration of production in a few centres. This prospect alarmed the Institute of Brewing, the great majority of whose members were operative and technical brewers. If concentration came about, a large number of these trained and skilled men might find themselves redundant, with no other comparable means of livelihood ready to hand. The Institute of Brewing accordingly appointed a 'Protection Committee' to represent the interests of skilled operative brewers, many of whom were away on active service; the purpose was *not* to oppose nationalization, but rather to secure adequate compensation for those who would return from the wars to find themselves without employment, and with little or no prospect of getting an equivalent job.

When it came to appointing the Committee, I felt myself, as a member of the Central Control Board, to be an object of some suspicion, inasmuch as the Carlisle experiment was regarded by some as the first instalment of State purchase. I imagined that many might think I was not wholehearted in supporting the interests of those whose livelihoods were in jeopardy. On the other hand, I was convinced that my position qualified me to serve the interests of the operative brewers. The Council of the Institute agreed that a small committee would be most efficient, and decided to ballot for the names. I have always made it a principle, in ballots in which I have had a vote, never to vote for myself, but on this occasion I was so convinced of the need to watch the interests of the members of the Institute, and so sure of my ability to give the kind of really practical help which was required, that I felt entitled to vote for myself. This was unfortunate, for when the votes were counted, out of twenty-four present, the whole twenty-four had voted for me—so I had given myself away! At our first meeting they voted me to the Chair; and so we set to work.

We began by going to see the accountant (who acted as honorary auditor to the Institute) Mr. A. E. de Peyer, senior partner of Peyer, Thomas and Miles, himself a member of the War Damage Committee. He admitted the justice of the claim of technical brewers for compensation; but when we asked his advice as to the line we should adopt, he startled us by suggesting that a year's notice would be reasonable. He even added his opinion that if this were guaranteed, those found redundant would probably see nothing against continuing their services during the period of notice! At this point we began to realize the magnitude of the difficulties facing us, and set about finding solutions.

Some of my constituents favoured the idea of a capital payment, but I got them to agree to basing our argument on the compensation given to engineers and other professional members of the staffs of independent concerns which had been taken over by various authorities, such as the London water companies and the docks. We consulted the chairman of the London Water Board and the chairman of the Dock Authority, and decided that our proposals should be based on the compensation paid in these two industries, with this variation: that whereas the engineers, solicitors, and other professional workers employed by these bodies would have an opportunity of securing employment in other water companies or docks, in the brewing industry there would be no such chance of finding suitable work, because the Government monopoly would be complete. We worked out our case with the assistance of our legal advisers, and made an application to be heard first by the English Committee, with myself as spokesman. We had a satisfactory hearing, and were fairly well pleased with the Committee's report.

I travelled to Edinburgh two or three times to discuss the position with the Scottish brewers, and to help in drawing up their evidence to be put before the Scottish Committee. We had no difficulty in agreeing on the same lines of evidence that had been presented in England, but when it came to giving the evidence I suggested that one of their own Scottish members should act; but even so, they asked me to represent them. My evidence before the Scottish Committee was received courteously enough, though a Labour member strongly criticized me for giving evidence only on behalf of the technical brewers and engineers in the industry and for disregarding the general labour employed. I answered that I was giving evidence on the instructions of those concerned; that I had received no instructions from the general labour employed. This did not seem to satisfy my questioner, although I should have thought that as a leader of a trades union he would have appreciated the point. The report was reasonably favourable, though rather less so than in the case of the English committee.

At this time I was also concerned in discussions with the London Brewers regarding their capital interests. It appeared that the valuation of the trade, and consequently the money to be received by the London brewers, would be based on average profits over some previous years. Now the profits of the London brewers had for some years been at a low level owing to their having provided a stronger beer at a lower price than the average in the country, and possibly lower than anywhere else in the world. Many of the public houses were on valuable sites, considerably above the average site value outside the Metropolis. Capital value based on profits alone would not, in their case, be a just basis. Therefore the London brewers decided to give evidence in addition to that given by the Brewers' Society on behalf of the whole trade; Cecil Lubbock, as Master of the Brewers' Company, and myself, were appointed to do this. We pressed the view that, considering the high capital value of the premises in which the Trade was conducted in London, compensation fixed on a basis of annual profits could not represent a just estimate. To some extent this argument was reflected in the report of the English committee, but by no means as effectively as we should have liked.

Whether the Government had any real intention of proceeding with the proposals of the report of the 1917 committees is not known; but the proposals were certainly supported by some members of the Government and (in a memorandum of July, 1917) by the Central Control Board, though I have reason to believe that this was opposed to Lord d'Abernon's personal view. From time to time, the subject was brought forward in the press and on the platform (nationalization of the coal mines was also in the picture) but on the 18th August the Prime Minister declared against it. Moreover, nationalization of the brewing industry was, I repeat, opposed not only by those who disliked nationalization in general but by such temperance advocates as regarded with horror the prospect of the State being engaged at first hand in the business they detested.

All the same, the supporters of State purchase appear to have influenced the Labour Party at about that time. A Labour campaign, with J. H. Thomas as its organizer, was now initiated, its object being to achieve State ownership and control of the liquor trade. In Carlisle as late as the 10th of November 1919, Thomas declared that the Government's proposal to appoint a commission was playing with the question. 'If you want to keep the drink question free of politics,' he said, 'you can only do so by taking the drink profit out of private ownership.'

Whatever may have been thought of the success of Carlisle as an experiment in State purchase, I have never considered that extension on a national basis would be anything but a public misfortune. The consumer likes to have a choice both of commodities and service. Although the supply of general refreshments was one of the original principles of the Control Board, full development has not been found practicable at Carlisle—far less so, in fact, than under private enterprise by progressive brewers when encouraged by sympathetic and enlightened licensing authorities. The standard of sobriety is no higher in Carlisle than in comparable cities. I am convinced that adequate regulation can be secured through the buffer of an independent trade with less irritation than through a public authority. The varied and changing requirements of the people, with regard to both services and amenities, cannot be adequately supplied by any public monopoly. I believe that the general prejudice against monopolies is well founded. A frequently-heard complaint at Carlisle has concerned lack of variety, and occasionally of quality. I cannot forget that in my early days, when I made frequent pleas for improved quality, I was met with the somewhat cynical argument, 'Does it really matter? They cannot get anything else'. The profits of Carlisle have been quoted as being greater than the average under private enterprise, and I have touched upon the reasons for this above. I still consider that the public is better served in the long run by competitive enterprise, and that if tax revenues and other financial considerations were carefully taken into account, the Exchequer would ultimately profit more extensively from private ownership than from the Carlisle scheme. However this may be, and whatever the truth of the matter (for it is still in dispute) it is an undeniable fact that the adoption of Lord d'Abernon's policy of improvement inspired much constructive effort in the Trade in the post-First War years.

* * *

In 1919 I was surprised, after a membership of the Committee of less than two years, to be asked if I would act as Chairman of the Brewers' Society. It was pointed out to me that as the Trade would be faced with serious problems during the next few years, my varied experience during the War and my contact with Government departments and, indeed, several Ministers, would be of service. Once again Brandon was kind enough to give his consent, so I was duly nominated by four past Chairmen from different parts of the country; but two days before the meeting I received a letter from Colonel Gretton (afterwards Lord Gretton), then the doyen of the Brewing Industry, saying that while he would strongly support the proposal, he assumed that as matter of course I would sever my connection with the Central Control Board as he for one would regard continuance as quite inappropriate. I heard he was joined by that shrewd commercial man, T. W. Thorpe, the Managing Director of one of the principal London Breweries, and Edward Lovibond, Chairman of the Family Trade Brewers, men who in other circumstances were unlikely to hold views which coincided, and men who were unlikely to find themselves in agreement with Colonel Gretton. As I held strongly that in any question affecting the control of the Trade the brewing industry should have a voice, I withdrew my name at the meeting at which the election was due, adding a touch of humour by remarking that I thought everyone would agree that I was probably the only man who could bring into common agreement three such widely differing personalities. This reminder served to inhibit the heated discussion which seemed likely between the Pros and the Cons.

Although not Chairman, I was usually asked to speak for the Society in representations to Ministers on the various thorny matters that arose. As can be imagined there were, during the transition from wartime regulations to peace conditions, many occasions when we had to discuss matters with the Government. A particular instance occurred when, after a period of restriction of the materials allowed us, necessitating very weak beer, the Government, while allowing a larger quantity to be brewed, announced their intention of increasing the beer duty and thus securing a portion of the profit resulting from the additional output. However, we were much concerned at being unable to supply beer of other than low quality, wages were falling, and we considered we should be allowed to devote to the brewing of better beer any profits which might accrue from selling the larger quantity. I was appointed to lead the deputation presenting this view to the Chancellor, then Mr. Austen Chamberlain. While I was doing so his attention was diverted by what was evidently an urgent note handed to him. Nevertheless, he asked me to continue, and when I had finished, thanked me for coming, and assured me that what the deputation had laid before him would be carefully considered. Then he added, 'If I am unable to agree to your suggestion, you will appreciate that I have to listen to many gentlemen who feel it would be better for other people to be taxed, and not themselves.'

This was a facer. So I rose, thanked him for receiving us, and apologized for wasting his time, since I had completely failed to put before him the advice I was instructed to tender. I had been asked to advise him that the poor quality of beer brewed was calculated to prejudice his revenue, as well as the interests of the Trade. We were not there to avoid taxation, but to stabilize our industry and his revenue. We had thought it our duty to give him our considered views. However, since I had failed, I must withdraw and not detain him further. This seemed to be a new aspect, and he asked me to sit down and continue the conversation. In the result, our advice was accepted, the proposal to increase the duty was dropped, and the different qualities of beer which were regulated under the Food and Descriptions Order then in force were modified so that we were able to supply better beer.

I found this strange interview both stimulating and instructive and it certainly confirmed my view that deputations to Ministers should take the form of tendering advice, rather than of asking for favours.

7

Planning of Constructive Policy 1917—Improved Prestige of the Trade—Policy adopted by Brewers' Society and developed by National Trade Defence Association—First Trade Bill, March 1920, Government Bill, November 1920—My letter to The Times *— Second Trade Bill, February 1921—Meeting with the Prime Minister at Downing Street—Trade Bill dropped on Government promise to introduce agreed measure—Government Bill introduced July and received Royal Consent August 1917—Bona fide traveller in Scotland—End of the Control Board, but continuance of Carlisle*

The end of the war did not narrow the scope of my public activities; indeed my most important work dates from then. Towards the end of 1917 I had received a letter from Sir Richard Garton, asking me to dine and to meet Edward Giffard, chairman of Barclay Perkins, to discuss the future policy of the brewing industry, about which I knew both men had strongly held and definite ideas. With the coming of peace, the industry would have to face great problems of reconstruction; and with the State purchase project fading into the background it was possible to look ahead and make plans. It meant much to me to take part; I gladly accepted Garton's invitation.

Richard Garton, though a man of few words, was one of those constructive industrialists who leave a lasting mark on British industry. His original interests were in sugar. He was senior partner in the firm of Garton, Hill and Company of Battersea, whose business was to supply brewers with refined fermentable sugar. He had made brewers' problems his particular study, had a wide knowledge of the technical aspects of brewing, and also held considerable interests in various breweries. Many of his customers were also his close and intimate friends. It was in the nature of things that so well-liked and knowledgeable a man should also have a powerful voice in Trade concerns. He was known also as an active supporter of various forward-looking philanthropic movements. He established the Garton Foundation to study international relationships with a view to lessening the possibility of war—an enterprise stimulated by the publication of Norman Angell's famous work, *The Great Illusion*, that pioneer attempt to drive home the lesson, now pretty well learnt, that the winner in modern war is little better off, sometimes is actually worse off than the loser. Garton was even more widely known as a founder, and a principal supporter, of the British Empire Cancer Campaign.

Edward Giffard was likewise a man of vision and political wisdom, and, though also a man of few words, was much valued as an adviser in Trade movements. They had both been members of the small group who—with Frank Whitbread, Cecil Lubbock, myself and others—had in previous days supported constructive proposals, as opposed to the sterile defensive policy which had contented the Trade organizations for many years. This group had not, however, under pre-war conditions, found it practicable to persuade the Trade to adopt a definite policy on a national basis: but now, with the end of the war approaching, they felt that the time was ripe for this.

When we met, Garton and Giffard told me they had been in consultation with several prominent leaders of the industry—John Gretton of Bass's, Lord Iveagh, head of the Guinness family, Frank Whitbread, Cecil Lubbock, and others—who agreed that, with the end of the war, an active and clear-cut policy of construction would be needed for all industries, especially our own. They asked me, in view of my pre-war activities, and war-time connections with Ministries, to join them in drafting an outline of a constructive policy. So we got to work and eventually put our proposals in a form which could be recommended both to the wholesale and retail trades. We did not forget the industry's duty to contribute to the rebuilding of the country after the upheavals of more than four years of a world war.

We dined together, we spent week-ends on Richard Garton's yacht *Morvern*, and at his home in Surrey, where we enjoyed the advantage of consultations with Garton's neighbour, Lord Justice Parker. Lord Parker was not unfamiliar with the Trade: an important and complicated income tax test case concerning Usher's Wiltshire Brewery Limited *v.* Bruce had come before him, in the course of which many sides of the industry's working had been disclosed to him.

The war had brought many changes, and had in fact thrown new light on many matters relevant to our business; we were fortunate in having men of the calibre of Garton and Giffard to lead us. A high standard of sobriety had been attained, thanks partly to restrictions and partly to public opinion (which is always the best lawmaker); this had gone far to confirm the apparently revolutionary opinion I had expressed ten years before: that the Trade could prosper more in England sober than in England drunken. The helpful attitude, too, of the industry during war had resulted in personal friendship and mutual respect between some of us in the Trade and the Government. Perhaps never before had brewers and the executive heads of Government departments worked so closely together—the gulf of suspicion and mistrust between the Trade and the Government and its various departments had been largely bridged.

The untimely attempt of the extreme temperance party to use the war to secure prohibition—and indeed they had openly declared: 'If we miss this chance we may never get another'—had embarrassed the Government by aggravating industrial difficulties. It had inspired Lloyd George to say in the House of Commons, on the 4th May, 1915, when referring to the Trade: 'There is no man in this House who has fought them harder than I have; but I am bound to say that they met the appeals which I made to them in a patriotic spirit, in an attitude of mind which could leave nothing to be desired from the point of view of anybody who is trying to help this country along. I feel bound to say that as an old political opponent of theirs. I say more than that. If there is a failure, I do not think the blame rests on them. I am bound to say so, and I think it is due to them.' Again, on the 11th May, 1916, Lloyd George said, 'The difficulties are not coming from the Trade; I have said that once before. I have been met in the fairest possible manner by representatives of the Trade, and they have not interposed insuperable obstacles. My greatest difficulties have been with those with fixed ideas'. This last reminder was especially addressed to Mr. Leif-Jones (later Lord Rhayader), then leader of the prohibitionist party, and we can best judge of Lloyd George's change of heart by contrasting these remarks with something he had said a mere eighteen months earlier to a deputation of ship owners urging him to introduce prohibition: 'We are fighting Germany, Austria, and Drink,' said he, 'and so far as I can see the greatest of these deadly foes is Drink.'

We were also encouraged by the policy of the Central Control Board, under d'Abernon's dominant chairmanship, of enlarging and improving the licensed houses under its control. This was the policy so long and so bitterly opposed by the prohibitionists and by many licensing benches under teetotal influence. The Board had a free hand, because the districts under their control were automatically removed from the jurisdiction of the licensing authorities (much to the latter's disapproval). It was with the obstructionist attitude of many licensing benches in mind that later, when drafting a Bill to be presented to Parliament, we proposed to remove licensing authority from the 'justices of the peace', who had administered it according to their varied and all too often prejudiced discretion, and to transfer these duties to a special body which could be trusted to maintain a more strictly judicial attitude. And so we set to work and drafted the following broad outline of policy on a sheet of foolscap. Our declaration's five principal pronouncements were:

(i) That measures which curtail freedom do not necessarily promote sobriety.
(ii) That the function of the State is to maintain public order and to punish drunkenness, but not to decide, except as

to the purity of the article supplied, what a man shall eat and drink.

(iii) That existing licensing machinery should be so modified as to provide a system which shall ensure uniformity of administration, and that such modification should be in the direction of setting up judicial tribunals operating over wide areas on uniform principles, with an appeal from their decisions to a single appeal authority presided over by a High Court Judge.

(iv) That, where the number of licences is excessive, reduction should be brought about with due regard to all interests affected, accompanied by facilities for the improvement of those licensed premises which remain, and for the removal of licences to developing districts.

(v) That improvements which involve an enlargement of premises and provide opportunities for greater amenities are more in the interests of temperance than a rigid adherence to existing restrictions on licensed premises.

Particular emphasis was directed to the following as the governing principles of the trade policy:

(i) Proposals emanating from the licensed Trade should be of a character to secure the approval of the majority of the public as well as the support of all sections of the Trade.

(ii) The policy should aim at attaining a high standard of efficiency in the public service, and thus secure commercial welfare, popular approval, and the active support of leaders of public opinion.

(iii) The existence of insobriety is directly inimical to the good service of the public, and to the commercial interests of the industry. The consideration of measures to suppress excess must find a place in Trade policy.

This note embodies in effect the tenets of the constructive movement first advocated in 1908 by our small group. It was submitted to the Brewers' Society, then referred by them to the

National Trade Defence Association, as representing all sections of the Trade. The N.T.D.A. appointed a sub-committee on which I sat and which, in due course, reported back to the Brewers' Society and to the leaders of the retail trade. A committee was appointed to draft a Bill to be introduced in the House of Commons, under the chairmanship of Edwyn Barclay, and enjoyed the assistance of that great man Randle Holme (later Sir Randle Holme) then Solicitor to the Society. This man of brilliant record was born in 1864, educated at Sherborne and Corpus Christi, Oxford, and took his law degree, with first-class honours, in 1887. He was a man of many parts and great influence. In his still early years he was made a Fellow of the Royal Geographical Society in recognition of the value of his explorations in Labrador. In 1914 he drafted an Income Tax Consolidation Bill, which became the Income Tax Act of 1918. He was President of the Law Society in 1940 and knighted in 1941. He made a special study of music and published an English version of Wagner's 'Ring' and 'Parsifal'. When compelled by age to give up his official connection with the Brewers' Society, he was elected to honorary membership. Until his death at the age of ninety-four he retained his interest in affairs, and attended his office several times a week. When, on his ninetieth birthday, he was congratulated by a man thirty years younger, who said he looked forward to being present at his centenary, Holme looked him up and down and replied, 'I don't see why not. You look pretty well!'

In our deliberations over the drafting of the Bill we found ourselves in a dilemma. There was intense public resentment against the continuance of restrictions long after the war had ended, aggravated by the knowledge that the temperance enthusiasts had tried to use the war to further the cause of prohibition; there was a conviction that it was the influence of social reformers that led to this prolonging of controls. We thought it possible that this resentment might lead to public and political agitation to enforce a complete return to pre-war conditions which we ourselves did not desire. While we wished for greater freedom in some respects, we did not want to reject all the experience which was the outcome of the war, nor yet to disregard those factors which had contributed to sobriety. As in everything that concerns the public as a whole, there was no isolated issue of support or dissent, but many warring opinions in regard to which we had to strike a balance between freedom and excessive regulation.

The general purpose of the Bill we drafted was to bring the Liquor Control Board to an end, to extend the facilities for service, and to ensure reasonable hours of sale—that is to say, considerably fewer than the pre-war hours which exceeded general requirements. Our most important reform, as I said just now, concerned licensing administration. We proposed that licensing should be taken away from the often prejudiced magistracy and thereafter become the responsibility of a special authority (with the County Courts as approximate model) administered by trained lawyers. We felt that the Control Board's record at Carlisle had shown the desirability of some such new licensing authority.

The drafting took time and labour, but its outcome was introduced by Colonel Gretton on the 2nd of March, 1920, as a Private Member's Bill. To judge by the number of copies of the Bill asked for by various Government departments and other interested bodies, it was almost a 'best seller'. Among others who were instructed by their departments to report on it was my friend J. S. Eagles, then a member of the Treasury Staff seconded to the Central Control Board. His witty and unofficial comment was: 'I can summarize this Bill in a paraphrase of the Litany—from the Injustices of the War, and the Justices of the Peace, O Parliament deliver us!' Thereafter, among the irreverent, it was called 'The Brewers' Litany Bill'.

Though this Bill did not get beyond its second reading, it still had served our interests valiantly. One immediate reaction was opposition from the general body of licensing justices who, whatever their politics or opinions about the Trade, were united in attaching great importance to their duties, which they most jealously guarded. This and other repercussions led us to think again, to trust to argument, gradual persuasion and steady propaganda to ensure a more reasonable attitude towards improvement in licensing administration. While our grievance was the obstructive attitude of many benches towards improvements, we felt that because of the increasing interest of the man in the street in the subtleties of the matter, and in public house improvement generally, not to mention the excellent results we were able to show wherever alterations had been allowed, we could persuade the benches to become more co-operative. With the passing of the years this change has, as we hoped, come about.

While we were considering our second Bill the Government, on the 13th November, 1920, introduced a Bill of its own. This was the 'Liquor Control (Temporary Provisions) Bill', presented by H. A. L. Fisher, then Minister of Education. The Government had not consulted the members of the Central Control Board and certainly not the Trade itself, but none the less Fisher claimed that there was considerable agreement for the proposals to be introduced. I have never been able to discover who had done this considerable agreeing!

The Bill simply proposed to transfer all the powers of the Central Control Board to the Home Office. I was furious, for I was convinced that what the country needed was an Act which would establish stable conditions, and this pernicious proposal would leave the industry as a political pawn. It would destroy all our hopes of a settled and constructive policy—at a time, too, when we had been assured that the helpful attitude of brewers during the war had merited consultations, just as soon as post-war legislation was contemplated, between the Government and what Lord d'Abernon used to call 'the best elements of the Trade'.

The day after the introduction of the Government Bill there was a meeting of the Control Board. I attended, and said that if it was felt I ought to resign, I would: but that in any event I intended to do my best to secure the rejection of this Bill, which I regarded as thoroughly inimical to the national interest as well as destructive to all sound policies and hopes. I had already drafted a letter to *The Times* and I had an appointment immediately after the meeting to discuss this letter with the redoubtable Mr. Boon, a *Times* staff reporter who foresaw a piquant story. I was not asked to resign by my colleagues on the Board, many of whom were as disturbed as I was, and it may be that my membership added some authority to my letter when it appeared on the 18th

12. MEMBERS OF OUR GROUP WHO DRAFTED THE CONSTRUCTIVE POLICY IN 1917

Colonel Oswald P. Serocold
We must do the right thing

Sir Richard Garton
We need a constructive policy

Francis P. Whitbread

Lord Justice Parker
You are wise to study the public interest

Edward Giffard
We need the respect of all right-minded men

13. Samuel Whitbread, the founder of Whitbread's Brewery

Sir Joshua Reynolds

14. Samuel Whitbread the Second, noted politician, who financed the rebuilding of the Drury Lane Theatre

Thomas Gainsborough

November. Such as it was, I think it may be worth recording in full in spite of its deficiencies.

To the Editor of *The Times*

Sir,

When the Central Control Board (Liquor Traffic) was appointed, Lord d'Abernon brought to the conduct of its affairs an entirely new policy in the history of the liquor controversy. I and others may not have agreed with all his views, but it was apparent that he brought to bear on the problem a broad common sense and a spirit of scientific inquiry hitherto entirely foreign to the discussion. Realizing this, I gladly accepted the invitation to join the Board, in the hope that my practical experience and knowledge would enable me to contribute towards such a balance between public convenience and restrictions as would satisfy the consumer, on the one hand, and ultimately reduce insobriety to negligible limits, on the other.

To several members of the Board the past two years have been full of disappointment. Of the Board's regulations some were obviously only suitable to war conditions, others did not secure the result hoped for, but others again contained important and valuable elements suitable for permanent adoption. It appeared to myself and others that the Board should at the conclusion of the war consider in the light of war experience what restrictions should be laid before the Government as the basis of a peace policy. Other members were unaccountably indisposed towards this course, and it ultimately transpired that they had received instructions from the Cabinet (the terms of which had not been disclosed to the Board as a whole) that restrictions, whether permanently desirable or not, should as far as possible be retained pending Government proposals for permanent legislation. As a result the Board was debarred from basing on the experience gained during the war a policy applicable to peace time which would be satisfactory to the consuming public and yet would secure a permanent social improvement.

The Government have now decided (again without consultation with the Board) to transfer the whole of the existing powers to a Government Department. This decision is greatly to be deplored. The drastic and far-reaching powers of the Board should not continue in peace time, and are not such as should be exercised by a purely official administration. Liquor regulation, affecting as it does the habits and customs of the great masses of the population, requires the support of the public as well as the co-operation of the industry if it is to be successful. The framing of suitable regulations requires more knowledge of the requirements of the public and more knowledge of the circumstances of the Trade than can be expected to be possessed by a departmental authority.

The leaders of the industry with whom I come in contact are fully prepared to accept and administer such regulation as will contribute to good service on the one hand, and sobriety on the other. But if Parliament accepts the proposed arrangements, in my opinion it is inevitable that ignorance of trade conditions and public requirements will result in such opposition from the general body of the Trade and such public dissatisfaction as will cause an outcry for freedom from all restrictions and a total reversion to pre-war conditions, whereas, had a wiser alternative been selected, it would have been found practicable to retain much of what has been gained by the war without impinging on the public convenience and without arousing public or trade hostility.

From the financial aspect the Government proposal is equally unsatisfactory. The success of the commercial operations of the Board, whilst primarily due to the outstanding ability and devotion of the heads of the staff, could not have been secured had it not been that when efficiency or economy was threatened by the difficulty of composing official methods with commercial practice the commercial members of the Board have been able to give sufficient weight to their opinion to enable commercial efficiency to be maintained. If the Government is to indulge in commercial trading, commercial methods must be adopted, and, as has been proved so often, the organization of Government Departments is not fitted successfully to engage in trading enterprise.

It has been suggested that the Department to which the Control Board work will be transferrred may have the advantage of an Advisory Committee. This will not meet the case. Government Departments never welcome and seldom accept advice, and it is hardly to be expected that an Advisory Committee will be either kept sufficiently informed of the facts or that sufficient attention will be paid to their opinion to secure satisfactory results.

For the reasons I have stated, the proposals of the Government are provocative in character and are undesirable both from the point of view of the consumer and from that of national sobriety, and it is to be hoped that they will either be withdrawn or that authority for the administration of this difficult work, which requires a broad knowledge of public requirements, as well as an intimate acquaintance with trade conditions, will be given.

Yours faithfully,

SYDNEY O. NEVILE.

*St. Stephen's Club, Westminster, S.W.*1.
1*7th November*, 1920.

This letter was something of a bombshell. In official circles my action in writing it was regarded as a grave breach of loyalty, but it won the approval of most of those engaged in seeking a permanent settlement of the question. I have since been told that it contributed to the hostility with which the Bill was received in Parliament, as a result of which it was withdrawn on the 14th December. I heard about this time (quite improperly) that my name was under consideration for an honour similar to that given to my Trade colleagues on the Board, Butler and Towle, but that it had been withdrawn on my plunge into open hostility to the Government Bill while still a member of the Board. Whether this was true or not, I was not greatly concerned.

It was not until the 18th of February, 1921, that Col. Gretton was able to introduce our second Bill. By that time, the war had been over for more than two years. The public were increasingly restive under the restrictions still exercised under the Defence of the Realm Act (popularly, or rather unpopularly, known as DORA), and more particularly with those imposed by the Central Control Board. It was believed by the Whips that the Government supporters would find themselves in difficulties if they opposed Gretton's Bill on the Government's instructions, and this led Lloyd George into taking active steps on his own. On the morning when the Bill was to be introduced, I received an SOS asking me to attend at Downing Street, where a discussion was to be presided over by the Prime Minister. I found several of my colleagues of the Control Board already assembled, including Henry Carter, Waters Butler, Sir John Pedder (acting chairman of the Control Board after d'Abernon's resignation) and several Ministers, including the Attorney General (Sir Gordon Hewart) and H. A. L. Fisher. The Prime Minister presided, and as I watched his handling of the meeting, I was impressed by the calm and deliberation he had retained in spite of the strain of the war years.

Lloyd George, Hewart and Fisher were discussing the public resentment at the continuance of restrictions so long after the end of the war, and were considering what course to take with regard to the Bill to be introduced that afternoon. The members of the Control Board spoke somewhat variously, according to their convictions. I said that, though many restrictions should be relaxed at the earliest possible moment, I was sure that the Trade would not wish for a complete return to pre-war conditions. Unless the public could be satisfied that substantial modifications would be made very soon, there might be agitation, which would not only embarrass the Government but would be against the public interest and in the long run be a misfortune to the Trade itself. I also emphasized the importance of stabilizing conditions by means of an Act of Parliament, so that the Trade and the public would know where they stood.

The proceedings did not take long. The Prime Minister announced his decision, which possibly he had reached beforehand. He asked Sir Gordon Hewart to make a placatory speech in the House, expressing the Government's appreciation of the need to give the matter their attention at the earliest possible date, but adding that in the Government's view this was not a question to be dealt with in a private member's Bill. The Government would feel bound to oppose the Bill as it stood; but, if its sponsors saw fit to withdraw it, they would undertake to bring in an 'agreed measure' at an early date.

Soon after this we all went across to the House, and there the matter fell out as arranged: Gretton introduced his Bill, which received strong support, Hewart spoke as agreed, and Gretton withdrew the measure on the understanding that an agreed Government Bill would follow. This was on the 22nd April 1921. The representatives of the retail Trade were angry at what they felt was a surrender, as they had hopes that the second reading would be carried and thus display what they termed 'the power of the Trade'. But I was sure that Gretton was right and my wiser friends agreed.

By mid-June, the Government had begun to fulfil its promise, for a round table conference of eighteen M.P.s of many shades of opinion was set up under Hewart's chairmanship, to consider the whole matter of licensing legislation. The conference consisted of four temperance representatives, four with knowledge of the Trade, two of clubs, four 'neutrals' to represent 'average public opinion', two members of the Government, and two of the Labour opposition. The terms of reference were clear and concise: 'To consider, with reference to the law of licensing, how best to adapt to times of peace the experience gained in time of war'. The Government, following common practice, appeared to think a strong panel of prohibitionists essential to the consideration of the regulation of the Trade whose purpose it was to serve the public. But at any rate it was a move forward to allot four seats to members who had an actual knowledge of the industry.

Not being an M.P. I was not a member of the conference, and no outside evidence was taken. But I was closely in touch with the Trade members, and so may claim to have had something to do, although indirectly, with the conference's final recommendations, which were embodied in the Government's Bill. This was officially termed 'The Licensing (No. 2) Bill, No. 177' and the

Attorney-General introduced it on the 19th July, with commendable promptness. Governments do not always keep their promises within three months of making them. The Bill was regarded as mainly non-controversial; it passed through all its stages with unusual rapidity, receiving the Royal Assent on August 17th. Its provisions have remained practically unaltered up to the present time.

The 1921 Act—like all licensing legislation—is a long and complicated measure. It would be inappropriate to discuss it here in detail. But as it is the basis of the main provisions of the law, I give an outline of it. First, it appointed eight hours outside London, and nine within the metropolitan area, as permitted hours for the sale of intoxicating liquors during week-days, in place of the 19 hours allowed in London in pre-1914 days. Next, it laid down certain rules regarding these 'permitted hours', which were not to commence earlier than 11 a.m. and were to end not later than 10 p.m. in the country and 11 p.m. in the metropolis, with a two-hour break in the afternoon, and with some latitude in certain circumstances, including late-suppers. Other clauses dealt with permitted hours in clubs, the sale of drinks in restaurants, the prohibition of the old 'long-pull' by which some publicans and especially off-licences sought to attract custom by giving 'a bit extra'; the dilution of spirits. A crucial clause dealt with the State Management districts. These were to continue until Parliament should decide otherwise; the Control Board was, of course, to be disbanded. Parliament has not so far abolished the State Management districts. There were other special provisions affecting Wales.

Another interesting change was the banishment of the 'bona fide traveller'. This thirsty but often fictitious personage made his first appearance in the nineteenth century, when restricted hours on Sunday were laid down. To make provision for tourists, licensees were allowed to serve, at any hour, 'bona fide travellers' who must not be less than three miles from the place where they had spent the previous night. On Sundays in particular, when the permitted hours were few, it was surprising how many people found themselves three miles from home during the course of an afternoon stroll, and accordingly qualified for a 'bona fide' drink. The closing of this loophole so far as England was concerned was regretted by few, as it had been much abused. The hardship was small as residents at licensed hotels could still, and can still today, be served with drink throughout the day; and the permitted hours still provide for drinks at lunch and dinner.

A provision of the Act which has puzzled many people was the compulsory break of at least two hours in the afternoon, during which drink might not be sold. This was resented by some; but it was thought that few people used public houses in the afternoon. This break was in fact one of the Central Board's orders which has genuinely contributed to sobriety. It appeared to be well established that, if sales were suspended during the afternoon, men otherwise inclined to 'make a day of it' would return to work.

There were one or two debatable points in the Act, and one or two anomalies too. The new 'permitted hours' represented a considerable increase on those allowed under Control Board Orders. But they were a great deal fewer than those in operation before the war, when, in London for example, sales were permitted from five in the morning until half an hour after midnight. Few people regretted the passing of these hours. A more controversial point was the inclusion of the English county of Monmouthshire as part of Wales, for Wales was subject to complete Sunday closing of public houses.

In order to make the new Act effective in Scotland, where the basic licensing laws are different, a separate Scottish Act was needed. In the framing of this, by some oversight, the abolition of the bona fide traveller was omitted. This omission produced the ridiculous position that whereas in Wales, with Sunday closing, travellers cannot get a drink even with meals, in Scotland, which also has Sunday closing, it is possible for travellers to be served. This discrimination is still bitterly resented in Wales. Another provision of the Act dealt with the supply of liquor in clubs, and for the first time brought them to some extent into line with the permitted hours applicable to public houses. But, while clubs could fix their own hours within the total number of 'permitted hours', those for licensed houses are defined by the justices and cannot be varied by individual licensees even if conditions make a change reasonable. This rigidity in regard to public house hours causes a good deal of resentment. Although well established and regulated clubs are careful to conform to the customary permitted hours, it is a matter of complaint by the retail licensed trade that there are many that do not. I remember the indignation of some acquaintances at a local club I would sometimes visit while a member of the Control Board. My connection with the Board became known to the club secretary, and so the steward began asking members, at ten o'clock, to finish their drinks. I found I should be more popular if I made a practice of leaving before 10 p.m!

There was one point of principle which may not be generally recognized. Whereas till 1914 legislation defined the hours during which licensed houses could be open, the new Act provided for 'permitted hours of sale' without ordaining that the house must be closed at other times. In practice, however, especially in industrial neighbourhoods, for various reasons (often at the instance of the police) houses are usually only open during 'permitted hours' for the sale of excisable beverages.

Although the 1921 Act was not perfect—what Act of Parliament is?—it provided a good piece of working legislation with which, except for minor points, no reasonable person could quarrel. And as a result of it, as mentioned above, the Central Control Board (Liquor Trade) was wound up and laid to rest, to popular satisfaction, in October 1921. Like all bodies engaged in restricting and controlling public activities, it was unpopular; it certainly made mistakes; but in general I believe that its labours were essential. I have never regretted the time I gave to it; I think we did useful work; but I was glad when it was all over. I wanted to forget war, and the things it had brought forth, and to concentrate on the problems of reconstruction.

However, one of the Board's activities, and a controversial one, continued still. The Government monopoly in Carlisle, commonly called 'The Carlisle Experiment', was retained, together with the Scottish areas, by a provision in the Act. With Butler and Towle, I was persuaded to continue to advise the Home Office. My principal reason for doing so was that the scheme represented the acceptance by the Government of the principle of public house improvement—my main preoccupation at that time outside my day-to-day commercial activities. So I became a member of the Council which directed the 'State Management Scheme' and continued in this until 1955, when, at the age of 82, I felt I had 'done my bit' after thirty-eight years' service to the Home Office as an honorary adviser.

8

Commercial conditions during War—Death of Chester Brandon—End of War—Invitation to join Whitbread's Board, 1919*—Tribute to the Whitbread Family and my Colleagues at Whitbread's—Early experience at Whitbread's—I join the Court of the Brewers' Company—Establishment of Research Scheme—Catalysts Club—Annual Dinner of Institute of Brewing, April* 1920

To go back to 1917: although my increasing participation in public affairs occupied much of my time, I still continued my responsibilities at the Putney brewery. But conditions in the war, to some extent, simplified management, as each brewer's output was limited; weekly brewings were standardized and each customer rationed with so much a week. There was thus no problem of adjusting output to demand or of arranging varying deliveries to individual houses. Nor was there any question of securing new business. So we carried on in spite of the absence of many of our people, including Brandon's son, Chester Brandon, who was serving as a Captain with his regiment, the 1st/4th Hampshires, in the Middle East. Then came the news that Chester was missing, believed killed, during fighting on the 21st January, 1916, at Hanna in Mesopotamia. His death was afterwards confirmed. This was a terrible blow to Brandon. Chester was his only son. It had been hoped he would succeed to the control of the Company, in which his father owned all the ordinary shares, and Chester had been trained with this future in view. He was born in 1885, educated at Uppingham and Merton

College, Oxford, and before joining the Company had taken two years' training in accountancy and general management; after this, he worked closely with me at Putney.

This tragedy set me thinking about the future of the business and its staff, for Brandon was by now of an age when men retire from active business. I ventured to ask him whether he had thought of arranging for the business to be continued on a permanent basis. If he contemplated retiring, I believed—from talks I had had with Cecil Lubbock—that Whitbread's might be interested. I knew that Lubbock thought highly of the business and might continue it as a separate entity, and felt sure that Whitbread's would treat the staff with kindness and liberality. I suggested to Brandon that he would be unlikely to find another buyer who would run the business as an independent concern; if it came into the open market it would almost inevitably be absorbed by another firm, perhaps one less considerate than Whitbread's.

Brandon told me his family had been urging him to retire, in view of his advancing age and the death of his son. He had not thought it practicable to dispose of the business at that time, but he authorized me to sound Whitbread's; so I had a chat with Lubbock, and found the suggestion appealed to him, partly because the business would be useful to Whitbread's (since they had few properties in the Brandon area) and partly because he would like to secure my help, not only with Brandon's, but with the Whitbread company itself. I explained that I should have to get the best possible value for Brandon's, and would find it difficult to act for both sides; this being so, I arranged a meeting between him and Brandon, and left them to come to their own agreement.

Brandon asked Reginald Mason, our accountant, to advise him on the terms for negotiating a transfer of ownership; and Mason set a high price on the business. However, Cecil Lubbock had experienced difficulties in those lean years around 1900, and these had made him somewhat pessimistic and unduly cautious. He found Brandon's price much higher than he had expected, so much higher in fact that there seemed little likelihood of a deal; and there, for the moment, matters rested. My position was difficult:

I could hardly intervene, either to ask Brandon to come down, or to ask Lubbock to push his offer higher. Accordingly I did nothing, though I hoped that later on agreement might be reached. Then one day Brandon told me he had received a letter from Cecil Lubbock regretting that he could not see his way to recommend his company to purchase on the terms advised by Mason. After saying he could not make an offer for the Putney Brewery, he went on to broach another matter of great importance to me; he told Brandon that he had been nominated for appointment as Deputy Governor of the Bank of England, an appointment which would occupy most of his time, and that it would be necessary for Whitbread's to reinforce their board. He knew he was asking a lot: but might he have leave to approach me and ask me to join Whitbread's Board? This opened up a most attractive vista for me, but I felt bound to tell Brandon that, after so many years of association with him, I could not bring myself to desert the ship just at the time when he might need me most. Brandon replied, typically, that he had decided to dispose of the business anyhow, and that, however much he would miss me, if I were his own son he would have seen nothing for it but to advise me to accept the opportunity. Within a few days Lubbock asked me to call and discuss the matter with Mr. Harry Whitbread and himself. The proposal accorded with my highest ambition, for of all the breweries in the country Whitbread's, although not the largest, enjoyed the greatest prestige. I had no hesitation in accepting the offer, although, to start with, the terms were little more than my remuneration at Putney. I knew that I should be in happy and congenial surroundings; and also felt sure that I could prove of sufficient value to justify more generous terms in the future. This being so, I took up the shares necessary to qualify me and was duly elected to the board. It was arranged that I should take up my duties as a Managing Director on the 1st of October, 1919.

I had hoped to retain my directorship of Brandon's in an advisory capacity until the business was sold, but since Brandon felt that those connected with the company should have a single interest, I resigned from the board, after twenty-nine years at Putney. The parting was a wrench, in spite of my having achieved my ambition of being connected with a really large concern. Moreover, my resignation at that time involved me in considerable sacrifice: had I waited until the company changed hands, I should have shared in the compensation customarily paid to members of a board in cases of amalgamation; in this case it amounted to an annuity of £1,000 which each of my fellow directors received. But I had no regrets then, and I have none now.

While these negotiations were in progress my mother died suddenly at the age of eighty-two; her death meant the break-up of our home at Putney. My sister Blanche and I decided to set up house together, so we began flat hunting with the aim of finding something within easier reach of Chiswell Street. After some weeks of fruitless search, we found an agent with something to offer: he had just been instructed to dispose of a lease which had several years to run, but at a much larger premium than I thought reasonable. Nevertheless we viewed the flat and finding it suitable, I returned to the agent, intending to offer a lower sum, only to learn that in the meantime the owner had decided to increase the premium. Still, as I had already been given the offer, I still could have it at the original figure; this clinched the matter, and I signed the contract. I was surprised and rather comforted to hear from the agent two days later that he had a client who was so anxious to secure the flat that he could get me £250 if I would surrender my option; but I could not face another search, so I stuck to my bargain.

It is curious to remember now that within two or three years after this so much building had taken place that large blocks of equally good flats were standing empty; in fact it was possible to obtain one at the cost of only the rates if one would agree to turn out at three months' notice if a more lucrative tenant arrived. At the rate building of this kind is taking place now I sometimes wonder if the same position may not arise after the present boom.

On the day I joined Whitbread's there was a strike which affected public transport, and so I arranged to enter by car upon the second, and longest, and most rewarding of the chapters in my life as a brewer. I felt deep satisfaction as I passed under the arch and entered the precincts of the brewery for the first time in a position of authority. Fine beers had been in continuous production on this spot for nearly two centuries, all under the care and control of a single remarkable family. The business was founded in London in 1742 by Samuel Whitbread, who had come up from the country at the age of fourteen to learn 'the mystery and art of brewing'. That was in 1734, and while still a very young man he established a brewhouse of his own in the City. About 1745 he began to brew on the present site in Chiswell Street, and indeed a number of the buildings still occupied by the company were built by the first Whitbread in the middle years of the eighteenth century. When whole streets immediately adjacent to the brewery were destroyed in the blitz, Samuel Whitbread's buildings survived almost unimpaired. It interested me to learn that the founder was the fifth son of a widow, for I was myself the fifth son of my father's family of fifteen children, and my mother was a widow. I found too that, like Samuel Whitbread, I had begun to learn the 'art and mystery' of our trade at fourteen; but there the parallel ends. I have never founded a famous brewery—but I have been proud to help to administer and maintain, for nearly forty busy and happy years, the one which he established.

Samuel Whitbread the first, who founded the firm, was a great personality of that eighteenth century which abounded in outstanding men. Besides building up a successful business he represented Bedford in Parliament for many years, and made brewing history by entertaining a reigning monarch at Chiswell Street. This was the occasion, described by Peter Pindar, when George III and Queen Charlotte spent several hours minutely inspecting the wonders of Mr. Whitbread's establishment: the great store, in which there were 'three thousand and seven barrels of beer; the mighty new steam-engine built by James Watt'. This 'mighty steam-engine' ultimately found its way to the Sydney Science Museum; it is the one I made a special point of seeing when I was in Australia. They also saw the cistern 'of such magnitude as to hold four thousand barrels of beer'; and 'the highest horse among His Majesty's subjects'—one of eighty horses assembled for inspection. All this and much more so impressed His Majesty that he postponed his breakfast so as not to miss anything—and made up for it by a hearty attack upon the provisions afterwards set before him. The honour thus paid to the brewery did not pass unchallenged, for in the aforementioned set of verses the satirist Peter Pindar gave a ludicrous account of the occasion. But he was on the other side politically. Today, for people who don't read forgotten satirists, there is a stone tablet on the brewery wall to commemorate the king's visit, designed by Professor Sir Albert Richardson, P.P.R.A.

It became traditional for the head of the Whitbread family to be head of the business, and Samuel Whitbread II (as he came to be called) succeeded to this position on the death of his father in 1796. The second Samuel was as active in politics as his father before him, and in the bitter party strife of the time was frequently lampooned and caricatured. It was he who commissioned Henry Holland to rebuild the family house, Southill near Bedford, regarded as an excellent specimen of Regency architecture, and filled with treasures. Some readers may know the book about the house which was published in 1951. The second Samuel Whitbread did not end his building activities with Southill: he was concerned with the rebuilding of Drury Lane Theatre after the disastrous fire of 1809. This brought him in his turn within range of the satirical poets, in his case James and Horace Smith, who found room for him in their series of parodies, *Rejected Addresses*—but this is carrying my story into a by-way.

Samuel II was a busy and influential politician in the years of the Napoleonic wars; the fourth Samuel Whitbread was at the peak of his political career in the days of Lord Palmerston, and held the office of Civil Lord of the Admiralty. He was on three occasions asked to be Speaker of the House of Commons. This is not the brewery's only connection with that office, for it is a tradition for Whitbread's to provide horses for the Speaker's coach on State occasions. This custom originated rather more than a hundred years ago, when another partner, Shaw Lefevre, was Speaker for the exceptionally long period of eighteen years, and on his retirement became Viscount Eversley.

I have touched on the public activities of the Whitbreads to emphasize a point I made earlier in the book: that in the great brewing families (the Whitbreads, the Barclays, the Grettons, the Youngers, the Guinnesses, and several others) were to be found men of public spirit, and not (as the teetotallers would sometimes have us believe) mere traders concentrating solely on selling beer and making money. From 1768 to 1910, with only brief gaps, there was always a Whitbread in the House of Commons; the family has also been prominent in philanthropy, in encouraging the arts, and in many other spheres of public life. The first Whitbread helped the prison reformer, John Howard, and was one of the first to point to the evils of the slave trade; his successors have followed the same tradition of disinterested public service. I had every reason to be proud at finding myself in such company.

When I joined Whitbread's the principal members of the board were the three sons of Samuel IV, and Cecil Lubbock. The chairman was Samuel Howard Whitbread, and Lubbock (who, as I have said, was a step-cousin of mine) was deputy chairman. The others were Henry William Whitbread ('Mr. Harry') and Francis Pelham Whitbread ('Mr. Frank'). Howard presided at board meetings and on other occasions when matters of major importance were involved, but did not interest himself in matters of detail. His time was much occupied otherwise: he had sat in Parliament, as a Liberal, for the Luton division of Bedfordshire from 1892 to 1895, and for Huntingdon from 1906 to 1910. He was also Chairman of Quarter Sessions, a county alderman, and Lord Lieutenant of Bedfordshire. Harry, the largest individual shareholder, and father of the present chairman, was the member of the family principally concerned with the control of the business, to which he was devoted. He was a great sportsman and a shrewd judge of men, whose qualities he could ably summarize in one or two phrases with a whimsicality I have never heard equalled. He was much loved by all who knew him. Chiswell Street was a fire danger area, the surroundings being largely occupied by small factories of two or three rooms in old, cramped and often worn-out buildings in which fires were all too frequent. As a result, Harry Whitbread had in his young days taken a practical interest in fire-fighting and had early organized a house fire-brigade, for which

15. MEMBERS OF THE WHITBREAD BOARD, 1919

S. Howard Whitbread, Chairman

Cecil Lubbock Henry W. Whitbread ("Mr. Harry")

My immediate colleagues

16. Aerial view of Whitbread's Hop Farm

17. A gift to a veteran hop picker

he retained the services of a retired chief of the County Council Fire Service. This officer trained and drilled our brigade until it ranked high among such organizations, and several times won the cup in the annual competition of house fire brigades. Harry Whitbread's foresight was amply justified in 1940; it saved the brewery in the incendiary raids at the end of that year, which left the brewery standing alone in the midst of a desert of destruction.

Frank Whitbread, the youngest of the three brothers, was also a Managing Director. He concentrated more particularly on the work of the various trade organizations: he had been Master of the Brewers' Company and, as far back as 1906, chairman of the Brewers' Society; he was for many years chairman of the Law Committee of the Society. The Institute of Brewing was also one of his great interests; he had twice been its president, and for many years was chairman of its Publications Committee. But he was principally known for his long chairmanship of the National Trade Defence Association, a position which he retained from 1907 until his death in 1941. The object of this body is to cultivate good relations between different sections of the Trade, and to represent the interests of both brewers and retailers whenever questions arise which affect the whole industry. I have already described Frank's notable contribution, when chairman of that body, towards the defeat of the notorious Licensing Bill of 1907. Apart from his activities within the public and political spheres of the Trade, he was a prominent figure in philanthropic enterprise. He was treasurer of Guy's Hospital, and chairman of both the Discharged Prisoners' Aid Society and the National Society for the Prevention of Cruelty to Children. So, although we did not see much of him at the brewery, he led a full and active life.

Cecil Lubbock, who had been Master of the Brewers' Company during the whole troublous time of the First World War, had been a distinguished scholar. He was a Fellow of Eton College, and a man outstanding in many ways. He had begun his career in the Home Office but had joined Whitbread's at the suggestion of his uncle, Edgar Lubbock, then a large shareholder, in 1914. It was the custom for the court of the Bank of England to be recruited from the younger partners of the large business concerns in the

City. Edgar Lubbock was himself Deputy Governor of the Bank, but on his death, which occurred before he was due for the Governorship, Cecil was invited to take his place on the board of the Bank; and by the time I joined Whitbread's, twelve years later, Cecil had proved his excellence and had been invited to become Deputy Governor. This appointment would entail practically full-time attendance at the Bank, first for two years as Deputy Governor, and then for two years as Governor, the usual terms of office; as I said, it was because of this that Whitbread's had found it necessary to strengthen their board by my own appointment. Cecil Lubbock never, in fact, became Governor, because Montagu Norman continued to be elected to that post until just before the Bank of England was nationalized in 1946.

Lubbock was also a director of the Northern Assurance Company and of other financial concerns. He became chairman of the City of London Income Tax Commissioners, and a member of the Council of Foreign Bond Holders. To all these interests he gave whole-hearted service, for he was a desperately hard worker. Considering how many other affairs he was concerned in, it was amazing what a grasp he had of Whitbread's affairs and how closely he was able to identify himself with the detail of the brewery. This singularly charming man was also one of H.M. Lieutenants for the City of London, and was closely associated with leaders of the Church. He had married Edith Furse, daughter of the Ven. C. W. Furse, Archdeacon of Westminster. Finally, he had been associated with the policy of public house improvement from its inception, so I had had much to do with him.

Thus it came about that I was to find myself for some years to come working side by side with four Etonians; in early days I sometimes wondered how I should fit in—especially as it was a favourite theory of Lubbock's that a classical education was the only foundation for a cultivated judgment in the larger affairs of life. In fact I had written to him expressing some doubt as to whether the rest of the Board would find me congenial; but his only reply was, 'I am quite convinced of the soundness of my views, but you happen to be a freak'.

There was one other member of the board, Percival Grundy,

who had been secretary of the Company for many years before being elected. At the time of my arrival he had been ill for some months and was beginning to come in for partial duties on about three days a week. He was one of the kindest-hearted men I ever met, and no trouble was too arduous for him if it would help his friends out of a difficulty. He was heart and soul devoted to Whitbread's, so that whereas in principle he favoured any improvement that might be suggested, in practice, when any particular proposal came up, he was grieved and hurt by any implication that the historic methods and usages of Whitbread's were less than perfect. I was deeply impressed by his phenomenal ability at casting up long columns of figures of thousands of pounds, shillings and pence correctly into one total, instead of using the laborious and elementary method of adding each column separately. He was a strong upholder of Whitbread's Liberal affinities, and worshipped the memory of Gladstone, deeply resenting any casual reflection upon the Grand Old Man. I am afraid I used to tease him by telling him of my sister's childish assessment, already mentioned, of his revered W. E. G. as the walking embodiment of wickedness.

When I arrived at the brewery on that October morning I already knew my new colleagues on the board—I had attended a board meeting some time earlier in order to be introduced. I had also met some senior members of the brewery staff, but by no means all. My first two or three days at Chiswell Street were passed in meeting others and in getting an idea of the general scope and constitution of the business. My name must have been pretty well known to the staff, on account of my work with official bodies during the war, and also because I was active at the Brewers' Society and the Institute of Brewing—this was the year I became President of the Institute. No doubt they awaited my advent with some curiosity, for I was known to have decided and perhaps radical views on the conduct and practice of the industry. For all that, I well remember the cordial welcome they gave me, and the total absence of the distrust and suspicion sometimes evident on such occasions. We quickly established a feeling of mutual trust which I have valued and fostered ever since.

In addition to owning, like other large concerns, many hundreds of tied houses in and around London, Whitbread's had a national trade in bottled beers distributed all over the country from Land's End to John o' Groats, through something over forty depots; a business in which they had been pioneers.

When I joined the company the war had been over for more than a year, but it had not yet been possible to do much in the way of reconstruction. Since 1914 little maintenance work had been carried out, either on the buildings or the plant, and of course the most able and active of the staff had been in the Services. We were faced with problems the like of which had never arisen before in anyone's experience—although they were to be repeated in an acute form twenty years later after a still more destructive war.

There was also a revolutionary change in the economics of brewing. The beer duty had been greatly increased, yet a new and more profitable price structure had come out of the shortage produced by war conditions, in place of the absurdly narrow margins of pre-war days. But apart from the price alterations, the character of the beer brewed was also different. The war-time shortage of materials had led to lighter beer, and it was found that the public had been more or less satisfied with a lower alcoholic content than in the past. Industrial beer, which before the war had an alcoholic content of about five per cent and sold at twopence a pint, had now disappeared. In its place the public was drinking, and was apparently satisfied with, a beer containing only about three per cent alcohol, and at a price of sixpence a pint. Indeed, a spectacular change. There were many worries, however, to counterbalance this happy circumstance, and one of the most trying was the suitable re-establishment of staff members now returned from active service. Their jobs had, of course, been guaranteed to them, but after an absence of four or five years they had naturally lost touch with brewing practice. Especially difficult were the cases of men of limited business ability, who had held minor positions in the company, yet whose unexpected aptitudes for soldiering had earned them commissioned rank. Such men as these now returned to their relatively modest posts to find in positions of responsibility others who had not shone in the army or navy, and who had been quite content to serve in the ranks or as N.C.O.s.

This, of course, led to curious situations. A demobilized private might take up his old administrative position to find himself exercising authority over one who had held field rank, perhaps even in the same regiment. I happened to mention to a fellow brewer a particular difficulty of this kind and he told me he had a problem acuter than mine—he had a cooper who had come back a brigadier, and what was he going to do about that? Afterwards, I heard that the brigadier, evidently also a philosopher, had returned happily to his job and was shortly afterwards promoted to foreman. He performed his new duties excellently.

Almost my first important job was to go with Lubbock to purchase a hop farm at Beltring, near Paddock Wood in Kent, for which the company was negotiating. This garden had for many years belonged to a hop-growing expert, almost a genius, named White, who had died some time previously. When White had originally taken over the land it was not thought to be even reasonably good soil for the growing of hops; but with exceptional ability he had produced a particular type of hops known as 'White's Goldings', with which he had won first prize at the annual Brewers' Exhibition on many occasions. It was the custom of most firms brewing fine beers to buy hops from the same gardens year after year. Each garden possessed its own peculiarities, and continuity of flavour, as I have said elsewhere, was thought to be essential. Whitbread's had taken most of White's hops for many years and when, at his death, the garden was put up for sale, it was feared that the first claim on these hops might pass into other hands, so the firm had decided to buy the property.

The farm was being run by White's adopted son, Waghorn, who had been closely connected with its management. Lubbock and I walked round with him and sat down to discuss the purchase. Waghorn named the figure asked by the vendors, and Lubbock and I retired to consider it. When I suggested making a lower offer, Lubbock explained that this was not Whitbread's way: their principle was to ask the price of anything they wished to secure and not to haggle, but say either 'yes' or 'no'. I had been brought up in a different school; experience had taught me that in such transactions it was not usual for the vendor to name the lowest price he was prepared to accept. Lubbock agreed with me so far as to tell Waghorn that if he would accept a figure standing at about ten thousand pounds less than he had asked, he could regard the farm as sold. If he could not accept it, we should have to consult our board in London and find out whether they would increase our offer. Waghorn said he would like a few minutes to think it over, and went into a little office where there was a telephone. I wondered whether he was retiring to pray for guidance or to telephone for instructions from the vendors or their agents. Before long he returned, and said he could accept the offer on behalf of the trustees; I have sometimes thought that even the decreased figure we had offered was something higher than the sum they had fixed as their lowest price. Anyway, I like to think that in this transaction I had pulled my weight, though on the face of it, it appeared to run contrary to Whitbread's usual method of dealing.

Like other hop growers we had our ups and downs but on the whole the gardens, besides producing the hops we like, have proved a satisfactory commercial proposition. In addition, since hops probably represent the most picturesque agricultural crop, many thousands of sightseers visit us each year; and our four thousand or so hop pickers who come from crowded districts of London carry back to their homes, or so they all tell us, happy recollections of their annual holiday with us.

The next landmark in my career was my introduction to the Court of the Brewers' Company, which I joined as one of Whitbread's representatives. The Company at that time consisted of the largest brewery concerns in London, each of which was entitled to a certain number of representatives. At Putney we had been outside its area, and I was delighted to be associated with one of the ancient City guilds. My friend Mr. D. R. Ledward, now managing director of Charrington's, and formerly clerk to the Brewers' Company, has been good enough to lend me an outline history of the Company. Its full title is *The Master, Keepers or*

Wardens and Commonalty of the Mystery or Art of Brewers of the City of London. The Company was probably formed at the end of the twelfth century as The Guild of our Lady and St. Thomas à Becket: Saint Thomas it claims as its founder. The medieval guilds were the backbone of commercial life in England, and similar bodies existed in all European countries. Their object was the protection of the trade interests and property of their members. They were voluntary associations, each of which built up its own body of rules and governing regulations. Centuries before the brewers and licensed victuallers were subject to parliamentary legislation, an elaborate system of self-government had been established by the Brewers' Company for the Trade in London. I have often felt that the public might have been better served if the control of the brewing industry had been allowed to remain in the hands of the Brewers' Company, instead of being subjected to the long series of differing restrictive laws and all the controversy attached thereto.

It is thought that guilds date back to Saxon times. After the Norman conquest they were accepted as the basis of civic government. The national exchequer was chronically short of funds and the guilds, representing the prosperous mercantile classes, were an obvious source of revenue. In return for substantial payments the Crown granted charters giving monopolies which were in fact contrary to the common law. But, while it is clear that from the sixteenth century onwards many of the London guilds had begun to decay as trade organizations and continued as purely social or charitable bodies, the Brewers' Company has always been primarily concerned with the affairs of its trade. In 1406, the Company was formally recognized as 'The Mystery of Free Brewers' and Master and Wardens were instituted. The directive was that eight Wardens should be appointed to act in all matters connected with the brewing trade, four from the district east of Walbrook and four from the west. In 1437, the Company was granted its first Royal Charter by Henry VI—the original document is now in the Guildhall. This Charter and subsequent grants gave the Company complete control over the Trade in London. All brewers could be compelled to become freemen of the Company, for which privilege they were obliged to pay—as they still are. From freeman, the next step up the ladder was election to the Livery, which carried with it certain voting rights and privileges. When in 1433 we adopted our present livery gown of gold and blue and cut the cloth, it is recorded that one member was so pleased with it that he not only bought a length for himself but also one for his wife!

However, the control of the Brewers' Company over the Trade does not appear to have been as complete as one might imagine from the comprehensive provisions of the Charter. It is on record that Richard Whityngton, Mayor, took offence against the brewers for 'having fat swans at their feast when he had none at his', and compelled them as a punishment to sell beer cheap, at one penny a gallon, all the following day. Contrary to popular belief, Whittington was an autocratic man. He decreed that every barrel used by brewers should be of a certain content and each marked by a cooper's mark, for each cooper had a different mark. A similar edict prescribed that pots used to serve beer must be sealed, and the smallest measure was a quart. The price of beer was fixed, and brewers who used inferior malt or sold beer by short measure or in unsealed pots were prosecuted in the Mayor's Court. The Brewers' Company was collectively responsible for seeing that brewers obeyed these regulations. It was the business of the Master and Wardens to make systematic searches of all premises used for brewing, and to bring offenders before the Lord Mayor or Chamberlain. To compensate them for these various duties, a payment known as 'Search and Quarterage' was levied by the Company on all brewers, calculated on the number of servants each employed. Today we still levy 'Quarterage', but base shares on each brewer's barrelage. The Masters and Wardens were sureties for the good behaviour of members, and if they failed to present defaulters at the Guildhall, the Company could be fined and the Masters imprisoned until the fine was paid.

Until the sixteenth century it was not regarded as respectable to use hops in brewing. The Company had struggled hard and unsuccessfully to suppress growing competition from foreign brewers. These came from the Low Countries and introduced hopped beer, which soon won popularity over the ale without hops brewed by members of the Brewers' Company. At that time the Company admitted as members only ale brewers, and therefore could, in theory, but evidently not in practice, prevent these beer brewers from trading in London, where the Company was reputed to enjoy a monopoly. According to the chronicler Stow, the foreign brewers established themselves in Southwark, and so successfully poached on the London trade that in 1626 there were only about a dozen brewer members of the Company. Soon after this, beer brewers were admitted to the Company, which thus regained its influence. The foreign hopped beer had by now so captured the taste of the public that at about this time the beer barrel of thirty-six gallons seems to have replaced the ale brewers' barrel of thirty-two gallons as the standard.

The Brewers' Company is now unique among City Livery Companies in two ways: first, because it has a rule that a member of the Court must be a director of a London brewery; and next, because it offers hospitality only on rare occasions and, curiously enough, is comparatively poor among City Companies. I attended my first Court in the Company's hall in Addle Street, built in 1670 to replace the one destroyed in the Great Fire. In old days it was the custom for the Master, the Wardens, and the Members, to file in in heavy brocaded robes and take their places in the panelled court room, with the sunlight falling through the narrow stained-glass windows, and the noise of the City dimmed by the tapestries and the curtains. The Clerk in his knee breeches cried three times 'Order for the Court in Session' before their deliberations began. It was not an occasion for dealing with defaulters and malefactors against the Mystery, but only for formal discussion of business policy. By the time I came to be elected, our proceedings were more informal and friendly. It was a great pleasure to me to be admitted to this historic circle and to wear the official cloak on being introduced—the only time I was to wear it except when welcoming new members during my Mastership.

The Company's hall was destroyed in the same incendiary raid that laid waste the area round Chiswell Street in 1940, and so far has not been rebuilt, although as this book goes to press the site is being cleared and rebuilding is imminent. At present we are in temporary offices, but the Company carries on its business according to its historic custom. It acts now mostly as a philanthropic body, but retains some elements of the commercial purposes for which it was founded. Among its philanthropic objects it maintains three schools, one of which is Aldenham, a boys' public school; the others are for both boys and girls and are known as the Dame Alice Owen secondary schools. The Company also administers various funds left by charitable brewers in the past with which we have established almshouses and annuities for old people. The members also conform to certain old-established rules for avoiding undue competition among themselves, perhaps a trifle less scrupulously now than in the old days. One of the rules embodies a ban on Company members calling on the customers of another member with a view to securing business. There is an ancient story that a partner of one of the largest brewing concerns was accused by another brewer of having been seen calling on one of the latter's valued customers. The accused admitted that he had visited the house, but insisted that he had been not to see the publican but to renew acquaintance with a barmaid! His explanation was accepted and the offence overlooked.

One of my early actions in this new sphere was to suggest, on 8th January, 1920, that the Brewers' Company should offer a prize to young architects for the best design of a public house. Such designs have to solve an intricate problem and, truth to tell, public house architecture had not then reached a very high standard. I felt this would not only encourage more earnest study of what was needed but would also show the world that brewers were genuinely interested in providing better houses. The Court agreed, with one dissentient, and offered a sum of 500 guineas for the best effort. The R.I.B.A. welcomed the proposal, undertook to organize the scheme and themselves added 200 guineas as a fee to the Assessor of the prizes. Plans were exhibited at the R.I.B.A. Galleries, opened by the President of the R.I.B.A. on the 14th of April, 1921, and later the plans were shown at the Building Exhibition at Olympia, both of which displays had good press notices. In this way our objects were achieved: we had not only attracted the attention of architects to the problem, we had also spread the gospel of improvement among the general public.

At the time of my joining Whitbread's I was President of the Institute of Brewing and still continued my activities there. A notable event during my Presidency was the establishment by the Institute of a Research Scheme which, although not initiated by me, occurred during my term of Presidency, so I was concerned with its inauguration. Originally suggested in 1918, my year of Vice-Presidency, on the basis of voluntary subscriptions, the Research Fund Committee was appointed in January 1920, under my own Chairmanship. The indefatigable W. H. Bird, Secretary of the Institute, visited most of the brewery concerns in the country and succeeded in securing subscriptions to the tune of about £9,000, a modest sum in comparison with similar funds today but at least it served as a beginning. The Research Scheme was ultimately developed under the inspiring leadership of Colonel Newbold of Guinness in 1946, since when it has been established at Little Hall with a more appropriate income of more than ten times the original sum. In the early days I recommended that since our funds were none too ample, we should not attempt to establish a centre; but when particular points arose on which we thought research was needed, we should interest whichever scientific establishment seemed most appropriate and delegate the work to them. As Chairman of the Research Committee, I achieved quite a spurious reputation for being a scientist myself, a qualification to which I have no claims, but it nevertheless resulted in my association with many great men in the scientific world. I served as Chairman from 1920 to 1923, being succeeded by that notable man, E. R. Moritz, Ph.D., then a leading scientist in the fermentation industries and adviser in that capacity to the Brewers' Society.

Years later, in fact not long after the Second World War, I was reminded that back in the 'twenties, when the mistaken impression that I was a scientist was still current, I was pressed to become, and did become, a founder member of a small dining club of scientific men, called the Catalysts, and was asked to preside at one of the dinners. As soon as I arrived I was persuaded to don a magnificent flowered waistcoat, bequeathed to the Club by that great man, Professor Armstrong. Though a giant in intellect, he could not compete with me in waist measurement, so I had to wear it unbuttoned as it would not meet by several inches.

The Annual Dinner of the Institute of Brewing, one of the year's principal events in the Trade in view of its scientific implications, had naturally been discontinued during the war, as well as the customary Council Meetings. As President of the Institute I was anxious to get the wheels going round again and thought it would be a good idea to make really memorable our first post-war dinner, to be held in April 1920. With this in mind, I invited the officers of each of the branches of the Institute to be my guests at the Great Central Hotel, Marylebone, as my own home was not equal to the occasion. We met for conversation on the previous day, dined together, and then went to a play; next day, we had a further talk prior to the Dinner itself. Although I had no intention, or indeed desire, to establish a precedent (as if I regarded my own presidency as something epoch-making in itself!) successive Presidents did in fact give similar parties for many ensuing years, and to these I was invited. As a result, I enjoyed far more hospitality than that which I had originally extended.

The Dinner itself was a success, and had a good press. Our guests included Lord d'Abernon, Lord Moulton, the scientist, the Rt. Hon. C. A. McCurdy, K.C., M.P., the Minister of Food, other members of Parliament, and some of the leading personalities of the Central Board, as well as representatives of the principal scientific societies.

9

The Licensed Trade as a Casual Industry—Birth of Scheme for Training Young Workers—Co-operation of the Sir John Cass Technical Institute—Education Project formulated; difficulties in finding Lecturers—Inaugural Lecture and Personalities involved—Criticism from the Old School—Students' Trips to Continent Project, and War's frustration—Revival of Efforts after War—The L.C.C. takes over responsibility

I have already related in Chapter Four that when our small Trade group began to consider improvement of standards, the staffing of public houses was not the least of our problems. Many of the less important houses were kept by elderly couples who 'took a pub' when the husband retired after spending most of his working life elsewhere. There were, of course, plenty of inn-keepers whose families had been in the business for generations and whose conscientious work was irreproachable; but far too many of the rest had passed their best years in other pursuits. Licensing legislation, unfortunately, might almost be said to have encouraged this attitude, for when a prospective licensee came before the justices to apply for a transfer of the licence to him, stringent inquiries by the police would be made into his personal character and past record but none at all by anybody into his qualifications for running a pub in the best interests of all concerned. His former career had indeed to be blameless, as the most trivial conviction for even a minor 'crime' was enough to prevent him, or was until quite recently, from holding a licence. Not so many years ago I myself had occasion to deal with a curious instance of this, in the case of a tenant who had had a licence transferred to him after the usual police inquiries, and had conducted the house for several years in an extremely exemplary manner. Then, through some accident, it was discovered that many years before when he was a boy he had been charged by his employer with a minor theft involving but a few shillings. It was a small matter, he had no opportunity of defending himself, and, though pleading 'Not Guilty' he was convicted, so was debarred for life from holding a licence. Yet his licence had been renewed to him for a period of years, and now that he had fallen from grace, the licence of the house was lost as well. The solicitors told us that our only course was to make an appeal to the Home Office, and they, satisfied that the facts were as put forward, secured a King's Pardon for the unfortunate man. It is one of the curious anomalies of the Law, that this involves not only forgiveness but also actual cancellation of the conviction, so all was well. Comparatively recently this anomaly has been recognized and adjusted. But this is digressing.

My attention was particularly directed to lack of training when studying the difficulties of the brewing trade during the early years of the century. At that time, as a result of minor research by way of systematic sampling from a number of houses during a period of some months, I found that the average quality of the beer offered to the customer fell far below standard. I found, too, that cellars were not always as clean as they should have been; they were often badly and uneconomically designed, in many, the temperatures (so important a consideration) were neither uniform nor consistent, and there were other defects traceable to the scanty knowledge of cellar management among those in charge and their unskilled employees. The natural result of such mismanagement of cellars already unsuitable was of course that the quality of the beer which reached the consumer was unsatisfactory. As I turned these things over in my mind, I began to deplore the lack of training which made these conditions inevitable.

So in 1910, there being a slack evening at one of the meetings of the Institute of Brewing, I opened a discussion detailing the facts as I myself had observed them and did not mince my words. Most of those present were practical brewers who already recognized the difficulty and had reason to regret the lack of proper handling to which the article they produced was too often subjected before it reached the customer. My condemnation of existing practices was too sweeping for publication in the Institute *Journal*, so I began to consider what could be done to develop greater knowledge in the handling of beer as well as raising the standard of the management of public houses in other directions.

At that time the Sir John Cass Institute in the East End of London was providing technical education for the benefit of brewery pupils and others interested in the scientific aspect of the fermentation industries. As I was a member of the Committee they had invited to advise them on the subject, it occurred to me it might be worth while enlisting the interest of the Institute, so I suggested to Dr. C. A. Keane, the Principal, that if he wished to strike a new note in technical education, here was the opportunity to do something of real public value. It would be a new development because, while technical education was much in the picture for the benefit of artisans in handicrafts and manufactures, it had not at that time been applied to any distributive industry. Dr. Keane was much interested and brought the idea before his governing body, who decided to adopt the scheme, provided I would undertake the preliminary steps of its organization, and so began my pioneer work in education for workers in public houses.

My first decision was to advise the Institute that, if the plan were to achieve success, it would be well to organize a tentative course of lectures, not so much for the workers of the industry, as for licensed victuallers and others interested, so as to give them an approximate idea of the kind of instruction we had in mind. So we planned the course of six lectures, the first being of an inaugural nature, with three lectures on the proper treatment of beer and other beverages, and the remainder on the provision of such food and refreshment as were appropriate to a public house.

Having got so far, I read a further paper before the Institute of Brewing (in this case in terms suitable for publication) which was heard at a meeting attended by a considerable number of directors and managers of brewery companies, and which included an outline of the proposed course at the Cass Institute. We made quite an event of the inaugural lecture, on the 15th of May, 1912, which I gave myself. Among those on the platform were Sir Owen Roberts, chairman of the governing body, and Dr. C. A. Keane, Principal of the Cass Institute, and another member of the governing body, Sir Richard Garton; the chairman of the Brewers' Society, C. H. Babington; the Master of the Brewers' Company, Cecil Lubbock; and the redoubtable Alderman Johnson, then chairman of the Central Board of London Licensed Victuallers. Alderman Johnson was not only a leader in the licensed trade, but also a notable orator; I had heard it said that he had endeavoured to model his style on that of Lord Palmerston, described as 'homely and unpretending, witty, tactically dexterous, always sensible and practical'. His acceptance of the invitation had been conditional—he must not be expected to speak for more than five minutes. We acceded, of course, but whether (as I like to think) I myself inspired him, or whether the cause was really close to his heart, he was moved to deliver an impassioned and eloquent address lasting over twenty-five minutes and rounded off by an excellent peroration on the Trade's duty towards its young entrants and the public at large. A piquant final sentence expressed the hope that he had not been too brief; this was maybe the only fraction remaining of the speech he originally planned.

This was followed by six lectures giving details of the instructions it was intended to give to the workers. The Food and Refreshments Course gave me a little difficulty and I enlisted the help of Mr. Herman Senn, then regarded as one of the high priests of cuisine. Indeed, so wide and so distinguished was his reputation, that he was retained not only as adviser to the kitchens of Buckingham Palace, but also to those of His Majesty's Prisons at Wormwood Scrubs and elsewhere. He was too big a noise to give the lectures himself, but he recommended one W. H. Taylor who, while possessing a wide knowledge of catering, was unluckily for him not endowed with sufficient commercial acumen to hold down a responsible post. Taylor gladly accepted, not only because the fees were welcome, but also because he hoped the assignment might lead to opportunities of making better use of his technical knowledge; but a few days before the date of his first lecture, to my horror, I had a note from him saying he would have to resign the contract as he could not think of anything to say! So I told him to come and see me. The first items on his syllabus were, naturally enough, the serving of tea and coffee, so I asked him how many cups of tea he would expect a pound of tea to yield. He promptly told me how many (I no longer recall the number), so I firmly said to him, 'Tell them that'. I went on to extort other answers from him. Would he, I inquired, buy the same quality of tea for the Grosvenor Hotel and for an East End café; would he, in given circumstances, do this or that? Each time his unhesitating answer was forthcoming, I reiterated my 'Well, tell them that' and in this way we ran through most of his subject-matter; thus, by displaying my own ignorance and inducing him to utter the answers which he had on the tip of his tongue, I proved to him that he had plenty to impart, and need not worry. I am glad for both his sake and ours to be able to report that he lectured well and helpfully.

As a result of this trial run, the Institute asked me to suggest an advisory committee on which prominent members of the retail trade would be included, and at which I was later invited to take the chair. Two of our most prominent members were Mr. H. C. Amendt, manager of the Great Eastern Railway Hotels, and Sir William Coxen, already mentioned in my fourth chapter, who had extensive interests in the licensed trade, and we got down to drafting a syllabus for the various types of weekly wage earner, barmen, cellarmen, etc.

The enterprise was not received without criticism. It was attacked by the old stagers who would not budge from their opinion that experience is not merely the best but is actually the only guide. Horatio Bottomley, in his periodical *John Bull*, paid me the compliment of devoting half a page to ridiculing the scheme. Most of the criticisms were based on suspicion that the real aim was to import a number of young men into the business, to the detriment of older 'experienced' men, and adopt the system of management instead of tenancy. This was a matter which called for decisive clearing-up, so Alderman Johnson asked Lubbock and myself to attend a meeting of the London Central Board at their offices in Russell Square. On this occasion I saw their boardroom for the first time, and was struck not only by its carefully planned décor but also by the formal dignity of the conduct of the meeting, somewhat different from the casual and friendly atmosphere in which brewers were wont to foregather. However, we were given a courteous reception, replied to all questions put, and left somewhat surprised and impressed with the manner in which the Central Board managed its meetings.

We drafted a syllabus for the autumn series of 1913 which was attended by a satisfactory number. After the first lecture, a deputation of some of those attending asked if there could be an examination in order that they might receive certificates which would be useful to them in after life. So we arranged this, designed certificates, and awarded a number of money prizes.

Thirty-seven candidates sat for that first examination, and twenty-six obtained certificates. This was a good send-off, and today almost all the students take the examination; and for some years the proportion of failures has not exceeded one per cent in the London area. As the standard is reasonably high, this record is a splendid testimony to the ability and lucidity of the lecturers.

In the early days our discussions were not unmarked by differences of opinion. One of our most valued and useful committee members was, as I have said, H. C. Amendt, a German by birth, upbringing and, if I may say so, conviction. His ideas and mine did not invariably coincide, and when I suggested a class or two for women, who were then beginning to be seen in the industry in increasing numbers, he was aghast. 'The men,' he said decisively, 'have brains. They have intelligence. They can learn. They can rise. But the women—bah! They are nothing but automatic machines.' For the time being this truly Teutonic 'Küche, Kirche, Kinder' concept prevailed, though after the First World War we admitted women, an innovation which increased the popularity of the enterprise. On the 5th November, 1914, I read another paper to the Birmingham section of the Institute of Brewing, giving a short history of the inception of the scheme.

Naturally the Trade as a whole watched these experimental classes with interest and I believe their success was an eye-opener to many. Our next move was to offer three special prizes enabling winners to spend a week on the Continent studying installations and organization there, and including visits to Amsterdam, Rotterdam, Antwerp and Brussels. I had suggested this as I knew from experience how illuminating such excursions can be. However, the tour was to have begun on the 6th of August, and the war broke out on the 4th, so that, for the time being, was that.

The war which upset this promising scheme for the prize-winners also frustrated us in other ways, and our scheme was in abeyance during those five years of difficulties for us in the Trade and almost everybody everywhere. The revival of this technical education was not one of the matters to which we were able to give priority after the war, and it was not until 1926 that we got a committee going to re-establish the courses. I again had the honour of being chairman, and once more had a band of willing helpers (although some familiar faces were seen no more in our midst). We re-opened the classes on lines similar to the original ones and before long revived the Continental trips scheme and other such ideas, making observation of European methods generally a possibility for outstanding students. However, after a year or two in our old surroundings, we learned that pressure on the restricted accommodation of the Cass Institute had compelled the governing body to decide on concentration on more scientific subjects, so for about a year the course had to be suspended while we cogitated on possibilities of resuming elsewhere.

As has been mentioned, I had much to do with those social workers who had formed an association for promoting the establishment of better public houses in poorer districts. One of their most prominent workers was the devoted and hard-working Miss Edith Neville, and when the Cass Institute was unable to continue the technical courses she suggested that they would fit in with her organization. So they were conducted in one of the Restaurant Association's public houses which was under the direction of Major Sotham (who with his wife had helped to found the movement). He suggested that it would be useful to recruit students from depressed areas where unemployment was rife, and then got in touch with the Ministry of Labour and secured grants covering part of the cost of this project. In such ways the scheme flourished until the Second World War compelled suspension. With the coming of the second peace we set about resuming activities, but now there was a new development to take into account. In the old days, various schemes for technical education were operated in direct connection with manufacturing industries, but they were barely known as I have hinted, in connection with distributive trades, before our 1912 innovation. Over the intervening years the L.C.C. had not been idle, but had established a college for the distributive trades in Charing Cross Road. We were able to arrange a conference at County Hall, under the chairmanship of the Assistant Education Officer to the L.C.C., Mr. E. N. Ritz, and at this conference the organizing secretary of the Restaurant Public Houses Association explained his society's present objectives. They hoped, he said, to interest trainees in learning the licensed victualler's business and to bring home to them the fact that it was a skilled calling and a real opportunity for public service. Trainees would 'live in' and would spend some part of the day actually assisting in pubs. It would be a progressive step if the L.C.C. could see its way to adopting the scheme in their technical college in Charing Cross Road, for the benefit of workers in the retail trades. For various reasons this plan was not acceptable in its entirety, but the co-operation of the L.C.C. was assured, and has ever since been a real boon.

The Charing Cross Road college offers education in many different industries and it is customary for each industry to appoint a liaison officer between itself and the college authorities. Major Sotham represented the Trade. When Major Sotham retired in 1947, Mr. A. J. Maddocks succeeded him. Mr. Maddocks had been in the licensed trade for over twenty years and was well known to its leading personalities. The Court of the Brewers' Company voted an annual sum for his services as contact between the Trade and the education authority, and thanks to his co-operative efforts the scheme has been smoothly and successfully run since 1947, and shows every promise of flourishing for many years to come. Each year there is a prize-giving, at which I have presided on one or two occasions, and it is deeply satisfying to see how well the plan has worked out in spite of frustrations and hindrances, not all of which I have dwelt upon.

One such hitch, however, caused a certain restrained amusement when I mentioned it again at one of the prize-day ceremonies. The vice-chairman of the Education Committee at one time was a lady social worker with strong temperance views; and although she agreed to the classes being held, she urged that a considerable part of the time should be devoted to the study of English. As I told my audience on this occasion, her idea was basically irreproachable, for one never knows when a sound and precise knowledge of our language is likely to come in useful. I thought this was the moment for re-telling the old story of Noah Webster's dilemma, a dilemma which his insistence on correct speech enabled him to resolve—at least to his own satisfaction. It is said that quite apart from being a great lexicographer, he had an eye for a pretty girl, and chanced to be kissing the housemaid one day when his wife, coming unexpectedly down the stairs, caught him in the act. 'Mr. Webster,' she exclaimed, 'I am surprised.' 'No, my darling,' he replied equably, 'I despair of ever succeeding in teaching you to have a proper respect for words. It is not YOU who are surprised. It is I who am surprised, whereas YOU are astonished.'

* * *

Although for many years these courses of instruction did not extend beyond the Metropolitan District, 1946 (the year of the L.C.C.'s adoption of the scheme) was to bring a notable extension under the auspices of the National Trade Development Association. This was at the instance of Mr. Peer Groves of the firm of Groves & Whitnall Ltd., the enthusiastic chairman of the Manchester Branch of the Association in connection with the Education Authorities of that district. Col. Charlier, M.C. was appointed National Education Organizer and proceeded to arrange similar schemes in rapid succession in various centres.

In 1950 the syllabus was accepted by the Hotel and Catering Institute, under Mr. Arthur Franks, Chairman of the Education Committee of that body. It was accepted by them as applicable to the whole country, and the course is now followed at forty-four widely scattered centres, with an intake of over seven hundred students a year. My hopes of 1912, that the Trade's various employments should rank as skilled occupations and careers demanding careful training, were shown not to have been illusory. Education for the Trade is now fully established along the lines we envisaged. I am often told that students who obtain diplomas are not without a post for long, and that many employers give preference to those who have successfully followed the course. There is a secure future in the licensed trade for thousands of today's young people, and I am glad to think that my pioneer efforts have helped to bring about this state of affairs. I often reflect that a mere twenty-six learners took the first certificate in 1912, so it is quite an occasion when one of these forerunners renews contact with me, and recalls early days. A few months ago I met Mr. Frederick Emberson, who has had a long and prosperous career in the Trade as licensee of a number of houses. He received his certificate, signed by myself, in May 1914 and still treasures it.

Two other recent incidents are just as pleasing to me. The first concerns Major-General Sir Reginald Scoones, K.B.E., C.B., D.S.O., who after his appointment as Director of the N.T.D.A. became so impressed with the value of this section of the Association's work that he made a typically courageous decision: in order to equip himself to speak with authority on these subjects, he enrolled for the London course under an assumed name, attended regularly, and passed out with honours.

The second was a more personal experience. In 1956 my old friend Peer Groves decided to celebrate the tenth anniversary of the opening of the Manchester classes, and invited me to a dinner party. At this party I was presented with a memento—an antique blue porcelain duck, of Persian origin—in recognition of my pioneer work of 1912.

10

Need for better Public Houses—Temperance Opposition—'The Rose and Crown, Tooting'—Cecil Whitely (practical difficulties of Counsel)—Development of Tied House System—Formation of Improved Public House Company—'The Welcome Inn', Eltham—'The Robin Hood', Becontree—'The White Hart', Tottenham—Address to London Diocesan Council—St. Giles, Cripplegate—Miss Edith Neville, Mrs. Sotham and the Restaurant Public Houses Association—Father Jellicoe and 'The Anchor', Tiverton Street—'The Bull', Guildford

By 1920 under peace conditions we were able actively to pursue our policy of public house improvement. By that time I was at Whitbread's, with the greater resources of a large organization behind me, and consequently more scope in this direction. Every public house presents interesting problems and I include a note of my experiences in respect of some of them.

We believed that a general improvement in tone and conduct would promote sobriety, and diminish the hostility of many social reformers. A school of more moderate thought was growing up, led by younger and less bigoted people than the temperance fanatics of pre-war years, though these still flourished. The Trade was beginning to recognize, too, that improvement was good business apart from its social importance. Although some trade might be lost, this loss would be more than balanced by the appeal of a good public house to a wider section of the community. There would be an increased income from the sale of soft drinks and refreshments that would outweigh any apparent loss on sales of alcohol.

In the early twenties we had three main sources of opposition—apart from a kernel of British apathy and the conservatism within the Trade itself. There was first the calculated policy of prohibitionists, who realized that improvement would popularize the public house. Those were the years of total prohibition in the United States, and its British supporters were reinforced by speakers and lecturers from America. 'Pussyfoot' Johnson was over here doing his best to spread the gospel; and he had the active support of many influential Church and social workers. They were shrewd enough to see that a clean, bright and spacious public house would be a liability to them—a dirty, small, overcrowded one, an asset to exploit; and so they opposed better houses and higher standards as means of popularizing the trade they wished to extinguish.

In the second place, there were the moderate social reformers, who might have been expected to take a more enlightened view of our intentions; but rather shortsightedly many of them preferred to think that behind our professed disinterestedness lurked a desire only to sell more drink; this was evidently the opinion of most of the justices, the third source of opposition. If we suggested that a particular house was overcrowded and that more room should be provided, they would often refuse an application on the ground that it would increase the 'drinking space'. It seemed impossible to convince many benches that better conditions would induce a higher standard of behaviour. There was indeed an almost general tendency to make the Trade pay dearly when they asked for permission to improve. An example of this lopsided manner of dispensing justice occurred in 1921, when we found it necessary to rebuild one of our houses in the Wandsworth area, in Tooting Bec Road—'The Rose and Crown'.

'The Rose and Crown' at Tooting was a fairly small but well-conducted house, the licence of which had been in the hands of the same family for nearly a hundred years. The local authorities found that the house lay in a direct line with some important road widening operations, and they gave notice to purchase half the area on which it stood. As we owned a considerable plot behind the house which would front the newly-made road, we decided to rebuild entirely. To do this would be a public service in more ways than one. It would permit the necessary road-widening; it would ensure the continued existence of a useful and popular licensed house at that spot; and it would provide improved modern amenities, with increased accommodation and facilities for supplying food and other refreshment, a service much needed as the house lay close to Tooting Common. So we prepared provisional plans, and, as we knew the local justices were wary of approving increased accommodation, we made the enterprise comparatively moderate; it was indeed a modest proposal in comparison with others we made later.

The sequence of events when a rebuilding is proposed is this: an application is made to the licensing bench to secure their provisional approval of plans of the future house. In most cases the justices adjourn their decision until a later date, and meanwhile study the plans and view the site. At the next meeting they give their decision for or against. In this case, when our counsel Cecil Whitely had made his application, the chairman of the bench asked him whether he had 'anything further to say'. This was a common though improper form by which benches were in the habit of inviting applicants to offer to surrender *other* licences in order to secure the approval of the plan under consideration. It was illegal, because the bench had no power to bargain in such matters; it was their business to consider the case before them on its merits. But many licensing benches, in their anxiety to reduce the number of licences, made it a practice to refuse leave for material alterations unless the applicants surrendered a licence. On this occasion, Whitely indicated that he had nothing further to say, and accordingly the bench retired to consider the application. On their return the chairman announced: 'This application is refused'; whereupon Cecil Whitely asked, 'Are we to understand that you would have reached a different conclusion had we offered a surrender?' The chairman was imprudent enough to say that this might have been so. Whitely at once gave notice of appeal.

The appeal came before the Lord Chief Justice in the High

Court on the 20th April, 1921; he ruled that the justices could not bargain for the surrender of another licence. Mr. Justice Darling and Mr. Justice Avery, who sat with him, agreed. The Lord Chief Justice then made absolute the rule of mandamus in the case. 'Mandamus' is the legal form whereby an inferior court is directed to perform some function it has neglected or improperly performed; in this case the Wandsworth justices were directed to hear and determine according to law the application made by Whitbread's. The words 'according to law' make it impossible for the bench to bargain or to do anything other than hear the case and adjudge it. They had on the re-hearing no alternative but to grant the application, and this they did on the 6th May, 1921. Even then they attempted to impose conditions, telling Whitely that the application was granted on the understanding that no liquor was to be sold in the coffee room except with meals. To this Whitely refused to agree; the bench surrendered and dropped their condition. So shortly afterwards a new, improved and enlarged 'Rose and Crown' was rebuilt a few yards further back; and Tooting got a new road as well as a better pub. I have thought this worth recording as one instance of the difficulties with which the policy of improvement had to contend. This kind of experience was almost general; it is an example of our setbacks which may come as a surprise to most people.

When discussing this case with Cecil Whitely I chaffed him about the ambiguity of many opinions received from Counsel, and he quoted one of his experiences showing that however wise and definite advice may be, it is sometimes not only unwelcome to the client but also costly to the Counsel who gave it. On one occasion, when asked his opinion he advised that his client had no case, advice which was unacceptable to a somewhat combative nature. Another opinion was obtained, which advised that while hazardous, the case, if argued this way and that, might possibly result in a favourable decision. So the case was taken to the courts and finally to the House of Lords, an adverse decision being given in each. Thus, as Whitely dryly remarked, he received a moderate fee, yet his friend who was retained throughout profited greatly.

At about this time I had come to the conclusion that it would be difficult to find retailers with sufficient capital to enable them to take over the really large houses which Whitbread's proposed to build in some districts. We were already thinking in terms of houses with a large room to seat say three hundred people for concerts, and perhaps half the number for meals, with other resources on a similar scale. My own views have since been modified by experience. I now believe that, although some large houses may be needed (especially when only one is to be provided in densely populated residential districts), the public is usually better served by several houses of moderate size rather than by the single super-house. However, at that time spectacular houses appeared to be one method of attracting attention to the new movement, and it was a puzzle to find tenants with sufficient practical knowledge as well as the capital needed for the tenants' 'ingoing'; so it became necessary to run these large houses under managers. In most cases licensing benches dislike this method, preferring an independent licensee living on his own premises. This is probably because of their suspicion that a brewer-owner would be mainly concerned in the sale of beer to the exclusion of general refreshment. Among the exceptions are the authorities in the Midland and Lancashire areas who, in fact, prefer managers: a preference derived, no doubt, from the fact that many large concerns in Birmingham and Liverpool were originally groups of retailers who became brewers to supply their houses, and consequently had ready-made departments to supervise and control the houses they owned.

Thus, partly to allay suspicion and partly to ensure a satisfactory standard, we decided to establish a separate company, with offices in a different part of London, to be solely concerned with the best methods of retail service. This was the Improved Public House Company Limited, and its business was to operate the large houses we began to build, mainly in the expanding suburbs of London. As managing director we appointed Major Denny, an enthusiast in catering, who as officer-in-charge had organized the canteen arrangements for the many thousands employed during the war at Woolwich Arsenal. He brought with him Theobalds, who had been his assistant, and some of his office staff no longer required at the Arsenal. Theobalds was a man of high character whose father, I was interested to learn later, had been a cooper at Brandon's for a number of years while I was there. We also secured the advice of Herman Senn, on whom I have already written in connection with technical education. To keep myself in the picture I joined the society known as the Food and Cookery Association and took sufficient interest in it to be adjudged worthy of the title of 'Fellow' of that body!

One of the first of the more ambitious houses we built was 'The Welcome Inn' at Eltham. This was an entirely new house, to which we transferred the licence of 'The Burrage Arms' at Woolwich, which—as in the case of 'The Rose and Crown'—was standing in the way of road widening. This transfer provided an opportunity for building a fine house in a developing neighbourhood, and we were fortunate here in being under the jurisdiction of a bench of enlightened justices who appreciated the need for good public houses, and were not limited by the absurd and all too common prejudice, that an increased floor area necessarily meant increased drunkenness. We decided, having the space, to make a bold experiment. Our first plan was to have no drinking at the bar, but to provide waiter service instead; the idea was that the customers should remain seated at tables; but this experiment was in the end found to be impracticable. For various reasons, the custom of getting what one needs at a bar is in Britain too deeply ingrained to be easily changed: perhaps this is due to the difficulty of attracting the attention of waiters, or to the feeling that it is necessary to tip those who attend to one's needs. It is also a fact that men, especially when unaccompanied by women, have a conservative prejudice in favour of what d'Abernon used to call 'perpendicular drinking'.

This was one of the houses where we provided a large club room or hall to be used for receptions, dinners and occasional concerts. I recollect that, as so often happens, we found that the cost of the house was likely to be considerably more than my board had agreed to spend; so I consulted the architect, Mr. F. T. Ingram, A.R.I.B.A., to see what economies might be made. He was troubled, and assured me that the only way of economizing without a drastic modification to the plan would be in respect of the concert room; and that if I insisted he believed it would much reduce the room's attractions and probably ruin the acoustics. However, there was nothing else for it, and I had to ask him to make the necessary economies.

Another feature of this house was the attention we paid to the accommodation for the resident staff. This allowed for a separate bedroom for every member, for the men at one end and for the barmaids and domestic staff at the other, with separate bathroom accommodation for each sex. For the manager and his family there was a separate flat. On paper, this arrangement seemed perfect; but in practice it was not found so, because large houses sometimes employ married couples, and for them this was perhaps not such a 'Welcome Inn' after all! In later rebuilding we found it better to make the staff accommodation more elastic; but the point to note here is that special care had been taken for staff living-in. Too often in the old houses the staff had been crowded into such little attics and back rooms as were available, with no real thought for their needs and comfort.

Later, as I wanted to find out how far the ample provision of bathrooms was appreciated, I made a careful inquiry; and the manager told me that so much were they approved that whenever a barmaid had rendered exceptionally good service it was his custom to allow her an extra bath as her reward!

The name 'Welcome Inn' is rather unusual, although very suitable for a pub. We advertised the house on a poster showing a cheerfully lighted inn lying back from a snow-covered road and inviting all to come in out of the cold and be refreshed. There is also the familiar quotation from the poem by the eighteenth-century poet William Shenstone:

Whoe'er has travell'd life's dull round,
Where'er his stages may have been,
May sigh to think he still has found
The warmest welcome, at the inn.

Perhaps I may add that only one other 'Welcome Inn' was

discovered in the whole country. This was at the gates of a cemetery in Swansea!

When the house was completed, Sir Kingsley Wood, the M.P. for the constituency, kindly agreed to perform the opening ceremony, in the presence of over three hundred guests, including Sir John Sykes, Miss Edith Neville, and four magistrates. It fell to me as chairman of the Improved Public House Company, to act as host to the speaker, and I took the opportunity to say something about our ideas and intentions. I shall not give my words in full, but I remember how in my speech of welcome to Sir Kingsley Wood and the other guests, I tried to impart a fair notion of what we meant by 'improvement', and to convey the idea that our present schemes were the result of long deliberation based on the conviction that a good public house, conscientiously and imaginatively run, is an asset to any community. I did not spare the obstructive authorities or the advocates of total suppression of the public house, who lacked any sort of constructive policy and had never asked themselves what kinds of mischief would soon be brewing in the pub-less land they longed for.

Ninety per cent of the population require fermented beverages and intend to get them, willy-nilly, so it was obviously our bounden duty, I pointed out, at long last to put into effect our policy envisaging 'good service plus sobriety'. The reader who has followed me thus far will not be surprised to learn that I took this opportunity for reiterating the truth upon which I have based so much of the Trade's planning, whenever I have been called upon to take a hand: the truth that for once in a way social duty and self-interest of the brewers actually coincide, since a contented, sober, well-catered-for public house population is a sure source of monetary profit as well as a commendable social unit.

Such overworked words as 'ideal' and 'reformed' I discarded out of hand. We were practical people trying to do a workmanlike job, although subject to hindrances and verbal assaults from which the real sincerity of our policy of improvement should have preserved us. One point well worth headlining, I said, was our certainty that we could sell just as much beer and make a far higher profit, in premises only a fraction of the size of the ones we were now occupying; all such amenities as roomy, comfortable, well-ventilated surroundings, and the provision of food and soft drinks to all who asked for them, were an extra, and we were proud of them. For the unfriendliness of various authorities and the errors of successive parliaments, I added, had made our task of improvement more costly and more nerve-racking than it need have been, and we looked to the weight of public opinion and the encouragement of liberal-minded men and women of good will to lighten our burden in the future.

One point I made, which was that even if the house had its full complement of 350 people each would enjoy his own 444 cubic feet of space, must have appealed strongly to Sir Kingsley, for in the course of his speech preceding his formal opening of 'The Welcome Inn', he remarked that this allowance was considerably greater than the space available to each Member of Parliament in the Chamber of the House of Commons. He said that this might explain the rowdy scenes which sometimes occurred there! (He was speaking, of course, of the old Chamber, destroyed in the blitz, and it may be worth adding that the new one shows a marked improvement in seating accommodation—almost as if the policy of improving public houses had been applied to the Mother of Parliaments!).

It will be remembered that I had been compelled to cut down the cost of the concert hall, and I was naturally anxious to find out how it would stand the test of a concert. When the opening ceremony was over we had some music; the room looked attractive enough, with its stage and seats to accommodate three hundred and fifty (as a dining room it seated two hundred) but—how about the acoustics? A well-known tenor sang for us, and to me it seemed that his performance was excellent; but as I thought his own views would be of interest, I went through into the green-room to find him walking up and down in a state of excitement. He shook me heartily by both hands and said he had never sung in a room that was so rewarding! If ever we needed a singer, and he had no other engagement, he would come and sing for the pleasure of hearing his own voice! Here was evidence that acoustics was an uncertain science indeed, but I understand that the challenge presented by broadcasting studios and modern festival and concert halls has resulted in spectacular advances over the last thirty years.

My next outstanding experience brought me in contact with the London County Council and centred round 'The Robin Hood' at Becontree. The L.C.C.'s first decision had been to have no public houses on their estates at all; but later, owing to pressure of public opinion, they decided to have a very few which must be really good and must be run on the so-called 'disinterested principle': that is to say, that those managing the houses must have no financial interest in promoting the sale of 'alcoholic liquor'.

We had owned a small cottage inn on the new housing site at Becontree which the Council now planned to develop as a new estate. I had asked them to allow us to retain the inn on lease at a handsome rent in view of the large number of building operatives who would be employed, but this they had refused, as their prejudice against tied houses was strong. However, they allowed the tenant to remain, so he became a free customer, and presently they asked us to tender for a new house to serve the expanding population. Rejoicing in this opportunity we planned one which I believed would be a first-class house, one which might serve as an example to later planners. The Valuer to the Council, Mr. Frank Hunt, C.V.O., informed me that while the plans were approved, in view of the large size of the proposed house, it was felt that a higher ground rent and premium would be appropriate. I replied that we had planned a house which I thought best suited to its purpose and something of which we could all be proud, but that since a smaller building would be more profitable, if the Council was determined to get more rent we would be willing to pay £50 more ground rent for every £1,000 saved by reducing the size of the building. In the face of this clear-cut proposal the Council decided to have the best public house and our terms were accepted.

When I asked about the licence, which, of course, was held by the tenant, whose consent would be essential if the existing licence

18. Some 'improved' public houses opened by the author: *The Welcome Inn*, *The White Hart*, *The Robin Hood* and *The Cherry Tree*

19. Father Basil Jellicoe

20. Dr. Cosmo Lang, Archbishop of Canterbury, at the opening of *The Anchor*

was to be used, I was assured that the Council had ample powers; but I had my doubts, and indeed three weeks before the application to the Justices was due, I heard that the legal advisers now thought otherwise, and wished me to undertake to arrange terms with the tenant. By that time, by reason of the great number of building operatives employed in the neighbourhood, this overcrowded cottage inn had proved so profitable that Mr. Hunt was startled when I told him I had been able to agree to terms based on one year's profits (a moderate basis in the circumstances) and that this amounted to more than £2,000. Hunt ruefully remarked 'And this is the man who persuaded us he could not pay more than £40 a year rent'. However, all went well, the justices granted the application, and we built the house, which is still regarded as a notable example, though I hold to my view that the provision of a larger number of moderate-sized houses is more in the public interest than a few very large establishments.

Another new house which offered some points of interest was the 'The White Hart' at Tottenham. This was a much more elaborate house even than 'The Welcome Inn'. It was planned in accordance with our principle that it would be well to build a few imposing houses to prove what could really be done when the authorities allowed us to do our best. We bought a large site in Tottenham near what seemed likely to develop into a popular district, to which we transferred a licence, at the same time surrendering that of 'The Spotted Dog' in order to secure the transfer. For the needs of a district change and sometimes we were willing to surrender licences if the project appeared to justify it. We decided to plan boldly, and in due course applied to the justices for provisional approval of plans for a house estimated to cost something like £35,000. We secured their approval; but when the estimates were submitted by several contractors we found, as one so often does, that even the lowest greatly exceeded our figure. I suggested to my board that we might reasonably ask the bench to allow us to modify the plans, but the board, mindful of the difficulties generally experienced with justices, thought it might create an unfortunate impression if, having received provisional consent, we began to amend the plans on the score of economy. So we decided to go ahead, and to spend more than appeared reasonable as a commercial enterprise. Our architect for this house was Mr. E. C. P. Monson, F.R.I.B.A., F.S.I.

It is usual, after a new house is completed, for a committee of the justices to approve the finished building as being in accordance with the plans they have passed. If they find it so, then the final consent is given which enables the excise licence to be taken up and the house to be opened for business. I well remember the day when the chairman of the justices arrived with two colleagues for this inspection. I took them over the house, explaining the different features and particularly the staff accommodation in some detail, while they maintained an unbroken silence. Although satisfied that everything was in order, I dreaded that they might find something to cavil at, for their present approval was vital for our future programme. All I could do was hope for the best, and when the time came for farewells the chairman, a rather dour individual, gave me his verdict. 'Mr. Nevile,' he said solemnly, 'you're not a businessman, you're a public benefactor.' This was a handsome compliment, though confound him, he was dead right; it was some years before we saw a return of even five per cent on the capital expended. Even so my board considered the enterprise worth while. It greatly helped to facilitate reasonable decisions when we sought approval for less ambitious projects. If I have laboured these early efforts it is to emphasize the problems and difficulties we had to face in those days.

A regrettable result of these activities was that I was called upon to speak in unfamiliar circles. Early in 1926 I was persuaded to do so in the austere precincts of Church House, on the occasion of the London Diocesan conference. The Bishop of London, though a critic of the Trade, had none the less invited Cecil Lubbock to speak at a meeting at which the 'drink question' was to be discussed, and Lubbock had passed the assignment to me. It was not one of my best efforts. There were to be three speakers: the first advocated State purchase, then it was my turn, and I was followed by Lord Astor, whose militant temperance proclivities I have already referred to. The Bishop, when introducing me, expressed the hope that I would not be controversial, so I sketched the history of our policy of improvement, all in rather a minor key, being oppressed by what seemed a patient but unfriendly audience.

I was followed, as I have said, by Lord Astor, who delivered an eloquent speech on the evils of alcohol and the Trade, quite uninhibited by the Bishop's instruction to me to avoid controversy. After a poorish discussion, a vote of thanks to the Bishop was proposed in popular and rather unusual terms, the tone of which would have helped me much had I heard it before I spoke. The speaker told a story about the Bishop of London in his younger days, when he was Bishop of Stepney: 'When the Bishop first arrived in Stepney and was seen walking the streets, the local people watched his gaitered figure and said to one another, "There's a bloody Bishop". But after a time, as he became a more familiar figure, people would say to one another "There's *the* bloody Bishop!" Finally, when they really knew him well, they would say with pride, "There's *our* bloody Bishop!" ' I feel that I should have been much happier if the crucial Shavian word had been used earlier on instead of following my contribution.

At that time I was closely in touch with the late E. R. Moritz, the consulting brewer I have already mentioned, and we often dined together. In his amusingly irreverent fashion, he had nicknamed me 'God'. One day, he told me, a friend had asked if he had seen lately 'that other friend he called "God".' His reply was, 'No, not lately. He is much too occupied in preparing his address for the London Diocesan Council'.

I was let in for an equally uncomfortable experience in 1925, when the City Churches were attracting some attention. There were practically no residents in the City, and thus no week-end congregations; so the idea was promulgated that a useful purpose would be served if there could be short week-day addresses in various churches on matters of public interest. Not unnaturally the 'drink question' was one such matter, and I was asked to speak one day in St. Giles', Cripplegate, which is adjacent to the brewery. I hesitated, but was persuaded to accept. I had a profound objection to going into the pulpit—I wanted to speak from the reading desk, but I was told that when somebody had spoken in this way the week before, none of the listeners had been able to hear him. There seemed to be nothing for it but to speak from the pulpit. It was an unfamiliar role to me: I felt most uncomfortable as I leant upon the purple cushion which was part of the stage property of the pulpit.

I outlined the policy of improvement, described some of my experiences on the Central Control Board, and gave reasons why I believed that better public houses would contribute to the sobriety and well-being of the nation. But I could not get away from the feeling that I was preaching a sermon; I had the utmost difficulty in avoiding the clerical pitch of voice all too often a feature of sermons. I have often felt that this rather unnatural tone is not so much willed by the parson himself as dictated by the position of the pulpit in relation to the congregation.

At the close of my remarks certain enthusiastic prohibitionists at once leapt to their feet, eager to ask questions; these, as a matter of fact, I should have been glad enough to answer, but the vicar promptly quashed the proceeding by saying that the purpose of the meeting was to listen to addresses and not to hold discussions; so that was that. Here again I produced one of my less successful efforts, and I have loathed purple plush cushions ever since.

While we at Whitbread's were pursuing our own policy of improving public houses—and, I must add, while other progressive companies were doing likewise—sympathy with our aims was growing among social workers. Many felt that however much they deplored drunkenness, the public house was a necessary part of the social scene and of the British way of life. I was naturally glad to do something to encourage this line of thought when the opportunity came my way.

About 1923 Mrs. Sotham, who during the war had helped with canteens and was prominent in social work, had joined Miss Edith Neville in an approach to Barclay Perkins. They said that they and their friends would like to operate public houses on new lines. Edward Giffard of Barclay's got in touch with Oswald Serocold of Watney's and myself, and the three breweries agreed each to make two houses available for this experiment. This was followed by several meetings between ourselves and Miss Neville, Mrs. Sotham (whose husband Major Sotham, as mentioned in the previous chapter, took a leading part in our educational schemes) and the Hon. Eleanor Plumer, later Warden of St. Andrews Hall, Reading University. It was agreed to form a body named the 'Association for the Provision of Restaurant Public Houses in Poor Districts', usually known as the Restaurant Public House Association.

To this association Whitbread's handed over two houses, and this marked the beginning of a close association with these ladies. The houses were to be leased to the Association as tenants who would then appoint their own managers, and it was here that the first difficulty arose; for, as I have said before, the London licensing benches were reluctant to transfer a licence from a tenant to a manager. However, when it was understood that the organization was controlled by persons notable for social work, including a number of well-known licensing magistrates, this particular difficulty was resolved.

So far as Whitbread's were concerned, it was decided to leave the running of the houses in all their social aspects entirely to the Association, but we promised assistance with the technical management, accounts and so on. We arranged that Theobalds, the Improved Public House Company's managing director, should attend their board and committee meetings to put his experience at their disposal. He was not to speak unless spoken to, as we had no wish to interfere with their affairs unless asked for advice. Theobalds happened himself to be interested in social work; he was in full sympathy with the R.P.H.A. and its aim. We told Miss Neville and her friends that we were willing to subsidize the project, and if necessary to lose money on it, as we regarded it as a matter of social research. This possibility of losses surprised them, because they fully expected to make a respectable profit; but, as any brewer could testify, a large and immediate financial return is not an inevitable consequence of operating a public house on new lines.

The Association aimed at making the 'local' into something nearer a family rendezvous by selling meals, refreshments, soft drinks, tea, and so on, and they met with a fair measure of success. Those of us who were concerned with the long-term development of our trade were glad to co-operate, and for a number of years we and the Association worked closely and happily together.

Miss Neville was a woman of resolution and personality. She was a daughter of Sir Ralph Neville, a Judge of the High Court, and all her life was devoted to social service. Though she became interested in public house 'reform', as she called it, this was only one preoccupation in a busy life given over to good works. She was a moving spirit in the Mary Ward Settlement in Bloomsbury; she was interested in the People's Theatre, the Somers Town Housing project, and other philanthropic enterprises.

The R.P.H.A. got under way, though sometimes there were misunderstandings as to their objects. My old friend, H. L. Grimston of Barclay's, reminds me of an experience he had in the early days, when the Association took over his firm's house, 'The Rose', near Camberwell Green. A woman came into the public bar, saw the changes that had been made, cried 'Gor lummy, the 'ouse of Lords', and promptly bolted. Grimston went after her, brought her back, and soothed her with a drink.

Miss Neville's connection with the People's Theatre at Somers Town brought her into contact with that dynamic personality and really great man, Father Basil Jellicoe, who was then working hard at his celebrated housing scheme in the district. Father Jellicoe was head of the Magdalen College Mission in St. Pancras, and was already celebrated for his fearless efforts in slum clearance and housing. He was under thirty, and full of driving energy and enthusiasm. He was born in 1899 at the Sussex vicarage of Chailey and at the age of two-and-a-half told Dr. Wilberforce that he meant to be a bishop when he grew up.

His first public appearance, while still a young schoolboy, was when he gave a lecture on Christian Socialism—it is interesting to recall, in the light of future events, that the lecture was delivered in a pub. After a brief period of war service in the R.N.V.R. in 1918 Basil Jellicoe went to Oxford, and was ordained in 1923. (Naval service had come naturally to him; his father was a cousin of the Admiral.) Almost all the rest of Basil Jellicoe's short but brilliant career confined him to St. Pancras, where he had been appointed head of the Magdalen Mission in 1921, before his ordination in fact—an unusual appointment for a layman, and one which he fully justified in fourteen crowded years. His early death, in 1935, was a grievous loss to the Church and to the people of St. Pancras and East London. The Archbishop of York wrote of him, 'No man ever so luminously exemplified the sacramental quality of the Christian religion as did Basil Jellicoe.' This was the man who at the time of which I write was turning his thoughts to the improved public house movement.

At Christmas, 1928, Father Jellicoe preached a remarkable sermon, the reports of which formed headlines in the popular press. He said that just as on the first Christmas Day there was no room for Christ in the inn at Bethlehem, so there was no room for Christ's people in the London inns of today. He said he had been struck by the need for comfort and entertainment in the average public house—as well as for a better atmosphere—and he wondered if there was any brewer who would be generous enough to give him an opportunity of showing what he could do. This challenge was too much for Lubbock and myself, and for our colleagues at Whitbread's. We asked Father Jellicoe to lunch, and (after talking the matter over) arranged to rebuild and hand over to him a house called 'The Anchor' in Stibbington Street, close to where the Somers Town Housing scheme (in which Father Jellicoe was a leading spirit) was demonstrating to the local authority that slum-clearance was a practical possibility. The tenants of 'The Anchor' were to be the Restaurant Public Houses Association, and the plans for the house were to be drawn up in consultation with Father Jellicoe. It was part of his creed that many who were unable to enter the Church were yet prepared to serve their fellow men; and that many of these would find a splendid outlet for their energies in a public house in which a Christian spirit could find a place. He hoped to show that there was room for the publican within the realm of practical Christianity, and the success of his experiment at 'The Anchor' went a long way to prove this.

The new 'Anchor' was a medium-sized house in keeping with

the style and character of the Somers Town housing estate, and in November 1929 it was opened for business. The experiment attracted wide attention, and many prominent people visited the house in its early days, including Queen Mary, the Prince of Wales and the Archbishop of Canterbury (who was present at the opening ceremony). The motive behind the enterprise was somewhat startling; but the house undoubtedly fulfilled its day-to-day function of providing rest and refreshment for the people of the district. Father Jellicoe himself, with some of his assistant priests, went to live at 'The Anchor' and became well-known to the customers at the bar. He used sometimes to say in his sermons that, if anyone in the congregation cared to take up any of his points with him, they would find him after the service in the bar at 'The Anchor'. He was an abstainer himself, but it was no embarrassment to him to chat with one of his flock with a pint of beer between them on the table.

Jellicoe and I differed on only one point. I felt it better not to be present when he was entertaining distinguished visitors and describing the house and its aims. I felt that the considerable public interest should be focused not on ourselves but on those running the social experiment; the presence of a brewery director might make the scheme appear to be something in the nature of a publicity stunt. The experiment and all its implications were too important to risk misunderstanding. Father Jellicoe's feeling about the experiment may be judged by his own words:

'I am much indebted to the spirit of adventure which has prompted Messrs. Whitbread and Company to allow me to make an experiment which has always been very near to my heart. I have always felt that if there is "trouble in the pub" it is not the fault of the pub itself. What is wrong sometimes and in some places is the *atmosphere*; and I believe that it is one of the chief duties of the Christian Church to strive to create the atmosphere of the family of God in industry as well as in Church, and also in recreation, for without wholesome recreation there can be no true bread-winning.

'I am sure that those who are not prejudiced against brewers must realize how very much has been done to improve public houses all over the country by the best firms at least. When a house is improved, I know that very often great pains are taken to find a first-class manager for the improved house. What my friends and I at "The Anchor" are anxious to do is to be allowed to train a few men who will be willing to go, not to improved houses necessarily, but often to the worst houses, and always to the worst districts! We want to do this because we believe that through the public house a really magnificent opportunity is opened up for social service. The slums have happened because men have failed to consecrate bread and bread-winning; and the Church is called to consecrate both bread and wine. This is what we are trying to do, and it is because of the spirit which animates our staff to a man that we are achieving the success which we knew must be ours if we would be faithful to what we believed.'

The influence of this gallant enterprise was far-reaching, but Father Jellicoe did not live to carry it beyond its early stages. His health broke down—he had never spared himself in spite of a delicate constitution—and in 1935 he died, honoured and mourned by everyone who knew him. I saw in him many of the qualities I had found in my uncle, Father Tooth: the same devotion to his Faith, the same will to follow his dedicated course, at whatever cost, and the same liberal spirit of love for all men, of whatever faith and creed. In every generation there are a few such men—but always, alas, too few. I look back on this experience as one of my happiest memories.

So far I have dwelt on the more outstanding instances of public house improvement, but we were engaged in many more modest efforts; though nearly every one possesses some point of interest. There was one case which showed that even difficult magistrates sometimes modify their prejudices, even if not quite aware that they are doing just that. We once took to the bench plans of a much-needed alteration, approval for which, after their viewing the house, was withheld. Two years later I was pressed to try again but suggesting a different design. I asked our advisers if this new design was any better, and was told that it was not. So I decided to present the same plans again on different paper. The application was adjourned, pending inspection, after which the same chairman remarked to our architect, 'Now, "Mr. Brown", this proposal is much better, why did you not bring this before?' There is much in the maxim 'If at first you don't succeed, try, try, try again'.

Apart from our London properties, we had many houses in Kent acquired by the purchase of Leney, of Wateringbury. Here our local managing director was John Marchant, who was enthusiastically bent on introducing features of human interest; one of his notions was that when houses were brought up-to-date we should drop their meaningless 'Red Lion' and 'Black Bull' designations, and seize the opportunity for commemorating some picturesque personality. This achieved, he liked to invite leading citizens to attend the opening. One case I remember was of the 'Railway Inn' at Hastings, which we re-named the 'G.I.' to commemorate the presence of the American Forces during the Second World War. The American Embassy was pleased and arranged for a representative contingent to attend. I remarked in my opening speech that, though they would shortly be leaving us, they would not go empty-handed, as some had married and would take home with them many of our prettiest girls; upon which the senior man among them called out, 'There are six of us here, and we've all married English girls.'

Another such inn was in a village, the principal resident of which had lost his son, who had won the Victoria Cross. This resident, and indeed his neighbours, were touched and delighted when we asked him to unveil the sign of 'John Brunt V.C.' as a tribute to his son's memory.

So far I have described our larger houses, and must include as a contrast a note on one of the smallest pubs we own, 'The Bull's Head' at Guildford. This house came into our possession as one of a small group of properties we acquired in 1951. It dated from the seventeenth century and contained architectural features in conformity with the picturesque style of neighbouring properties. Apparently worn out, and on a site too small to permit of rebuilding, it represented quite a problem. However our architect was convinced that restoration, though costly, might make it a museum piece worth our while. So the interior was replanned with old timbers, the elevation was restored, and as far as possible its antique features were retained. The proposal interested Professor Albert Richardson, P.R.A., who kindly offered to open the house when completed. Colonel Whitbread was abroad, and asked me to support Mrs. Whitbread, who was hostess on this occasion. Space was so restricted that the inn could hardly contain the number of guests who attended, so we used the space behind the bar as our platform. After a delightful speech Sir Albert performed the ceremony of drawing the first pint. Mrs. Whitbread entertained us later at a most happy luncheon party at her house at Warren Mere, when Sir Albert delighted my wife by giving to her, as well as to Mrs. Whitbread, one of his charming water colour sketches. In spite of our earlier conviction that this house would be like a museum piece, the unexpected happened; this small house has proved so popular that it returns quite a satisfactory profit, in spite of the large cost of restoration.

11

More Work at Whitbread's—Comparison Between Large and Small Breweries—Recruiting Staff—Visit to Brandon at Flowerdale—William H. Whitbread joins the Firm—Purchase of Breweries—J. E. Martineau—Problems of Bottled Beer—The Mackeson Story—Visit to Australia

Now I must return to my early experiences at Whitbread's which, from October 1919 onwards were to form the most important and eventful part of my life's work.

The exigencies of the First World War had caused us many a headache. Business had had to be carried on in spite of all the difficulties and it had been impossible to maintain the plant at peace-time standards; while the whole commercial pattern had changed. The increase of the duty from 7s. 9d. to 80s. per 'standard' barrel, and the restrictions arising from shortness of material and the need to produce the largest possible bulk even from what we had, had resulted in a considerable change in quality and a complete upheaval of the price structure. Whitbread's stout had disappeared from the market owing to the restriction imposed on English brewers, in March 1918, of an average gravity of 30 degrees, whereas the concession to Irish brewers to brew 45 degrees had resulted in their securing practically a monopoly of the stout trade.

My first object was to get a grasp of the business, which in many ways differed from my experience at Putney in both scope and structure, for the organization of a big brewery has little in common with that of smaller concerns. At Brandon's each of the three managing directors had taken care of a principal department and had exercised control over its details. I found Whitbread's to be administered rather differently. At Brandon's I had controlled production and managed relations with other breweries and with the Trade organizations. My colleague Alfred Palmer had been responsible for the tied houses and their accounts, and Sidney Foulsham had managed the bottling department in close collaboration with myself. Like many another moderate-sized concern we had no laboratory with specialized chemists, though a certain amount of control work was done by one or another of the under-brewers. For the more important scientific work we retained the services of the laboratory controlled by that great man Horace Brown, both for analytical work and for advice on special problems. We had no architect but employed a clerk of the works at a moderate salary to supervise decorations and repairs for our one hundred and fifty tied houses, and relied on outside architects and builders for major alterations.

At Whitbread's the organization was far otherwise. Each of the directors took a general interest in the whole of the business of the company. Under us we had the secretary as head of the office staff, and the head brewer (H. E. Field) was responsible for production and had several assistant under-brewers, chemists and engineers under his control. Our public houses, of which there were something like a thousand, were supervised by five outside managers, known in London breweries as 'Abroad-Coopers'. The head 'Abroad-Cooper' was W. F. Esse, upon whom, with his assistants, we relied for the general management of the properties. He had spent a lifetime in the industry and began, I believe, with experience actually in a public house, and was later on the staff of a brewery in Chelsea which had been bought by Whitbread's. I had first come across him in 1909, when he was chairman of the Outside Managers' Committee of London brewery companies during the period beset by difficulties arising from the 1909 Budget. For years he retained the leadership of this informal organization. A great supporter of public house improvement and an accomplished diplomat, he was of the greatest service in furthering this policy.

We also had a staff of architects who kept the properties in sound order and undertook all the structural work required, ranging from total rebuilding of a licensed house to the erection of bottling stores.

Our bottling department, even in those days, was numerically the most important in the business. It was conducted as an almost separate concern (since at its inception the bottling of beer was regarded as being somewhat beneath the dignity of the large wholesale brewers) with offices in Britannia Street, King's Cross. Walter Sharp, who was in control of this large establishment, was a great character and an excellent judge of men. He was assisted by his nephew, Granville Sharp, and by Arthur Grundy, brother of my co-director Percy Grundy, previously secretary to the company. The department he controlled, though not over-profitable owing to the keen competition of those days, was an example of excellent organization. On the other hand, he and his staff were singularly devoid of any technical training in brewing, and one of my early recommendations was to secure for him a technical adviser. I was fortunate to get one Carl Wootton, a trained brewer with specialist knowledge and enthusiasm, who for the next thirty years was to play a great part in technical development: he came to be regarded as one of the greatest authorities on bottling.

In this cabinet of executives Henry Field, the head brewer, with whom for years I had had much to do, took first place. He was popular throughout the Trade, though something of a martinet. When my term as president of the Institute of Brewing came to an end, I suggested him as my successor. Previously it had always been the custom for the president to be either a scientific consulting brewer or a well-known director of a brewery company. He was the first executive to be chosen for this post, but proved so popular that there have since been several instances of head brewers occupying this position with distinction. On his retirement from the presidency he succeeded Mr. A. H. Mure as treasurer, and retained that position for many years.

One of my early activities at Whitbread's was to do with transport. At that time the firm used no motor transport, but we owned, and stabled at Chiswell Street, two hundred and ninety horses, in the care of John Lomax, our transport manager, who had been with the company since 1896. It was quite a sight in the evening to watch the unharnessing of the horses and see them going each to its own stall in the brewery stables. The stalls were on three floors, with access by ramps which naturally had to be fairly steep. Each horse knew its own stall, but occasionally a newcomer might find its way into one belonging to another horse—this was apt to occur if the newcomer to the team arrived home early—and then there would be pandemonium; for when the rightful occupant appeared and found his stall had been filched from him, he would at once take the nearest one which captured his fancy and the result was something like a game of musical chairs, with horses charging here there and everywhere in search of empty stalls. On such evenings it took some time to stable them all to the general satisfaction.

It had become necessary to adopt motor transport, partly for reasons of economy and partly because the space occupied by stabling was more and more urgently in demand for other purposes. My co-directors were waiting for my advice about this, as I had had experience with transport in the early war years. The only use Whitbread's had so far made of mechanical transport was the hiring of steam wagons for delivering especially heavy consignments of beer in casks to various bottling depots in and around London. It was evident that a change-over to motor delivery of some kind was bound to come; the only question was, which kind? The petrol motor had not yet entirely superseded the steam wagon, and there were electric vans of the type we had used successfully at Brandon's. A problem was created by our large numbers of draymen, old servants of the company, who might not easily adapt themselves to the greater speeds of petrol-lorries after the leisurely pace of their horses. For this reason, I recommended a fleet of electric vehicles such as we had used at Brandon's; these had a speed of about ten miles an hour, at which rate our older drivers would feel more at home. Electric transport possessed many advantages within a limited area, though a transport manager likes to have vehicles of one pattern capable of going any distance at short notice. Later, as a new generation of drivers came along, we gradually turned over to petrol and diesel engines. Today we have a big fleet, including many large tank wagons which are now a familiar sight on the roads.

I also introduced tank vehicles. These tankers represented a startling advance on my first 'Heath Robinson' experiment, which I had designed about 1900; but they are a logical development from it. As at Brandon's, they were adopted to deliver beer in bulk to the bottling stores. The company had depots in London, as well as thirty or forty others up and down the country. In 1919 the beer was delivered to them in butts, each containing 108 gallons and weighing over half a ton when full. The handling of these presented a problem at the different stores; a regular gang was maintained for placing the butts in twos and sometimes threes in tiers. It was evident that if the beer were delivered in tanks on the principle I had originated at Putney, there would be a large saving in space and money and greater ease of handling.

We first tried out the system in one depot only, and the experiment proved so successful that we extended it elsewhere as opportunity arose. The first tankers were of modest dimensions—twenty barrels, representing a four-ton load—but later the size was progressively increased until we now employ several eighty-barrel tankers, each drawing a trailer. The practice which I initiated at Brandon's in 1900 has, as we all know, become general nowadays, not only for beer but for several other commodities.

Of course the change-over from horses to mechanical transport was not effected without regrets. For generations a brewer's horse had typified quality, and Whitbread's were rightly particularly proud of their fine animals. As I have written elsewhere, we had the privilege of providing horses for the Speaker's coach and we also horse the Lord Mayor's coach on State occasions so we still keep about thirty.

In the ordinary way the directors did not take any very active part in production, leaving this in the capable hands of my old friend H. E. Field. There were, however, occasions when I felt

21. *The North Yard of Whitbread's Brewery* by Sir Alfred J. Munnings

22. Gertrude Lawrence and Douglas Fairbanks, junior

23. Modern Inn Signs in Kent

called upon to take a hand; one such occurred in 1921 when, owing to a coal strike which had begun in April, the supply of fuel to London was much restricted. Early in May it emerged that our supply of available fuel was running out, and that we should be faced with complete stoppage if we did not ration our supplies and reduce the amount brewed.

Lubbock had quite a streak of fatalism in his make-up: an invaluable quality in times when irremediable emergencies threaten dislocation. At such moments his imperturbability and calm judgement saved rasher spirits from panic decisions. When this blow fell, he saw nothing for it but to brew less and ration our houses. He felt that all brewers would be in the same boat, as it were, and that we must all accept the situation.

Then I discovered, to my horror, that competitors of ours, some because they had larger fuel stocks and some because they could turn to oil fuel, were contemplating full production. The thought of Whitbread's being short of supply was unendurable, so I jumped into action and persuaded my colleagues to give me *carte blanche* for taking measures to avoid this catastrophe. I was first advised that it would take three months at least to obtain and install oil fuel and apparatus, but as desperate ills demand desperate remedies I sought for a shorter cut than this and consulted Sir John Thornycroft, head of the Thornycroft engineering firm, a connection of mine by marriage, and a most kindly man, and asked him about the possibilities of finding a set of oil-burning plant from a disused destroyer or other small naval vessel, many of which were available at the time. He was helpfulness itself, for while he dismissed as impracticable my idea of adapting disused naval plant, he told me that the Slipway Company had suitable oil burners available at Newcastle, that a firm of junk-dealers in the East End of London had disused boilers, one of which would serve as an oil reservoir, and that a suitable pressure pump might be obtained from Glasgow. Thornycroft also gave me the name of an expert in oil fuels who would advise us. I got this expert to the brewery that same afternoon; he considered the idea feasible if we could obtain the plant, and furnished precise details of equipment needed.

I telephoned to Newcastle and arranged for burners to be sent by special motor van to London. Next I instructed the manager of our bottling depot in Glasgow to purchase a suitable pump and arrange a special delivery for it also. Then I took our engineer to Bermondsey to see about a disused boiler, and booked a lorry capable of bringing the boiler next day, provided that we secured one.

The junk-dealer did in fact have several well suited to our purpose. He named his lowest price but added, looking anywhere but at me, that he would 'enter into any arrangement with me that would lead to business'. This enlightened me as to customary methods in that line of business; so I agreed his price, arranged with our engineer to make the pressure test, had the boiler delivered and placed in the open air on timber balks, and set every available man to preparing the necessary pipe-work. Thus we had oil fuel working in a week. I am sometimes told that I am lethargic but when suitably challenged I can put on quite a fair turn of speed.

I also applied myself to the business of recruiting the best type of staff. From about 1922 leading industrialists had tended to introduce recommended graduates from the universities into their organizations. This was in line with Lubbock's principle that a sound classical education was the best foundation for success in life. Although a man fresh from the 'Varsity might appear a long way behind those who had already had some years' experience in business, Lubbock held that by the time he was thirty he would be better equipped to bring a well-informed judgement to bear. We therefore approached the appointments board of one of the Universities and asked its secretary to recommend one or two likely applicants. The experiment did not meet with the success I had hoped for; perhaps it was before its time. I was not pleased with the type of applicant that appeared who, as often as not, gave small evidence of enthusiasm or ambition. I was particularly shocked by one. It was my custom during the conversation to ask the proposed recruit why he thought of entering commercial life, why the brewing industry attracted him, and why he thought Whitbread's would offer him the opportunities he looked for.

The languid reply to the first of my questions set the tone; the young man supposed he must have a job of some kind. When I asked him why he chose brewing, he said that when he met brewers they all seemed pretty well off, so brewing must be a good thing to be in. Finally when I asked him why he wished to come to Whitbread's, he showed a spark of real interest: everybody had told him Whitbread's was a good firm; he would never have to come in on Saturdays; they were good sportsmen and would always let him take time off when he had the chance of a bit of hunting or shooting!

This priceless example set me thinking, and I got in touch with the appointments secretary to make a few inquiries. We did not advance the subject very far. He said that, when he had secured appointments for many of his young men, their employers did not seem to take much trouble to encourage them. My reply was that when I was young nobody encouraged me. I found my encouragement in the need to equip myself with the necessary knowledge and experience if I was to do any good in the world. After a not too profitable talk I asked him about the after-history of those he introduced to jobs: how did they do, how many of them achieved distinction? There I drew a blank. He kept no records of that kind. The function of the educationalist was to educate; having educated the young idea and recommended them for appointments, all responsibility of the educators ceased. I am afraid that here again my reply was uncompromising: for I told him that as a brewer I found it necessary to keep samples of each brewing for a considerable period, to study its behaviour and to keep a continuous record of the results of our efforts. It seemed to me that the product of the Universities was the life blood of the nation, of far greater importance than beer; and I was surprised to hear that they took so little interest in the ultimate success of their work. I have no doubt that his verdict on me was that I was a typical industrialist, and I expect he often dined out on his version of our conversation.

Perhaps the proposal was, as I now feel, ahead of its time. I remember the explanation given by Granville Sharp, head of our bottling organization, who was himself a public-school boy. He said, 'If you go to the best public schools or to the 'Varsities for applicants you will not get the best. The educationalists want to keep the cleverest boys for high educational honours; others for the Army, the Navy, the Civil Service, the so-called learned professions, the Church, the law and so on; and then there are the boys who will inherit interests in family businesses. So the recruits recommended are bound to be the least promising; whereas, if you go to the grammar and secondary schools' (these were the days before the re-shuffle) 'the head masters will recommend their outstanding pupils for such jobs as Whitbread's have to offer, and such boys will know that they have everything to learn before they can be of much use.'

Yet when all was said and done, I was not unaware that the average graduate, not driven by sheer necessity as I was in my young days, must see his first few years in the competitive world of business as a grim and dreary prospect after a pleasant interlude. He has been working for only about half the year and much of his work has been arranged to suit his own inclinations. There has been plenty of sport, of social life, of long vacations. Office life, work from nine-thirty to five on week-days with as often as not a half-day's work on Saturdays; three weeks' holiday instead of six months; this was the abrupt change facing these young men I interviewed. Nowadays, of course, conditions are otherwise. The easy circumstances of the upper middle classes have disappeared. Many if not most undergraduates at the Universities are grant-aided and know they must work hard, having no inheritance to look forward to. A job upon graduation is a normal prospect, added to which the prejudice against commercial life, which was a heritage of the Victorian age, has largely disappeared together with other social distinctions. Some of our best men in recent years have been recruited from the Universities, though often they have come on to us after following some other calling.

As a diversion I had quite an interesting experience in September 1921. Brandon had taken Flowerdale, a sporting estate in Ross-shire, for the season, and asked me to stay with him for a fortnight. Later, he told me he was accommodating guests at the hotel instead of the house for reasons he would explain. I took the night train to Achnasheen and the somewhat antiquated bus to Gairloch. As we passed the lodge gates of Flowerdale, we had to stop for a few minutes, and saw quite a crowd assembled around a car in which was no less a person than Lloyd George, making a speech in reply to the welcome from those who had assembled. In the car with him I noticed Lord Riddell, one of his close friends. When I arrived at Gairloch, Brandon told me that, after settling his tenancy, the agents had approached him with the news that Lloyd George had set his heart on Flowerdale; could he (Brandon) be persuaded to release the house (they wanted to know) and some of the fishing. He had felt bound to do so and for that reason was entertaining his friends at the hotel instead of the house.

Two days after I arrived, the owner of the adjoining property called on Brandon to remind him that the fishing in the river separating the properties and shared by the two, was permissible only on alternate days. The Prime Minister, with his customary disregard for detail, had ignored this arrangement. I have forgotten now how the difficulty was adjusted, but anyway the next two or three days were to bring more exciting incidents. This was the time of the Irish troubles and one morning two destroyers appeared in the offing. These were bringing the leaders of the Irish insurgents, who had come to meet the Prime Minister for a conference. The delegates and their staffs stayed at the hotel, so the dining-room was filled with a varied and interesting company. One table was occupied by Brandon, his family and guests, another by the staff he had brought with him. At a third were the Irish delegates and their attendants; and, at a fourth, a party of plain clothes men from Scotland Yard, there to take care of the Prime Minister. After the Irish party had departed, an unprecedented event took place. An emergency Cabinet meeting was called at Inverness, the ministers being assembled by telegram from all over the country. Although not immediately successful, I believe that the gathering at Gairloch provided the beginning of the negotiations which finally led to the establishment of the Irish Republic. As might be expected, I had not much to do with the Irish delegates except to pass the time of day. There was little to indicate that they were the desperate characters popular opinion held them to be.

Sailing was still my favoured recreation, as I neither shoot nor stalk, but I had a pleasant time fishing in the loch and even tried my 'prentice hand at throwing a fly—but with little success.

* * *

In 1922, I was elected to the Council of the Federation of British Industries and served for some years on the taxation committee. This work led to my appointment as a lay member of the Board of Referees established under the Finance Acts of 1915/1927, and I sat from time to time in some dignity on panels at the Law Courts under the Chairmanship of a well-known K.C., with a distinguished accountant and two other ordinary business men, to adjudicate in cases when the revenue officials differed from the taxpayer as to the amounts chargeable for income and surtax. Most of our cases were concerned with the efforts of the taxpayer to utilize some loophole which enabled him to transfer income into capital. Many were so barefaced we had little difficulty, but I recollect one connected with a large group of Companies in which the issues, involving many thousands, were so complicated that my colleagues considered the decision for so long that in the end I hazarded an opinion in favour of the taxpayer, and this was agreed by my more expert colleague and given as our judgement. The revenue people were dissatisfied and took the case to the Courts; my view was upheld there, but next the case passed to the Lords who said I was wrong! I seldom sit nowadays and indeed have been too busy to do much at the Federation either, but whenever I have suggested to either body that the time has come for me to retire, they have asked me to let my name stand; and I verily believe I must be the oldest surviving member, both of the Grand Council of the Federation and the Court of Referees.[1]

January 1924 brought an important event in the arrival at Chiswell Street of William H. Whitbread (our present Chairman),

[1] Since these lines were written the Federation, at the instance of the President, Sir Hugh Beaver, has elected me a Vice-President in view of my long service on the Council.

son of Harry Whitbread. He had taken an accountancy course and worked a year's pupilage in the Burton brewery of Truman Hanbury and Buxton, with the intention of joining the Board as a Managing Director. One day I asked him whether he was satisfied with a general knowledge of the business, reinforced by his shrewd judgement of men and things, or whether he wished to acquire a thorough and more detailed grasp of the Industry as a whole and Whitbread's in particular. He left me in no doubt. He was devoted to the traditions he had inherited and was determined to secure as wide and comprehensive a knowledge as he possibly could of the Trade upon which his forefathers had left such an indelible mark; so I suggested he should join me in taking a group of our senior executives on the tour of the Continental breweries which I was contemplating. He jumped at the idea, cancelled all other engagements and shared the hectic fortnight we spent travelling through Belgium, Germany, Denmark, Sweden and Norway, moving on by night and working by day. This was the beginning of a friendship and co-operation between us of more than thirty years. I little foresaw in those days the quality of dynamic leadership he was destined to develop and devote to Whitbread's itself, the brewing industry generally, and indeed the whole wide field of commerce. I treasure as one of my most rewarding recollections his affectionate acknowledgement of the share I was able to take in displaying the interesting features of the industry in which he was to take so prominent a part when, after his service in the Great War, he succeeded to the Chairmanship on the death of his uncle, S. H. Whitbread.

While prominent in many fields of sport: polo, racing, yachting, shooting and hunting, his main interest and enthusiasm have been centred on the development of the business. My memories of the thirty-three years of our association and our work together have long been and will always be a source of keenest gratification to me.

The activities I have described at Chiswell Street, were, though important, matters of organization—they took place within the brewery walls. But expansion was necessary, and before long I was deeply concerned in negotiations for the purchase of other businesses. In 1924 I was busy on my first major purchase in the shape of the Forest Hill Brewery Company, the principal proprietors of which were the Venner family, well known in the retail trade in the earlier years of the century. The chairman, Mr. Edward Venner, had originally owned several large free licensed houses and with some of his friends had bought the brewery, then a small concern, to supply their requirements. Realizing that accountancy was a weak spot in the Trade, he had articled his son, Edwin Venner, to the firm of Edward Moore and Son. In the collapse that followed the boom in licensed property in the '90s, many mortgagees were driven to foreclose on their security and Edward Moore was in a large number of cases appointed receiver on their behalf. Edwin Venner consequently established an accountancy and stock-taking business to co-operate with the receivers in addition to acting as managing director of the family concern. In the early '20s he had been invited by Bass, Ratcliff and Gretton, the Burton brewers, to take care of their interests in the Wenlock brewery, a London concern of which they had acquired control; so the Venner family decided to dispose of the Forest Hill Brewery and I was asked if Whitbread's would be interested. I brought the suggestion to my colleagues, a price was arranged and the purchase concluded.

I had formed a high opinion of the character and ability of both the Venners, and remember the father telling me of the advice he made a practice of giving to those young men whom he helped to start in the licensed trade: 'Never drink with a customer, never lend a customer money'. I know from my own observations that drinking with customers has been the downfall of many publicans and, as the vicar of Wakefield discovered, lending money is the surest way of ending a friendship. Edwin Venner became Chairman of the Wenlock brewery, and when the firm joined the Brewers' Company at the invitation of Cecil Lubbock, he represented his company on the Court and in due course became Master. Frank Whitbread was so impressed with his character and ability that he nominated Venner to succeed him as chairman of the National Trade Defence Association, a post which I myself was to occupy on Venner's retirement.

On Sir William Butler's death the Home Secretary asked me to recommend an adviser to act with myself. Regarding Venner as the greatest expert in the country on wines and spirits as well as the licensed trade generally, I strongly recommended him and secured his acceptance. We served together until my retirement from the State management district. He received a knighthood in recognition of his services.

To return, now, to the Forest Hill Brewery, the purchase of which was to lead to issues more important than the mere acquisition of further property. For its size, the company had quite a considerable trade in bottled beers produced by the method of maturing and filtering before bottling (thus avoiding the sediment inevitable in beers matured in bottle). So we decided to equip a plant for producing this beer under its existing brand name, Forest Ale.

Now when Whitbread's had started bottling in the 'seventies they had adopted the best methods known at the time. They had used the finest materials and had exercised great care in both production and bottling. They had succeeded in producing beer of higher quality than the average, and as a result had secured a national output, in their own words, 'from Land's End to John o' Groats'. Their beer had for many years been advertised as 'matured in bottle' and when all went well their beer was unequalled. But there was one drawback. Bottled beers produced on these lines inevitably contain sediment. The demand was increasing for beers 'bright to the last drop', as some described it. Though we hesitated to change the character of Whitbread's beer, there was good reason for trying to discover how the new methods could be adopted without bringing about too fundamental a change in the character and flavour of our product. With this in mind, I took our leading technicians on a trip to the Continent to study the best methods abroad before planning our experimental plant. The party included our head brewer, our bottling manager and Carl Wootton, our bottling expert. We learnt much from the two great breweries in Copenhagen, and on our return we designed a small plant to produce beer of the variety previously supplied by the Forest Hill Brewery. I decided for this purpose to use the factory in Gray's Inn Road, Whitbread's original bottlery which had gone out of commission, because of its distance from most of our trade. It had had a chequered career, having been a non-conformist chapel, a horse dealer's yard, and a furniture repository before its acquisition by Whitbread's.

After some initial difficulties we found that Whitbread's beer, being brewed from exceptionally good material, took kindly to the new process and ranked higher than those of most if not all of our competitors (some of whom seemed to work on the principle that chilling and filtering sufficed to turn a bad beer into a good one). Before long we had made the momentous decision to apply the new method to Whitbread's brand. But the beer drinker is a conservative creature, and any suspicion that we were altering the process by which Whitbread's beer was produced was calculated to disaffect those who liked it just as it had been; so of course our chief object was to make the transfer without attracting attention. I arranged for the beer, after bottling, to be kept at least a month before supplying it to the distributors. The transfer from the one type to the other was thus successfully made. I believe that we only had one complaint, and that from someone who considered the sediment had a high medicinal value!

The limited size of the factory made it impossible to distribute direct to retailers from Gray's Inn Road, so I decided on a novel plan. We arranged for the beer to be transferred, as soon as bottled, to our distributing depots in various parts of London. The plant was organized so that when a lorry with empty bottles and cases arrived at the factory, the empties would be discharged on to the lower floor, transferred to the working floor above, and so arranged that the first full case could be reloaded by the time the last case of empty bottles and boxes had been unloaded. At first sight, this system might seem to necessitate costly extra transport to the distributing stores. In practice it was surprisingly economical. By concentrating the bottling in one centre, the efficiency and economy of labour and handling were greater than if the beer had been bottled piecemeal, in the different depots around London. I have gone into some detail here, because the transfer of Whitbread's bottled beer from the method of maturing in bottle to the more modern process was perhaps the most interesting technical experience in my whole career.

The next important transaction I was concerned with was the purchase in 1927 of the ordinary shares in Frederick Leney of Wateringbury in Kent, an old-established country business whose proprietors had ceased to take any active interest, and wished to realize their holdings. Their houses were principally in the rural districts of mid-Kent, with a considerable holding in the thickly populated Chatham district as well as some houses on the coast in the Hastings area. Whitbread's had few houses in those parts, so the purchase seemed worth while because it would spread the sale of Whitbread's bottled beers. Rural Kent was not at that time considered attractive to the large London brewers, so we got the business at a most moderate capital cost. In such a deal it is usual for the purchaser to have the right to close the brewery if he wishes. Since the debenture and preference shares had been issued on the understanding that the business would be continued as a separate entity, it became necessary to secure the consent of the holders of both, in exchange for which we offered an increase of interest. At the special general meeting called to secure the indispensable alteration to the articles of association, a not unusual attempt was made on the part of a few to get better terms. They opposed the resolution and demanded a poll, but the major interests were satisfied and the scheme was accepted by an overwhelming majority.

A year later we were approached by the auditors of another concern, Jude Hanbury and Company Limited, and asked if we would buy a block of properties in the Weald of Kent owned by that Company. Jude Hanbury had originally been close neighbours of Leney's in the small village of Wateringbury. Being convinced that the Channel Tunnel would be constructed and would bring great industrial development to East Kent, they had bought a brewery in Canterbury and had moved their business there. They proposed to dispose of their mid-Kent properties in order to raise part of the capital needed to complete the purchase of the old-established firm of Mackeson of Hythe, of which they had the offer. The price they asked for the Weald properties was far above our idea of their value, and it occurred to me that since our principal interest was in bottled beer, Whitbread's might help Jude Hanbury with finance; that Jude, Mackeson and Leney might be amalgamated with Whitbread's holding a majority interest; that the proprietors of Jude Hanbury should manage the business on handsome terms; and that Whitbread's should supply their bottled beers to the whole group in addition to those already bottled by its individual breweries.

This scheme was the first essay in what has become the Whitbread policy of keeping old-established businesses in existence and of selling our bottled beers in their houses, and also providing, in exchange for this concession, financial and technical assistance. But the world-wide financial blizzard of 1929 prevented the continuance of the original scheme; the remaining proprietors of Jude Hanbury wished to realize their interests, so Whitbread's acquired these and entered into sole control. There followed what I may call the Mackeson story, which I like to regard as one of my successes.

Some years before our acquisition of the brewery, the Mackeson company had taken up certain patents in connection with the use of lactose, a form of sugar obtained from milk, and had put on the market a stout sold as 'Mackeson's Milk Stout'. The merit of lactose lay in its being non-fermentable and it gave the stout a smooth taste as well as dietetic value. The output when we bought the business was small and at first there was doubt whether the product would be worth continuing. But presently inquiries came from different parts of the country, asking where Mackeson's Milk Stout could be got, the inquirers having been on holiday in Kent. It looked as if the demand might be greater than expected. I found on investigation that the quality was impaired by certain restrictions imposed by the customs authorities on the use of lactose, restrictions which seemed to me capable of revision. I was able to arrange with the heads of the Customs for these to be modified. This improved the product and we thought we might test the market in one district. We chose Sheffield for our first effort and met with such success that we decided to produce the stout on a larger scale and to organize a sales campaign. Before long we had secured a large and growing market throughout the country; in fact Mackeson Stout is now regarded as a national product, thanks to Colonel Whitbread's drive and enthusiasm.

The enterprise was so successful that many brewers in different parts of the country put on the market 'milk' stouts of various qualities. In 1946 I felt that this competition might hamper the sale of Mackeson and that the word 'Milk' should be dropped and the stout sold under the simple name of 'Mackeson'. In this way we could reduce the danger of people asking for 'Milk' stout and receiving varying qualities. However, our salesmen were unanimous that the demand for the stout depended on the word 'milk', and that to drop the term would be disastrous. This difference of opinion was resolved even while we deliberated, by a quite unexpected action by the Ministry of Food. After the end of the war the Ministry embarked on a campaign to ensure the correct terminology of foods sold for public consumption. They held that the word 'Milk' was an incorrect description, since 'whole' milk was not used, the 'milk' element—lactose—being merely a sugar obtained from whey, one of the by-products of cheese making. There was much criticism of the Ministry's action as officious interference, but they stuck to their guns and indicated that if the term were continued in use, a restrictive order would follow. So the word 'Milk' was dropped and, so far as we were concerned, the term 'Mackeson's Stout' was established in its place. Many of the other so-called 'milk stouts' disappeared altogether. But to return to 1927.

The tradition of Whitbread's had been to retain the principles of the old partnership, and from time to time to nominate a member of one of the families who comprised the principal shareholders to enter the business, pass through the different departments and join the management board in due course. I, in fact, provided the only instance in the history of the firm of the board being reinforced by somebody with purely outside experience. In accordance with this principle, John E. Martineau, whose family date their partnership from the early days of the firm, joined the company on January the 1st, 1927. As a result of my own experience, I had been able to convince him of the value of first obtaining an all-round working knowledge in a small firm, and on my advice he went for three months as a pupil to Mr. A. H. Mure of Hampstead who, although his brewery was small, had for many years been recognized as a leader in the application of scientific methods to his business. Indeed in the text book on brewing which was the bible of neophytes when I was a pupil in 1888, his name was constantly referred to in connection with scientific progress.

After leaving Eton, 'Jack' Martineau had been captain of his College boat club, and had obtained an honours degree at Oxford; he then plunged into brewing problems with an equal enthusiasm. On his return to Chiswell Street he became closely associated with me, and I owe much to his indefatigable help in many matters, a special instance being in the preparation of evidence which I gave before the Licensing Commission in 1930. As I mentioned, he sat with me on that occasion, together with our momentous documents, and I know how considerably his assistance contributed to the success which, they tell me, rewarded those efforts. He also joined me in many of the Continental trips I arranged from time to time for the benefit of the staff and the ultimate benefit of the firm. He has recently reminded me of some of our worthwhile encounters. On one occasion, when we were being entertained by that great man Dr. Almgren, then leader of the Swedish brewers, I had had something to say about my connection with the Carlisle experiment; and to this rashness I owed the invitation promptly extended to address a press conference. It happened that at about that time the Swedish government had been thinking seriously of extending to the brewing industry the control they already exercised over wines and spirits. Almgren thought an account of my experiences of government control of brewing and a summary of my views on the matter would be of interest, and later the principal Swedish papers published a report of this interview.

On another such tour, which took us to Berlin, I was asked by Lord d'Abernon, then our ambassador to Germany, to stay the night and give him an account of all that had occurred in England since his retirement from the Control Board. I agreed to do so if he could arrange train reservations to replace those we should have to sacrifice; for things were none too easy at the time. His suggestion was that I should borrow a member of his Embassy staff, and this official advised me that a tip to the railway people would be the best greaser of wheels in the circumstances. Sure that this was wise counsel I passed an amount which seemed quite generous to me, but the man who received it must have been of another mind, for he disappeared, never to return. My mentor then recommended trebling the *douceur* and trying my luck with another official, and this worked the oracle. When I went to bed that night, the exchange had been four thousand marks to the pound. In the morning this had fallen to eight thousand, which was adjusted by the simple expedient of doubling the price of everything in the hotel tariff. This brought home to me the tragedy of inflation for those living on fixed incomes.

I was eager to show my appreciation of the German Embassy clerk's good offices, but hesitated to offer a tip; and so I decided to ask him if his wife had ever seen one of our new English one-pound notes, and requested him to give her three with my compliments. The joy on his face at receiving something real and solid in the way of money was both moving and revealing, and I often think its intensity would be a lesson to some of those who seem content with the fairyland of inflation in which we live today.

* * *

In the late autumn months of 1929 I began to show signs of overwork and was advised to take a real rest. I decided to take a trip to Australia to see one of my brothers who had lived there for many years, and also to meet my friends at Tooth's Brewery, which had been founded by my mother's brothers nearly a century before. I had corresponded with my Australian connections from time to time and had occasionally done some business for them over here. I wondered whether I ought to leave this country for I was Master of the Brewers' Company, but my very kind friend, Sir Edward Mann, senior past Master of the Company, willingly agreed to my absenting myself, and explained that it would not be necessary for me to resign the mastership.

So I joined the P. & O. ship *Mooltan* on a gloomy afternoon at Tilbury in November 1929. Harry Whitbread had whimsically promised to get his vicar to have the hymn 'For those in peril on the sea' sung during my absence, but when I joined the ship at Tilbury and surveyed the gloomy countenances of the comparatively few passengers who were joining the ship on that foggy day at London instead of Marseilles, I sent him a post card 'No perils on board, no need to sing hymn.'

I was going from Tilbury because I thought the longer voyage would give me more rest than travelling across France. We had an uneventful passage though we met with fairly rough weather in the Bay. I was a good sailor and was not inconvenienced, and duly reached Marseilles on a wonderful autumn day. As usual, the smarter and more exciting of the ship's passengers joined us there. I was so struck with the beauty and charm of many of my fellow-voyagers that I climbed to the wireless cabin and asked the operator to telegraph to Harry Whitbread 'Many perils on board, please sing hymn twice!'

This interested my nieces in Australia, who, when asked by their many friends what I was like, repeated this story as a thumbnail picture of my character.

I had suffered from the delusion that time might hang heavy on my hands and, as I was a very indifferent bridge player, took steps to improve my knowledge. Before I set out, I had enlisted the help of a teacher who had been recommended to me as able to put me wise to some of the intricacies of the game. Now, I have sometimes seen inquiries in newspapers as to the most terrifying experiences which their readers have ever endured in their lives, and unlikely as it seems, have always felt that my contact with this amiable man led to one of my most racking, if not exactly terrifying, experiences. He was blind, and had taken up the teaching of bridge to supplement his income. The cards were marked in some secret way to enable him to distinguish the ones in his own hand, and all he needed was to hear someone read the cards out in the dummy hand once only and he never made a mistake.

He had a charming and attentive wife who helped him with his teaching. After a few lessons I learned that she would have to go to the Continent to meet a brother who had been absent abroad for some years. She told me that it would be a kindness if I could, during her absence, call on her husband for an occasional evening's conversation, and this I promised to do. Then I was shocked to hear from a lady with some experience of the world that my friend's wife would not come back—a blind man was so exacting that few women could permanently stand the strain. My anxiety grew as the days went by bringing still no letters from the wife. She was believed to be following her brother about somewhere on the Continent. I was with the husband one evening when the post arrived; he asked me to look at the letters, and there was one from Holland, which he asked me to open and read to him. I was terrified—I felt sure that the letter would tell the unfortunate husband never to expect his wife again. But it had to be done, and to my intense relief the letter contained nothing of the kind: it was merely to say that she had had great difficulty in finding her brother and would be away for another week. I breathed again.

I imagine that the voyage was the same as most voyages. One day, in a dead calm in the Red Sea, the ship stopped in response to signals of distress from a native craft. It appeared that they were without food and water, so the *Mooltan* stopped to provide them with water and rice. I was told that there had been instances of native craft starting empty and gradually collecting a useful cargo as their voyage proceeded, so our wireless operator immediately broadcast particulars of the latitude and longitude, the name of the craft, and the fact that we had supplied them with necessaries.

Some of my fellow passengers were in the Indian services and in business, others were going further east. I was particularly struck with the qualities of the captain. On Sunday he read the service better than I had ever heard it read in church. One day I told him as much. He told me in reply that when he was a young apprentice in sail, and had been ashore in San Francisco, he had been entertained by a group who made it their business to protect young sailors from the errors into which they were apt to fall after a long voyage. On Sunday they were taken to a prayer meeting and every apprentice was pressed to make an extempore prayer. When it came to his turn he repeated the General Confession from the English Church service which he knew by heart; but they were nonconformists, and did not know it. It filled them with admiration, as well it might.

My trip to Australia was in the middle of the slump of 1929 to 1930, when there was great scarcity of sovereigns in England. But when I went to the bank manager at Melbourne to cash some travellers' cheques for my expenses on the way home, he asked me if I would like some sovereigns—he seemed willing to let me have as many as I wanted. It occurred to me afterwards that Australia had to make heavy payments to England in gold. While the amounts in the case of individual passengers might be small, the collective result saved transport and insurance costs. But the difficulties of the times were evident in other ways. One of my Australian fellow passengers told me that he had called on his bank a couple of days before sailing and asked them to transfer £1,000 to London to cover his expenses and purchases in this country. He was warned that this was impossible; the utmost that the bank could manage was £100. My acquaintance found that the only way to finance his trip to England was to buy wool in Australia, pay for its transport to England, and arrange for its sale in England on arrival. I got to know him quite well on the voyage and found that his business interests included totalisators, which he claimed to be the best of their kind—one object of his trip to England was to push their sale over here. Now, the chairman of the Betting Control Board, which handled all totalisators in this country, was Lord d'Abernon. 'Smith', as I shall call him, expressed a great desire to meet d'Abernon. After our arrival in England I asked them both to lunch. When Smith explained that there was a particular racecourse on which his associates wished to erect their totalisator, d'Abernon promised him careful consideration. To my indignation Smith's answer was that, if permission were refused, his associates would have questions asked in Parliament. I was furious at this discourtesy, but d'Abernon did not turn a hair. This was a lesson to me, and I resolved never again to try to oblige an Australian of that type who is apt to confuse rugged individualism with downright rudeness.

I arrived at Sydney in time to reach my brother, who lived about forty miles outside, on Christmas Eve. Later I was welcomed by the board of Tooth's Brewery who promptly made me an honorary member of the Union Club. I made a point of visiting the Sydney Science Museum to pay homage to a treasured relic of Whitbread's—their first steam engine built in 1785 by the great engineer James Watt. After a century of use it was somehow or other bought in 1887 by the Sydney Museum. It may be far from home, but at least it has not been broken up for scrap—the regrettable fate of many of Whitbread's historic relics.

The commercial and technical efficiency of the breweries I visited in Australia left nothing to be desired, and I imagine that this high level is the happy result of the brewery concerns' custom of sending their chief executives 'home' to England and the Continent periodically, so that the newest and best methods are not overlooked. They also study American techniques and developments closely. At first the almost inevitable 'toughness' of the average Australian startled me, but the toughest as well as the more urbane demonstrated a real affection for England, in spite of racily expressed disapproval of almost everything England said or did. I became particularly friendly with some of the vignerons, and was surprised to find that in spite of the poor reputation which Australian wines had in England, they managed to offer me some of truly remarkable quality. I had often thought that there must be room in our country for a better and more representative market for Australian wines, and I attributed their comparative failure to the lack of attention given to the selling and maintaining of a uniform quality. The customer likes to know in advance just what is going to come out of the bottle. Whereas the production of continental wines, port, sherry, champagne, and so on, are concentrated in well defined districts, of known soils and climates, Australian wines seemed to have no distinctive mark of origin. There was a tendency to try to grow several varieties of wine in one vineyard. All too often the quality shipped was indifferent, and I fear that much of it was used as an adulterant of continental wines and therefore secured but a poor price. I suggested to a few growers the advantage of combining and establishing a name for a really high class wine such as they were able to give me, and also initiating a collective publicity scheme; but the average Australian is exceedingly independent, and the notion of combining with their competitors and making a collective effort did not appeal to them.

Altogether I enjoyed my trip, I had some difficulty over my reservation for the home journey, for although I had tried to book a single cabin for my return before leaving London, I had been told that this must be arranged in Australia. When I went to the P. & O. offices in Sydney I found they had no single cabins to offer me. They offered me a double one, for my single use as far as Ceylon. But I did not fancy risking a possibly uncongenial cabin mate for the rest of the voyage. Before I left London I had, through Lubbock's good offices, obtained a letter of introduction from Sir Alan Anderson, a director of the Orient Line, to his management in Sydney. I used this letter and was able to get what I wanted at the cost of finding myself a V.I.P. on the voyage home, breathing in the glorified atmosphere of the Captain's table, and being persuaded to act as chairman of the entertainments committee—no sinecure.

12

A 'prentice hand in Advertising—My growing Interest in Publicity—'House of Whitbread' (House Magazine)—Getting Whitbread on the Sideboard—Gertrude Lawrence—National Advertising of Beer—Chairman of Brewers' Society Publicity Committee—Advertisement in War-time—Pictures—Londoners' England—Hop Festival

However valuable, however badly needed a commodity may be, publicity and salesmanship are necessary if its merits are to become known and utilized. I have had quite a bit to do with the subject and have found some of my experiences sufficiently interesting to recall them here.

Fifty years ago the approach was almost blatant, and as often as not didactic. One merely considered whether or not a suggested advertisement would catch the attention of the prospective customer. There was little attempt at persuasion, certainly no subtlety of approach. It was thought enough to say 'Buy Jones's Beer' or 'Brown's Brew the Best Beer', and leave it at that. The term 'public relations' had not been coined. There was no planning of elaborate campaigns, as there is today, and the press—now one of the principal media for advertising—was little used by the brewing industry, which expended its effort in large and overpowering display boards outside licensed houses, posters on railways, and in similar exposed positions. Indeed, some houses were so plastered over with the name of the brewer that the upper windows were obscured. The change is very marked nowadays: some houses even appear, at first sight, to carry no brewer's name at all, even on the signboard; almost everywhere the prominence and the size of the advertising boards are greatly reduced, and yet there has been no loss of effectiveness.

I have lived to see this primitive art of advertising transformed. Today publicity in all its implications has become a skilled profession, employing many of the best brains in industry; it is now regarded more as an element in carefully-planned schemes under the general term 'public relations' than as an objective in itself.

My first incursion into advertising happened in this way. In 1905 Brandon suggested that in order to make our new bottling department a success, we should produce some speciality. The Russo-Japanese war was in progress, and the sympathies of the British people were largely with the Japanese. Brandon thought we might brew a beer principally from rice and call it 'saki' after the well-known Japanese drink. After much thought during the night watches, I concluded that this would not be beer, and also that, since national affections and enthusiasms are fickle, it did not follow that Japan would always be popular with the British. My alternative suggestion was that we should do something to catch the popular fancy and brew from malt and hops only, for such a beer was then well-nigh unknown. Sugar and other malt adjuncts were then almost universally used to surmount the difficulty of haziness (due to the protein content of the barley). Now the new processes of chilling and filtering beer before bottling were to a great extent eliminating those elements that produced haziness, and I considered that with this process an all-malt beer would be practicable. I made a trial brew, and the result justified my expectations.

The next point was the marketing and salesmanship. There was great competition at the time, often at the cost of quality, as brewers were striving to cut the price of their bottled beers, and many were economizing in the actual brewing; consequently the beers were not all they should have been. I decided that it would be foolish to attempt to produce something cheaper still; on the contrary, there was a good chance of success for a better product. We should use the best possible materials, achieve the highest possible quality, and charge a correspondingly good price.

We had a battle-royal at the next board meeting. Two of my colleagues insisted on the necessity of cutting the price to meet competition, whereas I argued that it was bad policy to tell the public that our beer was inferior to our competitors' in the only language the consumer would understand: the language of price. My critics tried to convince me that unless we cut the price we shouldn't sell a bottle; I retorted that as we didn't sell a bottle then, we hadn't much to lose. The discussion became so heated that Brandon adjourned the meeting. His uncle, Mr. Chester Foulsham, then aged eighty-four and always ready to express himself bluntly, remarked, 'Mr. Nevile, you know everything and I only know one thing: I know that you are wrong!' a phrase I sometimes find useful in difficult discussions today. But before we resumed our wrangling, Brandon said to me, 'Don't listen to Uncle, I believe you are right after all!' So when the meeting was resumed, we agreed to brew a beer of malt and hops only, using the best materials we could buy, aiming at the highest quality, and achieving individuality by charging more than our competitors.

We needed a name for this new product, so we organized a competition among the children of the employees, one of whom suggested 'Rustic Ale'; and 'Rustic' was registered as a trade name in 1906. Then came publicity; I argued that, as we were a small concern, we ought to have large advertisements, even if this meant having fewer. An almost unknown name would be lost among dozens of other competing products—one bold poster would be more telling than a host of small ones. I had been struck by the effectiveness of a huge poster in Fleet Street advertising *John Bull* on an unoccupied site where no other advertisement competed with it. In Paris, too, I had noticed the large and solitary advertisements of 'Savon Bleu'. So I got in touch with the contractors owning the large hoardings which were—and still are—a feature of the railway line east of Clapham Junction, and offered to rent the whole of one of these hoardings, in order to take a single advertisement for our new 'Rustic Ale'. The bill poster insisted that my proposal was contrary to the whole field of accepted opinion and at first refused to accept my offer. However, I stuck to my guns as I felt convinced that few people could read a tithe of these advertisements as the trains sped by. Finding me determined, he eventually surrendered and rented me the hoarding. In due course, therefore, the plain, blunt announcement 'Rustic Ale Stands Alone' appeared on one of these long hoardings. I don't seem to have been wrong after all, for I have noticed for many years that those hoardings are nearly all used to display a single poster.

It was not until I came to Whitbread's that I began to enjoy my most interesting experiences in publicity. Soon after joining the Board I made a tour of the forty-odd factories spread over the United Kingdom in which our beer was bottled. Everywhere I was pleased to see the excellent organization, and the goodwill and loyalty of the staffs, yet few of the rank and file seemed to know anything of the scope and achievements of the firm for which they worked: to the vast majority their employment was merely a daily job without personal interest. I realized how important it was that they should acquire a wider knowledge of the business they served, and an increased awareness of the activities and interests of their fellow workers, and I was sure the encouragement of a team spirit not only benefits the firm but also the individual worker. It makes him feel that he is engaged in a worthwhile enterprise, and it shows the ambitious man how many openings there are for him in a large organization.

In the early 'twenties the practice of issuing house magazines was in its infancy. My colleagues and I were convinced that something of the kind would be of value to the firm and the staff, so in December 1920, the first number of *The House of Whitbread* appeared, under the editorship of C. H. Adams, Secretary of the Company. I had written to Mr. Howard Whitbread, the Chairman, asking if he would contribute the first article, and since I felt he might be at sea as to what was needed or what was the purpose of the magazine, I also sent him a rough draft of what I had in mind. In those days I did not know the Chairman well, and I waited several days for his reply. He agreed to write the article, but did not adopt a single word of my suggestions! The inspiring article he did write admirably suited its purpose and was indeed infinitely better than what I had outlined.

The early issues of the magazine contained articles on the nature and extent of the business, the personalities of the board (I find my own face gravely confronting me as I turn those early pages, accompanied by my life history in briefer form than this present one), news of our various company activities, and references to individuals on the staff and to employees at all levels. We covered a wide field; we made a feature of our policy of the improvement of public houses and included pictures of houses we had rebuilt or improved. As we had a flourishing sports club, their achievements formed a popular section.

I was delighted with the welcome given to *The House of Whitbread*. In after years, when its care has passed into more professional hands, I am told it is one of the best examples of its kind; and indeed I believe it is now regarded as a model. In its early days such a high level was not aimed at; our first object was to interest our own people, so naturally we introduced much material of no particular interest to a larger public. For example, I discovered that one of the young ladies who bottled our beers had gone to a fancy dress ball cleverly tricked out as 'A bottle of Whitbread's'; she was photographed in this costume and we published the result. We let it be known that we would publish photographs of any other of our employees who chose to follow her example, and bottles of Whitbread's began to appear at parties and balls all over the country. This was not only good fun for our workers, but valuable publicity for the firm.

I am reminded in this connection of one curious incident. A young worker from our Hove depot got herself up tastefully as a bottle of stout and was a great success at the dance. When it came to the time for the prizes to be awarded, the master of ceremonies called her forward and announced that though it was impossible for the judges to include her name in the regular prize list, since this happened to be a temperance dance, she was to receive a special prize. We all enjoyed this dazzling triumph!

About this time I was confronted with another problem. A big market of Whitbread's had been, for many years, the sale of bottled beers for home consumption, supplied through the off-licences (or grocers' licences, as they were often called) established by Mr. Gladstone a generation earlier; the point of those was that they enabled the householder of modest means to get a bottle of beer to drink at home without having to enter what was then the rather undesirable atmosphere of the public house. This beer had been costing him twopence ha'penny a bottle, but the war had brought changes of habit, increased taxation had made higher prices inevitable, so that although our sales in industrial neighbourhoods had declined, there was a tendency towards the increased popularity of beer among those still called in those days the 'upper classes'. So it was of importance to us to take advantage of this change and to advance our beer several rungs up the social ladder, on to the sideboards and tables of the middle classes and on to restaurant tables: but many of the better-type restaurants, especially the smart and fashionable, either did not supply or discouraged the serving of beer. Thinking it over, I decided to try an advertising campaign in the six principal illustrated weekly journals which, although of comparatively small circulation, were to be found in clubs, in the waiting rooms of professional men, in country houses, in fact everywhere where comfortably-off prospective customers were to be found. I conceived the idea of getting celebrated people to be photographed while dining at well-known restaurants and with Whitbread's boldly replacing the carafes and decanters which usually appear in such illustrations. I had a little difficulty with our advertising agents at first, as they doubted whether the celebrated people would consent, and thought that professional models would carry the thing off better; but the whole point of my scheme would then have been lost, for I was not interested in an obviously contrived situation and I depended on names of celebrities for my effect. So I persuaded our agents at least to try, and asked them who was the most popular stage favourite at that time. The vote was unanimous for Gertrude Lawrence, then at the height of her fame. I considered that, after all, this would be publicity for her as well, and naturally for the restaurant concerned.

So Gertrude Lawrence was approached and, since we hesitated to offer her a fee, we suggested our sending instead a cheque to any stage charity she would care to name, and were pleased when she willingly accepted. We then asked her to let us know her choice of fellow-diner, and she suggested Ronald Squire. Everything being fixed at last, we had to select a restaurant, and it was at this stage that we encountered a check. Most of the best restaurants had no wish to sell beer, and although they were willing for Gertrude Lawrence and Ronald Squire to be photographed at dinner, they were not so pleased when we said we wanted a bottle of Whitbread's on the table. Indeed, when I approached Sir Francis Towle, managing director of Gordon Hotels, and son of my old colleague on the Central Control Board, Sir William Towle, to offer him a free advertisement for one of the restaurants under his control, I met with a categorical refusal, on the ground that he didn't want to sell beer, only wines.

However, at last we found a restaurant that was not so angular, and on the 21st March 1934, we published our first full-page all-colour advertisement, showing that most charming lady Gertrude Lawrence, and Ronald Squire, refreshing themselves with Whitbread's bottled beer after a dance. The element of advertising material was limited to the recognizable bottle of Whitbread's beer on the restaurant table, but before the advertisement appeared our publicity agents suggested that we should invite these two renowned people to luncheon in the historic dining-room at the brewery, an invitation which they accepted with pleasure. At this stage William Whitbread began to wonder what view his uncle, Howard Whitbread, the chairman, would take of this rather startling innovation, but the chairman quickly dispelled all doubts by his eager 'How interesting! When is she coming?—I want to be there to meet her!' So we had a most enjoyable luncheon party. Afterwards, the visitors were taken round the brewery and shown its historic features—just as King George III had been taken a century-and-a-quarter earlier, and many famous people since. They were fascinated by the complex process by which we turn malt and hops into beer, and, as we claim, the best beer at that. As Gertrude Lawrence was signing the Visitors' Book, she exclaimed: 'This reminds me of my wedding day—where's the best man?' I can't think now why I failed to rise to the occasion.

Our publicity agents had arranged for photographers to be there, and everyone was delighted when Gertrude Lawrence insisted on being photographed driving one of the drays with its team of horses of which we are so proud. With surprising agility, she mounted to the lofty and rather inaccessible driver's perch, and was photographed not only handling the reins, but also wearing the driver's traditional top-hat in place of her own elegant toque which she tossed down to him. Our drayman's face as he carefully dusted his hat before throwing it up to her was a sight to see.

I had no reason to regret pressing forward with this idea. It attracted much attention, and we subsequently published similar illustrations of other famous stage stars, including Heather Thatcher and Owen Nares, Winifred Shotter and Ralph Lynn, and Gertrude Lawrence again, this time with Douglas Fairbanks, junior. We also published advertisements featuring other distinguished personalities, so that altogether this proved a dazzlingly bright excursion into the world of publicity.

Another recollection I enjoy is connected with the Royal Academy. Our advertising agents told me that the Academy proposed to have one advertisement on the back of the catalogue; the price would be high but the advertisement would carry great prestige. After ascertaining the cost, I instructed them to reserve it for Whitbread's; but this was premature, for the design must be approved and perhaps a brewers' advertisement would not be accepted. I was soon able to assure them that they would not refuse what I had in mind—a reproduction of Samuel Whitbread's portrait painted by Sir Joshua Reynolds, the first President of the Academy; the only element of advertisement would be a note to remind people that he was the founder in 1742 of the firm of Whitbread's. The advertisement was accepted and we were well satisfied, though the main value was as an enhancement of what the publicity agents term prestige.

As time went on we began to feel the need for an organized planning of publicity and a skilled professional adviser on our own staff, in addition to the outside firm who were already helping us. Now one of the difficulties in securing a head of a publicity department is that in the nature of things these gentlemen are great experts at selling themselves, and our first two appointments were unsuccessful—the practitioners could not attain the dignity and high tone we wished for. But at the third attempt we secured H. Douglas Thomson, who was then working for a group of national newspapers. We were indeed 'third time lucky' when we appointed him. Although it took a little time to organize our publicity activities under his leadership, I like to think it is no exaggeration to say that Whitbread's publicity and public relations are regarded as being among the great achievements in this field, both in good taste and sheer efficiency, not only in so far as the brewing industry is concerned but in the whole realm of advertisement.

* * *

Though my first loyalty was to Whitbread's my interest in trade organizations led me to wonder whether collective advertising of beer as the national drink would not be beneficial to the industry as a whole. I had noticed that certain other commodities were already the subjects of collective publicity. Early in the 'twenties I had been favourably impressed by the gas industry's creation of 'Mr. Therm'—which was, I think, the first venture of its kind in this country. As it happened, accident brought me in touch with the lady whom I believe to have been largely responsible for the plan; then not long after I was asked to meet a representative of the Spanish Embassy. It appeared that his Government was concerned over the falling imports of sherry into this country and wanted to do something to arrest the decline. His reason for meeting me was to seek the support of the licensed trade in the hope that they would provide a better market. Later the conversation turned to collective publicity and, whether or not as a result of this talk, the Spanish Government and the sherry industry together initiated a campaign for popularizing sherry as sherry, with no reference to this brand or that. I was interested to see that, in a comparatively short time, sherry became increasingly popular as an aperitif and its import increased considerably. I also noted a similar campaign for currants, sponsored either by the Greek Government, or by the exporters, or by both. Thus whenever the subject of falling sales arose in brewing circles I suggested that some such plan would be worth while in the case of beer which, owing to high taxation, was losing its popularity as the national drink.

In 1933 F. A. Simonds, then chairman of the Brewers' Society, asked me to preside over a small committee to consider the proposal. I had the able assistance of Sir Edgar Sanders, the director of the Society, who was not only an enthusiast of advertising, but had had great experience when managing director of Lord Leverhulme's vast enterprises. We were to consider the possibilities and report to the Society. Our report was adopted, I became chairman of the advertising committee, and our next step was to invite brewers to subscribe on a voluntary basis, according to their output, towards a collective fund. Sir Edgar Sanders made it his business to attend various meetings of county associations and explain the scheme to them. But then, just as the plan was about to be launched, an unexpected difficulty arose. Several who had attended the meetings were struck by the force of arguments and suggested that Sanders' summary of the scheme should be printed and circulated. There were two points in his paper which, if taken out of their context, were capable of arousing criticism: one was the possible appeal to young people, the other was that money spent on advertisement would influence editorial opinion. These matters raised a storm: first among prohibitionists, who misrepresented the trade as trying to popularize beer among those of tender years and, second, among the newspaper associations which resented the idea that press opinion on matters of public interest was in any sense modified by its advertisement revenue: so much so, that the matter was referred to in both Houses of Parliament.

Some of the weaker spirits suggested that it would be better to drop or suspend the scheme in view of press and other criticism. Others insisted that to retreat at the first attack would be an admission that our motives were dubious. The advertisement committee had next to consider how to advise the Council of the Society, and I expected a difficult, if not tempestuous meeting. As chairman, I felt that to abandon the project would place us in a position of having hatched a plot which had been discovered and defeated; on the other hand, to hasten the scheme forward might entail a risk of inefficiency or lack of taste. So I recommended that we should advise the Society to proceed with the scheme, but to be careful of its substance and to avoid giving any opportunity for such charges. The majority favoured this proposal, and I asked the committee to realize that, since the Council needed a direct line from us, a unanimous report was essential. I urged the minority to reconsider whether they could not agree to the continuance of the plan, and the result of the second vote was a unanimous decision that in all the circumstances the scheme should go forward.

There was great competition among advertising firms to secure the business, and we invited some of the leading concerns to put forward their ideas. Eventually the suggestions made by the London Press Exchange appeared the most promising, and we agreed to appoint them on condition that the scheme would be under the personal supervision of their managing director. All advertisement schemes depend on a central idea, or slogan, and our first task was to choose one; after considering and rejecting many we adopted the words 'Beer is Best'. I think that it is generally accepted today that these words successfully conveyed the message we wanted, capable of being illustrated in a multitude of ways. Nonetheless at first it was rather a shock to see the words 'Beer is Best' on posters with 'Left Alone' added by amateur temperance enthusiasts; but I doubt whether the addition lessened the value of the posters; it may have attracted more attention to them by raising a laugh and making a talking-point.

The chairmanship of such a committee is a harassing job indeed, for most people have ideas on publicity and all think their ideas should be accepted. On the other hand, if a campaign is to be effective it is necessary to keep continuity of theme and to rule out many attractive ideas if irrelevant to the main message. I had another difficulty in that the scheme was voluntary, and it was essential to maintain the subscribers' good will, and allow them to feel that any proposal they made would be adequately considered. While the executive committee consisted of more or less knowledgeable people I also invited a consultative committee containing representatives of the various county associations to meet at regular intervals. This committee was regularly informed of the policy and methods of publicity and the reasons why this and that suggestion might or might not be suitable for adoption just at that moment. My mind went back to the Central Control Board meetings, at which d'Abernon used to ask every member of the board for his opinion. There might be eighteen or twenty members present, and after each had contributed his view, which usually did not agree in all particulars with any other, d'Abernon would say, 'Well, I think we all agree; let us decide to do this'—'this' being a solution which nobody had suggested or even thought of, and quite strange to one and all. Nevertheless he always got away with it. I followed this example on numerous occasions and it rarely let me down.

For several years the 'Beer is Best' campaign developed effectively and was generally admitted to be a useful and helpful extension of individual brewers' advertising. When war broke out in 1939, many of us were in two minds as to the advisability of keeping this collective advertising going. It was felt that the juxtaposition of a beer advertisement and a list of war casualties would be tasteless and inappropriate. On the other hand, some believed in 'business as usual'. There was also a case for taking into account the hardship to the advertising industry if publicity were generally abandoned. So I felt this to be an important point of policy. I had little time for consultation, but when the committee met I proposed that we should retain all the spaces booked and offer these—both in the press and on posters—to the Ministry of Information, which would often have occasion to make nationwide appeals or statements. This rather unforeseen suggestion was received with unanimous approval, in that patriotic spirit which seems always to animate the Trade in time of real national emergency. Before long I learned that the Ministry would certainly accept this suggestion, and I thought that we should write a letter making the formal offer to the Minister. Doing it in this way did not satisfy Sir William Crawford, our then genial chief advertising adviser. In a matter of such magnitude, it seemed

24. Whitbread's Brewery '. . . standing in a desert of destruction'

25. Desolation in the City after the incendiary raid, December 1940

26. Lord Woolton

The Brewers always met my requests. I never had to make a formal order

27. Hugh Paul—my link with Lord Woolton

fitting that we should ask the Minister to lunch, with one or two of his principal advisers, and make the hand-over a matter of some little ceremony. So I invited the Minister, then Duff Cooper, with one or two of his principal lieutenants, to lunch at the Connaught Hotel and meet the advertisement committee. He came, and formally accepted our offer. In this way we obtained some kudos for the brewing industry. In putting forward the proposal I did suggest two small conditions—one, that we should have some voice in the nature of advertisements that might appear, and two, that in small print at the bottom of any press advertisement might appear the words 'This space is given by the Brewers' Society'.

This was one of my most pleasant experiences in the sphere of publicity, especially because it brought us into friendly contact with nearly every department of the Government—for when some particular occasion arose and their own ration of publicity space had been expended, the Society's space supplied what they needed. I had rather hoped that the brewers' example would be followed by other large advertisers; but so far as I am aware this did not happen.

When the idea first occurred to me, I had felt that here, at any rate, was something which could not be criticized by anybody: but I was wrong. For from time to time the Government, in Parliament and elsewhere, were accused by our prohibitionist friends of having accepted a 'bribe from the liquor traffic'.

While the collective advertising scheme was getting under way I had not forgotten the advertising of Whitbread's in particular. It seemed to me that as we now had a number of fine 'improved public houses', we might help their interior decoration by employing some of the most prominent artists. Although Whitbread's were not the largest owners of licensed property houses they had always been regarded as leaders and thoughtful innovators, thanks to Frank Whitbread's chairmanship of the National Trade Development Association, whose function it was to represent the interests of both brewers and retailers. We were always looking for an opportunity to introduce new ideas, not only for raising the standards and prestige of the public house but also for attracting favourable attention to ourselves and our policy. Public houses in general, I thought, needed some more inspired embellishment than the usual display of price lists and advertisements, so in 1937, on Douglas Thomson's suggestion, we decided to prove that fine art would not be out of place in the public house by commissioning four really distinguished artists to paint pictures which could be reproduced for our houses.

The first picture of the series was one of horses in the brewery yard, by A. J. (later Sir Alfred) Munnings, R.A. Munnings produced a wonderful picture which he has since told me was 'the cheapest picture he ever painted'. When he began work he found the task so congenial that he put far more into the picture than he had contracted to do. The picture is one of our treasured possessions, and this was for me the beginning of an acquaintanceship with both the painter and Lady Munnings which has lasted to this day. Lady Munnings is of course almost as well-known as her husband, not only for her charm and wit but also on account of her tiny Pekinese, 'Black Knight', which she was in the habit of carrying about in her black bag with only its nose showing. This was pleasant for both but not always convenient: there was an occasion when my wife and I asked her to dinner at the Royal Thames Yacht Club, where unfortunately it is an inflexible rule not to admit dogs, and as Lady Munnings would not be parted from hers we had to take her next door, to the Hyde Park Hotel, where the management had no such prejudices. I think one of my most amusing experiences with 'A.J.' was when he was President of the R.A., and invited us to lunch on Private View Day. He declaimed against the absurdities of modern painting, and afterwards took us into the galleries and displayed with delight a picture which the Hanging Committee had succeeded in hanging upside down. On the way he collected one or two representatives of the press, who gave the incident full publicity.

The other subjects painted for us were a picture of 'The Woolpack Inn' by Stanhope A. Forbes, R.A., our Oasthouses on our Hop Farm by Algernon Talmage, R.A., and Hop Picking on our Hop Farm by T. C. Dugdale, A.R.A., all exhibited at the Royal Academy in 1938. We made an occasion of this enterprise and organized an exhibition at the New Burlington Galleries during April, 1938, with a luncheon and a 'private view' on the 6th of April. However, four pictures painted by artists, however eminent the names, seemed hardly to justify the dignity of an exhibition all to themselves, so we supplemented them with a number of plans and pictures of our improved public houses and especially of our sign boards, many the work of well known painters and designers. Our chairman, Mr. Howard Whitbread, naturally presided at the luncheon, and made a characteristically distinguished speech. He was followed by Professor Richardson, Professor of Architecture at the University of London and later President of the Royal Academy.

My own contribution to the proceedings was to propose the toast of 'The Public House'. As I read it twenty years later, my speech appears to reflect faithfully our frame of mind at that time, so I repeat it here, for what it is worth:

'For various reasons the policy of public house improvement was not found practicable before the war. But in 1919 several considerations appeared to justify the adoption of the policy; these were that drunkenness was found to be less inevitable than had previously been thought to be the case, that the general policy of reconstruction was much in the public mind, but more than anything that the Government had adopted the improvement of public houses as an essential element in the Carlisle district which was taken over by them during the war.

'Under these circumstances the owners of licensed houses throughout the country decided that there was a reasonable hope of securing public approval of a constructive policy which was roughly defined as "good service plus sobriety": so they tried to "hitch their wagon to a star", they "put their shoulders to the wheel", and, to complete a rather mixed metaphor, they "put their hands in their pockets".

'Every human enterprise must have a material foundation, and you are familiar with the material aspect of this movement in the improved public houses that are being built throughout the country; and those who go inside will see that a much larger range of food and commodities is being served.

'After providing the material needs of the people, the public house cannot be said to fulfil its destiny without what (for want of a better term) I will call "social amenities". A good deal of progress has been made in this direction. Wherever authorities permit, games are supplied. In many houses either music is available in the public rooms or musical societies meet in the club-rooms. Comparatively recently a Society having for its object the popularizing of good literature and verse, suggested the public house might be a centre, and in many houses throughout the country recitations in club rooms are given at regular intervals and are popular. (This Society later sponsored the amateur company, 'The Taverners', who give regular performances of first-rate plays in public houses.)

'And then we come to Art. We need something to decorate the walls of our houses instead of concentrating on advertisement of commodities. The first step was the reproduction of good prints for this purpose. A year ago we decided to make another step forward, and it is that step you are asked to celebrate today: and that is to start a movement to bring customers of the public house face to face with examples of the best modern art.

'It is impossible to visualize the limit of the possible scope for developing licensed houses into real community centres, and is equally impossible to estimate the value to the nation. That it is in the public interest we have no doubt, but we need the support of public opinion, and for that reason we are grateful to you for coming here today. If I may say so, there is one particular problem where the support of public opinion can help us more than anything else. One of our great difficulties is the staffing of these new establishments. We cannot be really successful until we make service in the licensed house a trained, skilled, lifelong calling. A certain prejudice hangs around it, and it is only by the help of public opinion that we can secure the right type of staff.'

The toast was acknowledged by Mr. T. C. Dugdale, A.R.A., who applauded the introduction of art into the public house, and in his plea for better and more imaginative cooking, urged the revival of traditional English dishes.

Apart from well known people in the art world, we had quite

a distinguished company of guests, including prominent members of licensing benches and social workers, altogether numbering some two hundred.

A few years later I once again found myself enrolled among the patrons of art, when I became concerned in an enterprise which, if not 'publicity' in the narrower sense, was certainly 'public relations', nowadays publicity's big brother. One of my friends, who is interested in public house improvement, told me that the Pilgrim Trust had in the early part of the war voted a sum of money to commission artists, many of whom, as can be imagined, were in sore straits as a result of the war. Their scheme was called 'Recording Britain'. The fund had just run out, and he suggested the brewing industry might take it over. This continuation could fairly be called a contribution to the improved public house movement; it would again be bringing art into the public house.

I suggested the idea to the Brewers' Society without success, as many members felt that the scheme was too uncommercial for the Society's funds. The Brewers' Company gave the idea just as chilly a reception, but as I had previously obtained the consent of my own board, I was able to say that if the business did not interest the Court as a whole, Whitbread's would carry on the proposal alone, though we would gladly accept the co-operation of anyone else. Watney's, Barclay's and Courage's, all pioneer supporters of the improved public house movement, asked to collaborate, and together we put up a fund of about £10,000.

As we were all London brewers we decided to limit the commissions to artists living in or near London. They would be invited to go into any district that appealed to them, and if they saw anything which appeared to them a worthy subject, paint it. If it happened to be an inn, so much the better. I had no artistic qualifications myself, and was very busy elsewhere, so M. V. Courage, then acting chairman of that well-known family brewery, willingly agreed to act as chairman. We obtained the help of several leading artists, and a small committee was formed. The scheme was carried out in association with the Central Institute of Art and Design, of which Sir Charles Tennyson and

T. A. Fennemore were respectively chairman and director. The choice of the artists was made by P. H. Jowett, Principal of the Royal College of Art, Sir Kenneth Clark, then Director of the National Gallery, and Sir W. Russell Flint, R.A., President of the Royal Society of Painters in Water Colours. Sir Kenneth Clark urged us to stick to water colours (and not commission oil paintings), if only because British artists had been supremely successful in this medium.

We hoped to continue the scheme under the title 'Recording Britain' adopted by the Pilgrim Trust; but as they were reluctant to allow this, we had to think of a new name. The title 'Londoners' England' occurred to me as a possibility, since the subjects were to be whatever a London painter might find inspiring and paintable, wherever he might be. This is the title we adopted.

The amount of the artists' fees was the next point, and we felt that by paying a larger sum, which worked out at an average of twenty guineas per picture, we should secure better results than if we adhered to the smaller figure paid by the Pilgrim Trust. We were somewhat disappointed at some of the earlier pictures submitted, and a rather curious explanation for their inadequacy was offered by Sir Kenneth Clark. He thought that the larger sum we were offering, large, that is, by the standards of pre-war years, might be the reason for our disappointment. The Pilgrim Trust's smaller fee meant that the artist was less likely to overpaint his subject, more likely to register merely his first impressions; but at our figure there was a tendency to give 'value for money' by adding excessive detail, which in some cases destroyed the worth of the painting. However, the quality improved as time went by, and we were entirely satisfied with the general result.

Through Sir Kenneth's kind offices we hoped to have an exhibition at the National Gallery, for the permanent collection had, of course, been removed for safe keeping during the war; but by the time our pictures were collected for exhibition the war was over and the Gallery was being prepared for normal use. We held our first show in the Suffolk Galleries, with of course a celebratory luncheon, and Mr. Herbert Morrison, the Home Secretary, as chief guest and opener of the exhibition. Before the paintings were dispersed, we again exhibited them in Charing Cross Underground station. Dr. A. C. Don, Dean of Westminster, kindly and charmingly presided for us on this occasion.

After the exhibitions the pictures were divided among the four partners in the undertaking, and in accordance with the original plan various shows were organized in public houses throughout London. These smaller exhibitions were opened by various distinguished people, who amongst others included my friend Mrs. L'Estrange Malone, a prominent member of the L.C.C., and the great Augustus John; on other occasions we frequently called the Mayor of the Borough, or chairman of the licensing justices, to officiate. The pictures found permanent homes in various public houses, where they are still on view.

I enjoyed every minute of my role as art patron. As with so many of my undertakings, what appeared at first sight to be an altruistic action, came to have commercial value as an element in public relations. Here again one would hardly have expected criticism from anybody over this very innocent excursion into the realms of art; indeed, the press were uniformly kind. Yet some of the prohibitionist party, true to their 'policy of beastliness' (as a friend called it) with regard to public houses, took the opportunity to attack us. As an example, a temperance paper calling itself *The Christian* ended its article on the subject with these words:

'It is to be feared that many people who have hitherto shrunk from entering such buildings will excuse themselves on the grounds that they only wanted to see the pictures. Is it not time that the temperance forces of this country, which should be synonymous for the membership of the Christian Churches, called the bluff of the Brewers?' . . . Well, well!

* * *

The hop growing industry is so picturesque and attracts so much public interest that our doings at the hop farm merit inclusion in the term 'Public Relations'. It has been the practice of Whitbread's to hold a hop festival each year, partly for the entertainment of the four thousand pickers who journey to Kent to pick the crop, partly for publicity, and partly for the interest of our many guests. For several years I acted as host on this occasion, which involves various sporting contests for the hop pickers and a concert by performers of note, and only once have had cause to wish I had been elsewhere. This was the year when we followed the fashion of electing a Beauty Queen, and I was pressed to be Chairman of the Adjudicating Committee. This duty was difficult enough, especially at the point where we had to eliminate nine from our short list chosen from the large number who had entered the competition; for the nine we had to disappoint viewed the judge with ill-concealed disfavour. Not only this, but I was told that it was my duty to kiss the winner, and was infuriated when one of the papers reported, with journalistic fervour, that I had performed the task with 'almost unnecessary warmth'.

13

Government Committees and my Contacts—English and Scottish State Purchase Committees—Preservatives in Food—Royal Commission on Licensing 1930*—Morris Committee* 1942

Ours is a trade almost constantly in the public eye, so it is inevitable that over the years I should have been involved in many official inquiries, either by Royal Commission or Government Committees; sometimes giving evidence, sometimes serving as member of one or the other.

Some of my readers may wonder what difference there is between a Royal Commission and a Departmental Committee, and why a problem is referred sometimes to the one and sometimes to the other. I think the distinction is that a Royal Commission is appointed by the Sovereign on the advice of the Cabinet and is as a rule open to the public. Departmental Committees are appointed by the Minister concerned and their meetings may or may not be open to the public: this is as the Minister or chairman of the Committee may determine.

A rather cynical friend has told me that if a government decides to introduce legislation, it appoints a departmental committee to recommend the lines it should take; but that when a matter arises which may lead to political conflict, a Royal Commission is more suitable. A Royal Commission may be trusted to deliberate at some length before producing its report, and during this lapse of time public opinion may be tested; or, what is more likely and often more satisfactory, the subject may cease to be a matter of public interest and action may then be deferred indefinitely! Nevertheless, it still remains a matter of importance to those whose interests may be affected: a report may be shelved and almost forgotten, but sooner or later the subject may be revived, in which case unwise or undesirable recommendations made several years earlier could result in legislative blunders.

My first experience with such committees was in 1917 (and here again I have to repeat myself). This was soon after discussions between Lord Milner and the committee of the Brewers' Society on the proposal to nationalize the brewing, distilling and licensed industries. I had been appointed to represent the large interests of brewers in London and the surrounding area. These discussions disclosed that the scheme involved unforeseen complications. Consequently Lloyd George appointed three committees, for England and Wales, Scotland and Ireland respectively. Evidence of a general nature was given by the Brewers' Society, but the London brewers considered that their interests differed in many respects from those prevailing over the rest of the country. They felt that separate evidence should be given on their behalf, and asked Lubbock and myself to undertake this responsibility: Lubbock as Master of the Brewers' Company and myself as having been appointed by the London brewers to represent their interests on the original trade committee.

For the benefit of some of my readers who may be unfamiliar with the procedure of such inquiries, I should explain that the number and qualifications of the committee vary according to the nature and importance of the subject. In my experience the number varies from ten to twenty, sometimes consisting of people with expert knowledge and sometimes of persons capable of forming an unprejudiced opinion on evidence brought before them. It usually happens, of course, that both types of committee member are chosen. When the subject is one of general concern, and almost certain to admit of conflicting views, a committee sometimes contains representatives of the various protagonists, in the hope that some compromise may be reached. The members sit round a horseshoe table, the chairman in the centre with his colleagues on either side of him on the longer curve. While giving evidence, the witness sits at a table at the open end of the horseshoe with accommodation for the shorthand writers who take down evidence *verbatim*. It is usual for the witness to submit a précis containing a statement of his qualifications and the heads of the evidence he proposes to give; this is circulated to the members in advance.

The chairman first leads the witness through his précis, giving both witness and committee time to adjust themselves. He then invites the witness to develop his argument, during which development he himself, or occasionally another member, may interject a question or two. At the conclusion of the witness's evidence he is subjected to cross-examination: first by the chairman and then, at the chairman's invitation, by the individual members in turn if they so wish. This is the most trying part of the proceedings for the inexperienced witness. He has had time to prepare his evidence, but he has had no notice of the subjects that may be raised in questions. Some witnesses rely on their prepared evidence and ask to be excused from amplifying it; indeed, this may be advisable if the speaker is acting on definite instructions from a trade organization. He thereby saves time and avoids the risk of expressing opinions which may afterwards be criticized. In my view this is bad policy if the witness is satisfied with the propriety of his evidence, for a testimony is far likelier to carry conviction if the members realize that the witness is expressing his own opinion candidly as well as speaking in the public interest.

The committee which Lubbock and I had to face contained no representatives of our industry. We made our points, received a courteous reception and were fairly well satisfied with the record of our evidence, though the report of the committee did not, to our mind, give our opinions the weight they merited. Had the Government proceeded with the proposed scheme, the particular points we had brought forward could have been considered when the Bill came before Parliament, and the fact that we had put them before the committee would have made adjustment possible.

I appeared again before the same committee when (as mentioned in an earlier reference to the Institute of Brewing) I pressed the claims of the technical brewers for reasonable compensation. On this occasion I had to face considerable cross-examination, but seemed to have made my points, as the report was regarded as satisfactory by my constituents. The same considerations had to be laid before the similar committee appointed for Scotland. As chairman of the Institute's protection committee I had recommended that evidence on behalf of technical staffs in Scotland would be more fittingly given by a Scottish brewer, but (as I have said) I was nonetheless pressed to act for them. I agreed, on condition that two of the Scottish members should sit with me and supplement my evidence if desirable. Although my Scottish colleagues recorded their gratitude for my efforts, we were not as successful in Scotland as in London, principally, as I have recorded, on account of the curiously hostile attitude of the labour members. Nevertheless, our reasonable claims and opposition thereto might have been adjusted had the Bill appeared in Parliament.

My next work with a major committee, in 1923, was concerned with a technical matter, for the question of preservatives in food products began to concern the authorities. Although only moderate quantities were used in beer, it was felt that unlimited freedom might result in excessive amounts being used, to the prejudice of health, and that permissible limits should be specified by law. A departmental committee of dietitians and other experts was appointed to consider suitable limits for all food products. As beer had achieved the dignity of a food, evidence was required as to how much preservative should be allowed.

The Brewers' Society and the Institute of Brewing appointed a joint committee to consider the subject, and I was asked to join E. R. Moritz, scientific adviser to the Brewers' Society and founder of the Institute of Brewing, to give evidence. He and I faced the music together, with the result that when legislation emerged, the limit allowed to brewers was sufficient for our purpose—though curiously enough the producers of cider were granted three times the amount regarded as the maximum permissible in beer.

I had asked our head chemist to have a survey made of our

own position with regard to preservatives and to let me have a report. When this report came I was much impressed by its competence. I asked the name of its author, and was told it was by one of the assistant 'testers' who had been appointed on the instruction of the directors. He had previously been chemist to a concern that had been amalgamated, had become redundant, and, being unable to secure another post, had been glad to accept the modest salary offered for routine work. At that time difficulties were arising in connection with our bottled beers, and as these called for investigation by a qualified researcher, we promoted this assistant to do the work, on the strength of his able paper on preservatives. His discoveries contributed greatly to maintenance of the high quality which was and is our objective.

The year 1930 brought another notable experience, indeed my most memorable, I think, when I gave evidence in an independent capacity to the Royal Commission on Licensing of 1929 to 1930, which the Labour Government had pledged itself to appoint if returned to power (as it was) in the General Election of 1929. The Members of the Commission, as is usual in such cases, were of all sorts and conditions of men, representing the various interests and opinions commonly supposed to be concerned. As usual, there was a strong temperance element represented by the Rev. Henry Carter and Gerald France; social workers in Edith Neville and Miss Eleanor Barton; Arthur Sherwell, who worked hard for securing legislation for State Purchase; also representatives of Labour and of registered clubs. The Trade itself had three members on the Commission—Thomas Skurray, chairman of the Brewers' Society (as owners of licensed houses), John Morgan, chairman of the National Consultative Council of the retail trade, and Frank Whitbread, chairman of the National Trade Defence Association whose function was to represent the Trade as a whole, both retail and wholesale. Licensing authorities were especially represented in the person of Mr. George A. Bryson of Birmingham, who acted as vice-chairman on the occasional absences of Lord Amulree, the chairman. Bryson was a great authority on licensing and, unlike many licensing justices, he had established an understanding with the Trade in his district (led by Sir Waters

Butler), and had helped to formulate with them the celebrated policy of 'fewer and better' in the Birmingham area. Perhaps most important of all was Sir John Pedder, Permanent Assistant Secretary at the Home Office (the Government Department responsible for licensing) who had been the most prominent member of the Central Control Board after its chairman Lord d'Abernon, and had been chairman since 1921 of the Council administering the State management district.

The Proceedings of the Commission were regarded as of the first importance to the brewing industry. Evidence on behalf of the trade was given by Frank (later Sir Frank) Nicholson, who had been chairman of the Society from 1921 to 1925, and by Cecil Lubbock, who had been Master of the Brewers' Company from 1913 to 1919 and chairman of the London Brewers' Council from 1916 to 1922. They were followed by Sir Randle Holme, solicitor to the Society, whose evidence was concerned with law and licensing procedure. Their evidence was given in the early stages of the inquiry and was mostly of a factual nature. To my mind they had not dealt adequately with the change-over by brewers after the war from the defensive to the constructive policy of 'good service plus sobriety'. They had, too, been followed by a number of witnesses prejudiced against the Trade, some of whom had made fantastic statements, so far uncorrected, calculated to arouse much prejudice.

I became more and more convinced that the Trade's policy of public house improvement should be brought to the Commission's attention; also that, since there was no means of discovering to what extent the damaging statements made in antagonists' testimonies had influenced the minds of the members, some at least of the misstatements should be corrected. As I had myself been intimately concerned with the new policy, also with the Central Control Board, I felt I could give useful evidence, but the suggestion was met with criticism, almost horror, from many of my influential friends in the Society. 'The Trade,' they pointed out, 'had offered its evidence already, through its official spokesmen—Frank Nicholson, Cecil Lubbock and others—and had made known the views of the Society. Surely no more was necessary.'

And so on. Also behind the scenes there was much concern as to what I might say, in view of my individualistic attitude towards Trade matters. Accordingly, as I became increasingly persuaded of the value of the information I could give to the Commission, I decided to give my evidence as an individual, unsponsored, and in no way an accredited representative of the Trade. I was encouraged in this resolve by a conversation I had with John Pedder, who agreed that my evidence would be useful, although there was something to be said for not adding to the already long list of witnesses. In the matter of tactics, he suggested that it would be better for the Commission to invite me rather than for me to ask to be heard, and undertook to arrange this. Having reached this point, I consulted Richard Garton, Cecil Lubbock and one or two others with whom I have been closely connected in the constructive policy. I suggested that I should go over the outline of my proposed evidence with a legal expert; I had two or three consultations with Sir Reginald Mitchell Banks, a distinguished counsel, at which Garton was good enough to be present. Then I got busy on the précis of the evidence I was proposing to give, to be circulated to the Commission. In this task I had the assistance of my younger colleague, J. E. Martineau, who helped me with the drafting and also sat with me at the Commission to lend a hand with the various documents I should need to refer to.

I was asked to give evidence on Wednesday, the 12th of November, 1930, so I handed in my précis and was invited by the chairman to elaborate the points it contained. There was no means of knowing, before I started, how long it would take me to do so, because on every point there was much to be said, and I had also to reply to the many questions put to me. I was questioned by every Commissioner present at the session. My appointment was for 10.30 a.m.; the Commission adjourned at 1 p.m. and reassembled at 2.15 p.m.; but it was not until 3.30 p.m. that I finished my evidence and my cross-examination began. In all, I took up seven hours of the Commission's time and was surprised at the patience of its members and gratified by their interest. One of my points was more weightily illustrated than most, for wishing to have some evidence of improvements in structure and design, I had asked many of my friends to supply me with photographs and plans of what they had done. This produced such a deluge of material that I was puzzled as to how to deal with it, so I decided to take the whole lot with me and I had it stacked in a corner of the room. It seemed to me that the very bulk of the material and number of the photographs would be practical evidence that the improved public house policy was supported as a general movement, and was not merely the province of a handful of pioneers. At the appropriate moment I directed the Commissioners' attention to this stack, and offered to leave it for them to examine and criticize later.

In my evidence I first reminded the Commission of circumstances from the turn of the century up to the first war, of early achievements based on the principle of the improved public houses, of which the various Trust Companies were early supporters. Much had been done, I told them, but results had been less spectacular than they might have been because of the Trust Companies' refusal to work with brewers. I described the accomplishments of the small group which had promoted the policy of improvement in the early years of the century, the discouragement offered by many, if not most, licensing benches, and the determined opposition of the militant temperance organizations. I quoted many instances where improvement had been prevented by such agencies as these, and made a special point of my original contention that insobriety was detrimental to the permanent interest of the Trade itself. It also seemed to me necessary to refer to many instances of evidence previously given by prejudiced witnesses, which were contrary to known facts which I could substantiate. In conclusion, I made suggestions as to how improvement could be furthered, and expressed the hope that the report of the Commission would include recommendations along these lines. I was a little embarrassed by my association with the Carlisle experiment, for although I made no secret of my objection to nationalization as not conducing to the best public service, I had been persuaded to continue my association with the monopoly, as adviser. This difficulty I had previously mentioned to John

28. Herbert Morrison

29. James Chuter Ede

30. Colonel W. H. Whitbread

Pedder, and we had agreed that I should be quite frank about it and state that although I disapproved of the principle, it was my duty to accept and do my best for the accomplished fact. At the same time, Pedder advised me to avoid reference to any related experience, however amusing, which might furnish the press with undesirable copy. One fortuitous circumstance favoured me on this day: the two 'temperance' members, one of whom was my old colleague on the Central Control Board, Henry Carter, and the other Gerald France, chanced to sit on the left-hand side of the Chairman. When inviting his colleagues to cross-examine me, the chairman began with those on his right-hand side; so that it was not until I had been there nearly seven hours that these formidable critics had their turn. By this time I was pretty tired, but I remember Carter asking me whom I had in mind when I employed my 'elegant' term of 'enemies', and seizing this opportunity of reminding him of one of my last conversations with him some ten years before, when I had asked him to lunch at Whitbread's and he had answered 'Possibly, but even if I do I shall still remain an enemy'. This passage I eliminated from the official record.

The meetings of the Commission were held in public. So I had quite a little audience of the press, the Trade and teetotal enthusiasts, although comparatively few lasted the course. Space does not enable me to elaborate; but one little incident called for ingenuity. Miss Edith Neville, though an abstainer, regarded the public house as a necessity, but had strong temperance views and was opposed to 'alcohol' being advertised. She asked me whether I did not realize that the advertisement that '. . . . is good for You' must give offence to many thoughtful people. Although I was allowed to delete this passage from the printed record of my evidence, my reply was that I felt diffident about criticizing the taste of one of our most important competitors, especially as they were 'listening attentively to everything I was saying'!

Although they say I stood the ordeal pretty well, I retired at the end of the day exhausted and, as usual, apprehensive as to whether my evidence had been worth while. I was intensely gratified to receive a telegram from Richard Garton within two hours of its conclusion, saying: 'Congratulations, you did well.' The next day a most charming letter came from T. B. Case, managing director of Guinness, who although not directly interested in the ownership of licensed houses, were inspired with a great sense of citizenship and were warm supporters of the 'improvement' policy. A third letter, from Captain Dyer, the chairman of the London Central Board, was to the effect that although he was not able to agree with everything I said, he felt all the same that the progressive spirits with the best interests of the licensed trade at heart were pleased and grateful.

Each witness is sent a proof of the evidence he has given for correction before printing. I spent a long afternoon, with invaluable help from that distinguished barrister W. E. Montgomery, K.C., correcting inaccuracies and also drafting a supplementary note. Later, I was pleased to hear from various members of the Commission with whom I was personally acquainted that my account of the constructive policy of the Trade had given the Commission a different picture from the one implanted in their minds. The assurance that so many in the Trade were actively engaged in improving public service considerably affected the Royal Commission's majority Report. So ended what I look on as one of the most important occasions in my career, though perhaps 'ended' is not entirely appropriate; for it seems that my evidence has been, and still is, commended as a useful epitome of a significant chapter in the Trade's history.

Through all the years separating the two wars, I was closely connected with the inner politics of the Trade and had frequent contacts either as a representative of the Brewers' Society, or in a personal capacity, with Ministers and Departments. In 1942 I was engaged, this time as a member of a Committee, in helping to solve a problem unlike any we had ever had to face. It arose in this way. During the intensive bombing of England, public houses suffered severely and many were destroyed. This led to a difficulty over the continuation of the licences, for, as is well known, these have to be renewed each year at the Annual Licensing Sessions. If renewal had been neglected, applications for new licences with all the attendant expense and complications would become necessary before the house could be rebuilt. For the first year the licences were renewed without question, but as time went on both the licensing justices and the Trade began to be worried; for it is a condition under the licensing law that no full licence can be attached to premises unless they have at least two rooms available for public service. Licensing justices began to doubt whether they could properly renew licences for premises which consisted of a hole in the ground, often full of water! It might be held that 'renewal' in such cases would contravene the law and that in fact no licence existed. So what was to be done?

We asked for an interview with the Home Secretary, then Mr. Herbert Morrison, at which I was deputed to speak for the Brewers' Society. I outlined the situation, which no doubt had been explained to him already, and he told us that he appreciated the difficulty and would see what could be arranged. Since (he said) there would be extensive replanning and transfer of population after the war, brewers must not expect to be able to rebuild their houses necessarily in the same position. He asked for a resolution from the Brewers' Society recognizing this. I replied that there would be no difficulty in securing such a resolution, for no one would want to build a house where it was not needed. Thus, in December 1941, the Council of the Society passed a resolution (previously agreed with him), recognizing that it would be in the interests both of the public and the Trade that the replacement of bombed licensed houses should be determined in accordance with considered schemes of restoration, especially where redistribution and reduction of licences were necessary or desirable in the light of local circumstances. I remember that in presenting our case to him I reminded him that I was not only speaking for brewers as owners of licensed houses but also for many owners who leased public houses to brewers and to other tenants. There were charitable institutions whose properties included public houses, among them the Ecclesiastical Commissioners; indeed, my own company rented a house from the Baptists (to which denomination I believed Herbert Morrison himself belonged) and we found them to be excellent property owners, in fact easier to deal with than the Ecclesiastical Commissioners.

As we were leaving, Mr. Morrison asked me to wait behind for a minute, and told me: 'I used to work for your company. I was your telephone clerk and you paid me thirty shillings a week.' He went on to speak appreciatively of the firm and especially of the freedom they allowed their staff in the spheres of religion and politics; he himself, for example, had always been a convinced Socialist and had often spoken in his young days in Hyde Park. He referred to one still on the staff, John Kent, who had in his day been a sound Socialist, but who unfortunately had 'gone to the dogs and had become chairman of the Conservative Association of Acton. Still, for all that, a very good fellow.' He told me that from time to time some of his old friends at Whitbread's had asked him to Trade dinners but that, being in politics, he had felt unable to go. He asked me to remember him to any such former colleagues as might still be in the company; and asked if they still lunched in the room which the managers of the bottling stores used; he would hate it to be thought that now he had come up in the world he had forgotten his friends, and he would love to go and have lunch there. I told him that he must certainly come to lunch at Whitbread's, but that he must come to the board room for more than one reason: first, because none of his former immediate associates was any longer in evidence, and second, because I wanted him to meet Cecil Lubbock. When he was at Whitbread's Lubbock was at the Home Office, and now Lubbock was at Chiswell Street and he himself was at the Home Office.

The invitation was cordially sent and duly accepted. The day before the luncheon I had a telephone call from his secretary who said that it would be an added pleasure to the Minister if his eldest brother, who was still in Whitbread's service in an engineers' department, might be included in the party. We gladly agreed, especially as it had been at the request of Henry Morrison that Herbert had originally been engaged.

One of Herbert's reminiscences was that he was in charge of the telephone switchboard at the time of the great fight over the Licensing Bill of 1907, when his own sympathies as a Socialist were much against the Trade; he was kind enough to add that, if the whole Trade had been modelled on Whitbread's lines, he might have thought differently. As I have said before, Frank Whitbread (as chairman of the National Trade Defence Association) was, with Waters Butler, the joint Commander-in-Chief of the opposition; and, as the bottling stores had tentacles all over the country, the telephone wires were pretty busy on that occasion, and Herbert Morrison was well in the middle of it all.

To return to our licensing problem. After a week or two the Home Secretary told me that, though licensing legislation was regarded as political dynamite, he was convinced of the need to adjust the difficulty. To this end he appointed a committee, in August 1942, under the chairmanship of Mr. John Morris, K.C. (now Sir John, a Lord Justice of Appeal) to consider how the functions of the various authorities could be co-ordinated. The vice-chairman was Mr. G. A. Bryson, chairman of the Birmingham justices, who had in fact been in the chair on the day I gave evidence in 1930 before the Royal Commission on Licensing. Other members included Miss J. I. Wall of the Home Office, Mr. F. B. Gillie of the Ministry of Planning, Mr. I. J. Hayward and Mrs. L'Estrange Malone, both representing Labour on the L.C.C., Mr. Frank Hunt, for many years assessor to the L.C.C., Sir Miles Mitchell (late Lord Mayor of Manchester), Mr. H. T. Edwards, and Mr. F. Jones. He appointed myself and Mr. H. G. Griffiths, managing director of Bents Brewery, Liverpool, to represent the owners; and, at my suggestion, Captain A. J. Dyer, the doyen of the retailers and chairman of both the London Central Board and the National Consultative Council of the retail licensed trade, was invited to complete the party. So we were a mixed assembly, representing many different points of view.

As I wished to know something about my fellow members of the Committee, and to gain thereby an idea of their varying angles of approach, I asked one of my knowledgeable friends to make inquiries and let me have a report, one which in due course I found most helpful. Noticing that one lady was characterized as brilliant, with strong Socialist tendencies and apt to be difficult, I asked for further information and was shown the original comment by the authority consulted, whose over-critical opinion of the lady turned out to be wholly unfair. I asked her to lunch and quickly discovered she was inspired by a high sense of citizenship and by the wish to do the right thing. If at times she appeared unreasonable, it was due to the misconception of those who disagreed with her, allied with her determination to maintain her own point of view. (This is my diagnosis, not hers.)

I have reason to think that the Minister had appreciated my sincerity when I assured him that we would aim at securing only what was reasonable and just; and had passed a word to this effect to his representative. I found myself seated on the right hand side of the chairman though, as Trade interests were concerned, I did not act as vice-chairman in his absence. Licensing can always be trusted to attract the attention of a host of people, whatever their qualifications, but even I was astonished at the number who wished to give evidence and air their views.

As the local authorities were in charge of replanning the redistribution of population, it was evident to me that they must work closely with the licensing authorities who had the power to decide if a licence should exist and where it should be. So when the time came I proposed that in any district declared by the Minister to be a devastated area, the replacement of destroyed public houses should be determined by licensing-planning committees representing both the justices and the planning authorities, instead of each operating in a practically watertight compartment as hitherto. This, to me, was plain common sense. But licensing authorities were strongly prejudiced against any interference by, or transfer of their powers to, the local authorities. In many districts, too, the licensing and local authorities were drawn from different classes with differing political ideas, and I was told that any endeavour to get them to work together would prove as unsatisfactory as trying to mix oil and water. I was not convinced.

Our first meeting, as I expected, presented an immediate and practical problem. Restaurants were then so busy that it was difficult to get a seat for lunch. It was all very well to adjourn for lunch, but it was not going to help friendly deliberation if the majority of the Committee, when it reassembled, had been unable to obtain anything to eat, or at any rate had eaten only in discomfort. This drawback had to be overcome so I made a habit of ordering a table at the Café Royal on the days of meetings, to which I invited various members of the Committee. I cannot help thinking that these lunch-time opportunities for meeting each other contributed to the unvarying friendliness with which our discussions were conducted, though I must not undervalue the invariable tact and patience shown by our chairman. During the whole course of the proceedings I do not recollect a single instance of any personal friction, although naturally there were many points of difference. Our work extended over a far wider field than I imagined possible when we started. We listened to sixty-six witnesses representing all shades of opinion and a good many whose views in the ordinary way would not have been regarded as relevant. We listened to authorities on licensing and on planning, labour representatives, prohibitionists, solicitors, owners and occupiers of property. The Committee was appointed in August 1942, but it was not until February 1944 that we issued our report. I was pleasurably surprised at the friendly attitude of some of my fellow members who might have been expected to be critical of the brewing industry. There was, for example, Frank Hunt, who owed his position on the committee to his long experience on the London County Council as assessor; I had had quite a bit to do with him in the 'twenties over houses we built on the L.C.C. housing estates. I remember that when some question arose about the difficulty of negotiating with brewers, he said that in all his experience on the L.C.C. he had found brewers the easiest of all owners to deal with.

When the report was published the Society passed a resolution 'That the Council of the Brewers' Society, having considered the report of the Home Office Departmental Committee on War Damaged Licensed Premises and Reconstruction, resolves that it welcomes the report and that the Home Secretary should be informed accordingly and further that, if the Government introduced legislation on the general lines recommended by the Committee, it will advise the members of the Society to do everything in their power to co-operate throughout in making the scheme a success.'

The report of the Committee is too long to detail here. The

main recommendation established the right of the owners of war-damaged licensed houses to have an opportunity of rebuilding their properties with due consideration for replanning. It introduced the rather novel principle that the authority responsible should be a combination of the planning authority and the licensing justices, with an independent chairman. In the event 'licensing-planning' took much longer than was expected and the duration of the Act has had to be extended; indeed it is in operation today.

Nothing seemed to happen for a time, but the Minister told me that he had accepted the report of the committee and that he was satisfied with the resolution passed by the Brewers' Society. He intended to introduce legislation before the next licensing sessions and he was determined that the Bill should become law without material alterations. It was introduced in October 1944, under the title 'Licensing Planning Temporary Provisions Act 1945', with Miss Ellen Wilkinson, Parliamentary Secretary to the Home Office, in charge. I naturally took a keen interest in the progress of this Bill and went to the House several times. I was much impressed with the ability shown by this fascinating lady in handling the various difficulties that arose and in piloting the Bill through without any material alteration, and I felt a sense of almost personal responsibility for it.

I like to think that, broadly speaking, the provisions for which I was largely responsible proved satisfactory and that, on the whole, the Act has worked smoothly. In certain districts unexpected difficulties have arisen. In London, owing to the vast extent of replanning and of the redistribution of population, it was impossible to find a chairman willing and able to give the time adequate for dealing with the intricate problems involved. But in general the Act has worked well enough. I had much hoped, too, that the principle of licensing-planning would be extended beyond the war-damaged areas; but here I was sadly disappointed.

Apart from my work on or with committees, and my part in formal deputations to Ministers, I have often acted in a personal capacity. My association with Lubbock and others had convinced me of the futility of regarding the Government and the various Departments as potential enemies to be kept at arm's length. I can sympathize with the feeling of those who run trade organizations, that they may be hampered by personal contacts between their members and the powers that be. But on the whole I am satisfied that individuals should never refuse such contacts, provided they make it quite clear that conversations are to be purely personal and in no way representative of the official organizations. In the early stages of the First World War I remember Lubbock, who was on friendly terms with Lloyd George (then Chancellor of the Exchequer), being vigorously attacked by the chairman of a large London brewery (not, I may add, one of the old family concerns) for 'tittle-tattling with the Chancellor of the Exchequer'. On one occasion Lloyd George had asked Lubbock to meet Leif-Jones, the leader of the prohibitionist party, at breakfast. While they were waiting for a fourth guest to arrive, Lubbock sat down to the piano and played a few notes. Lloyd George thereupon insisted on having a song, produced a book, turned to 'Beer, Beer, Glorious Beer', and insisted on Leif-Jones joining in.

Whenever I had been invited to confer with either a Cabinet Minister or a Government Department on a matter of importance, I made it my custom to consult one or two of those members of the Trade whose sagacity I respected, without necessarily committing myself to taking their advice. I only once got into hot water, and then through no fault of my own. In 1934 I was asked on the telephone whether I would call on Walter Elliot, then Minister of Agriculture, and have a personal conversation on the general set-up and needs of the brewing industry. The prices and marketing of barley were under review at that time and he felt he knew nothing about the Trade and wanted information. I naturally agreed and was asked if I would have any objection to being accompanied by Thomas Skurray (who had been chairman of the Brewers' Society and also a member of the Licensing Commission of 1929). I of course agreed, on the understanding that it was to be a purely personal conversation. Later John Gretton asked to come and introduce us—he was a close friend of Elliot's. When we arrived we found quite a few of his principal officials with the Minister. I said I found this surprising, since I had been assured that this was to be a personal and private conversation, in no sense representing the voice of the Brewers' Society or brewers as a whole; but my doubts were set at rest with the reiteration that all this was fully understood.

It turned out, however, that a note was taken of the conversation, and circulated, as is sometimes done, to the Heads of other Government Departments—but without our knowledge or consent. Consequently I was taken aback when Eric Simonds, without any notice to either Skurray or myself, roundly reproved us at a Council meeting for approaching the Minister behind the backs of the Society. I felt resentment that this course should have been taken without a private word with us beforehand, but after conferring with Skurray, I decided not to make a personal issue of it.

I like to think that the old suspicion and distrust between industry and Government Departments, so prevalent fifty years ago, has been largely dispersed—I have never known anything but good to come from friendly discussion. I also feel that it is a mistake to regard anyone who appears critical as an inveterate enemy. My inclination, as every reader must know by now, is to ask him to lunch, and I have almost invariably found the ensuing discussion helpful, provided that one's approach is that industry's function is to serve the community and not merely to make quick profits irrespective of the public interest. I am also certain that it is not only wrong but foolish for trade organizations to pin their faith to one political party. The result is that the one party hesitates to help an industry for fear of being charged with favouring its friends, and that the other becomes prejudiced against it. The function of collective organizations is to secure for their industry conditions under which they can grow in usefulness, no matter which Government may be in power.

14

Chairmanship of Brewers' Society, 1937—Outbreak of Second World War—Ministry of Food—Whitbread's Problems—The great raid of 1940—My Knighthood—End of Second World War

I have referred in the past to the invitations I had received to become Chairman of the Brewers' Society, first in 1919, when I refused owing to the objection of some to anyone holding that position who was a member of the Central Control Board; and again in 1930 after my evidence before the Licensing Commission when I was again compelled to refuse owing to pressure of work. In 1937 my friends returned to the subject and asked me to serve as Vice-Chairman under Sir George Courthope, then Chairman of Ind, Coope and Company, and Member of Parliament for Burton-on-Trent, with the view to succeeding him after his period of service.

On this occasion I was in fairly smooth water and accepted the responsibility. Courthope had many calls on his time, and I had to take a greater share of the work than usually falls to a Vice-Chairman. Although it had become a custom for the Chairman to occupy the position for two years, Courthope decided not to continue a second year, so I was duly elected to follow him at the Annual General Meeting of the Society in November 1938, with Sir Richard Wells, M.P., of the firm of Charles Wells Limited of Bedford, as my Vice-Chairman.

I little thought that during my term of office a second world war would break out and that we would have to face the inevitable difficulties and complications which would arise as a result, to affect the brewing industry in general and Whitbread's in particular. Although the experiences of the 1914 to 1918 War were helpful, in some ways our problems were different. There seemed to be no question of prohibition, which move had been so strongly pressed by prohibitionists in the first war. There was no serious drunkenness. The industrial troubles occasioned by the intemperate and untimely advocacy of the temperance enthusiast had not been forgotten; indeed, the usefulness of beer as an element in industrial contentment was recognized; and its value as part of the diet of the nation had been established by the scientific committee which had found during the First World War that barley brewed into beer returned in terms of calories a greater food value than when it was fed to livestock. On the other hand, it was obvious that in time of real shortage the greatest food value was derived from barley by using it as an ingredient of bread. This being so, it was clear to us that strict economy would be necessary if we were to utilize wisely the barley made available.

The Government department which was to govern our production was naturally the Ministry of Food, but other elements were concerned, such as the Treasury, the Board of Trade, the Home Office, the Ministry of Supply, the Ministry of Transport, and so forth. We were disturbed when we learnt that the Government proposed to appoint a joint committee of representatives of those various departments to deal with our affairs. This troubled us as we felt that such a Committee would have insufficient knowledge of the details of our trade to enable us both to accept their rulings and to function to the best advantage; so I asked Sir Henry French, Secretary of the Ministry of Food, to meet some of our principal members at lunch to discuss the position, as we felt the need of one individual at the Ministry of Food to whom we could look for guidance and who would be our channel of communication with these various departments.

Sir Henry French took the line that, while undoubtedly we should have to face considerable difficulties, the Minister would probably agree, provided the requirements of the situation were met. At least he himself would advise him to do so.

Now Hugh Paul, to whom I have referred in my chapter on the first war, and in whom I had the greatest confidence, was well known to the industry and had already offered his services to the Minister. This offer had been accepted, although without his being given special responsibility at that time. We suggested that he might be appointed as the link between the Trade and the Government.

By this time Lord Woolton had become Minister of Food, and he agreed to the suggestion. There is no need for me to emphasize the qualities of that great man, the confidence he inspired, or the genius with which he secured the co-operation of those with whom he came in contact. He appointed an Advisory Committee, of which he asked me to take the chair, and we worked in close co-operation with Paul at solving the manifold problems that arose during the war years.

In times of difficulty we were asked to meet the Minister who would indicate the difficulty that had arisen, detail the advice he had received as to how it should be met (which often was the result of conversations between Paul and myself), and add that if anyone could suggest a better method, he would willingly consider it. In every case we succeeded in working along the lines which the Minister proposed, and as a result were gratified at Lord Woolton's public statement, at the close of the war, that the brewing industry had met his requirements without the need of a single formal order. I believe he has also said that it was the only industry under his control that had succeeded in doing so.

While there was at first but little reduction in the total tonnage of materials allowed us, we had to make use of un-malted grain and to adjust our process to an extent that in the ordinary way we should have regarded as out of the question. But the most spectacular change was in the duty we were asked by the Chancellor of the Exchequer to collect from the beer drinker, which rose in various stages from roughly £62,000,000 in 1939 to no less than £295,000,000 in 1946. However, as I have said before, war is a thirsty business, wages were high, luxuries were few, there was little industrial unrest, and I like to think we came out of the war with our prestige undiminished.

The earliest question had been whether or not to continue our collective advertisement scheme, a doubt we resolved by handing over our booked space to the Ministry of Information; and then later came the difficulty of the renewal of licences of destroyed public houses, to both of which episodes I have referred in my chapters on publicity and on Government committees.

At the end of my first year of office I was asked, and agreed, to continue for a second year. I am not sure that my activities met with universal approval. In ordinary circumstances, the Chairman of a trade organization leaves the day-to-day negotiations with Government departments to his high administrative staff, as instructed by the various Committees from time to time. My association with Ministers and head officials had been so friendly and had existed for so long, that in the emergencies of war I was rather apt to neglect formal procedure and act personally and promptly. I thought then, and still believe, that my breaches of custom were justified in the result, but it was not everybody who agreed with me at that time.

Fuel was one of our difficulties, and in this sphere my old study of the subject was useful; and, indeed, I found myself for the second time Chairman of a committee set up for devising means of economizing on fuel in the industry, and in this, as in other directions, we had to modify old-established methods to a degree which would have horrified us in ordinary circumstances.

Meanwhile, while part of my responsibility was centred in the Brewers' Society, Whitbread's were going through hectic experiences. The two younger and most active members of the Board, Col. W. H. Whitbread, now Chairman of the Company, and J. E. Martineau, together with several of the leading members of our staff, had naturally joined up at the outbreak of war, leaving Lubbock, Gilbert Dunning and myself, with unfailing encouragement and support from Harry Whitbread, then in his eighties, to carry on as best we could.

When bombing began and passenger transport to the brewery was difficult, we housed many of our workers in the cellars and indeed opened these cellars to many in the neighbourhood who sought refuge. The provision of sleeping accommodation at short notice taxed our ingenuity, and provision of proper beds was out of the question. However, we had plenty of scaffold poles, so we called our scaffolders together and with the aid of hop pockets (the sacks in which hops are baled) which happened to be of exactly the width needed, we erected several hundred berths in two tiers in the cellars in less than forty-eight hours, and this met the occasion. Roughly two hundred of our men slept in this part of the cellars, while in other corners many of our staff and usually two directors also remained in case of emergency.

Perhaps the most notable incident as far as Whitbread's was concerned was the great incendiary raid in December 1940. I myself was out of town that night and, as there was temporary destruction on the railway, drove myself up to town with two acquaintances similarly placed. My customary route was over Battersea Bridge, then along the Embankment, but when I reached the Embankment I was informed by the police that the Embankment was impassable and that my way to the City was over Westminster Bridge and then by London Bridge. By that time traffic was chaotic and it took me two hours to reach London Bridge, only to be told the Bridge was closed, and directed that the way to the City was back over Westminster Bridge and along the Embankment! So it resulted in my going north; and being pretty exhausted, I called at our bottling stores at King's Cross for refreshment.

When I got near Chiswell Street, I was stopped by the police and told that the whole district had been devastated and there was nothing left. However, they let me through so that I could judge the extent of the disaster. Before I reached it I saw the Brewery standing practically undamaged, amid a desert of still blazing ruins. Harry Whitbread's foresight in establishing a House Fire Brigade had indeed paid big dividends. The area around the Brewery had consisted of many small factories and businesses, conducted in two or three rooms apiece, with no fire protection, and these provided an easy prey. Our Fire Brigade had worked like heroes, without cessation throughout the night, dealing with each incendiary bomb as it dropped, so the Brewery was saved, though, since the multitude of Council Fire Engines had taken all the water, we lost a Hop Store with something like £40,000 worth of hops.

Although without serious damage, we had no water, gas, electricity or telephone for some days, so brewing was suspended. But we got going again in a surprisingly short time.

I still recall one strange incident of that night of destruction. Some of the horses were released from their stables owing to the proximity of a fire, and galloped away, soon to be lost sight of. In the morning they not only all returned in twos and threes, but brought along with them quite a number of friends picked up during the night. These friends made themselves at home in various stalls and we were able to return them to their owners within a few days.

Two days later, when I arrived at the Brewery, I discovered almost a mountain of malt in the Brewery yard. It emerged that an incendiary bomb had, unbeknown, dropped several feet into one of our large bins of malt and having been discovered during the night, the whole of the bin stock had been emptied into the yard. Though much of the malt was untouched, a considerable amount had been burnt black, and while it was lying in the yard, the rain had further damaged it, rendering it unfit for brewing. I understand that it was later bought by a firm of biscuit makers, and not wasted!

No one had contemplated that the Brewery would become so prominent a feature in the landscape, standing as it did in a desert of destruction; and indeed it still does, though large blocks of offices and industrial buildings are now steadily being built round it.

We have often been congratulated on our 'good fortune' in escaping the surrounding destruction, and have had occasion to point out that it was not so much the result of good luck as the reward of foresight, and the devoted efforts of our fire brigade, that saved the brewery.

While this was our narrowest escape, we had naturally many excursions and alarums, one of which was to do with transport, as so much of our Trade was at a distance, especially in the North; but I heard of a disused brewery in Lancashire which, though in working condition, had been closed owing to an amalgamation. We acquired this, got it going again, and were thus enabled to supply our North Country Trade, which otherwise would have had to be abandoned. In certain parts of the country we also saved transport by the mutual exchange of trade with other breweries. Although this was not always appreciated by our customers, the shortage of beer was so acute that no serious complaint arose.

In the meantime my two years' Chairmanship of the Brewers' Society had expired and I was able to take a larger share in the day-to-day difficulties at Chiswell Street. These were mostly concerned with our partially and completely demolished properties. Some had simply vanished, others were damaged sufficiently to put them out of commission for a time. We were told it was important from the point of view of the morale of the neighbourhood to keep the 'local' functioning, if possible, so after each raid, we took steps to ascertain the extent of the damage both in London and the country and made every effort to help the tenants to get their houses trading again, even if, as often happened, there was no living accommodation for them on the premises. I often feel that insufficient tribute has been paid to the courage and devoted service of those many publicans who, with their wives, contributed to the maintenance of public morale, by carrying on in circumstances of the greatest difficulty.

In the autumn of 1941 I received a letter from the Lord Chamberlain telling me that my name had been submitted to His Majesty as I had been deemed worthy of a knighthood; and asking whether, if the suggestion were approved, I would accept the honour.

As far back as 1920 I had heard a rumour that my name was being considered, as had been the case with my other colleagues on the Control Board, but had been removed from the list as a result of my naughtiness in writing to *The Times* condemning what I considered the thoroughly bad bill proposing to transfer all powers of the Board to the Home Office. I have no idea whether there was truth in this rumour, which in any case should not have reached me, as these matters are rightly regarded as strictly confidential. On that occasion I had not been much concerned, there being so much criticism at the time of the liberal granting of honours that a knighthood conferred on a commercial man did not at that time carry much 'kudos', even though it might be granted for personal work rendered in the public service. But in 1941 a knighthood carried greater dignity, so I wrote accepting the suggestion with grateful appreciation.

As is customary, I heard nothing more until the 1942 New Year's Honours were announced in the press, and in these my name was included. I was touched by the large number of personal and business friends, numbering nearly two hundred, who were kind enough to send me their congratulations; especially was I pleased with the one received from Sir Alexander Maxwell, Permanent Secretary of the Home Office, referring to the unanimous satisfaction with which the suggestion had been received by the various Government departments, with whom I had had contact from time to time.

Many of my friends addressed me as 'Sir Sydney', which was technically premature, as an honour does not become effective until one has attended and received the accolade. I remember inquiring of my old friend, Sir John Sykes, what the etiquette was, and even he seemed somewhat doubtful; but told me that when his own K.C.B. was announced a friend who should know addressed his letter to him as J. C. Sykes, Esq., K.C.B., which appears to me to be a compromise, anyway there may be doubt as to what is technically correct, or it may be possibly a matter of courtesy.

In due course I received the Royal command to attend an Investiture at Buckingham Palace. Each recipient has the privilege of inviting a limited number of friends to view the ceremony, so I duly arrived at the Palace well before time with two of my sisters. We were separated on arrival, for they were conducted with the other guests to the room in which the Investiture was to take place, while I was shepherded into a reception room where most of the prospective recipients were already gathered. I was glad to meet two friends whose names were in the same Honours List—Sir Guy Locock, Director of the Federation of British Industries, and Sir George Aylwen, later Lord Mayor of London.

Mr. Herbert Morrison, then Home Secretary, who was in attendance on the King, looked in for a few minutes and made a short speech to us collectively, and had a specially kind personal word with myself. We were carefully instructed by an official on the details of procedure, and in due course the signal was given that His Majesty was ready, and we entered the large room where the Investiture was to take place. His Majesty, with the Home Secretary and others in attendance, occupied a platform at the side of the large chamber, while those privileged to witness the ceremony were seated in rows before him. We received our honours according to the instructions given us, and I in my turn rose as 'Sir Sydney', K.B. Afterwards I met my sisters and celebrated the occasion by as good a lunch as war conditions permitted.

At the end of hostilities we had some little difficulty in securing the release of Colonel Whitbread, our present Chairman, and later J. E. Martineau, who had been serving in the R.A.F., and those leading members of our Staff who were in one or other of the Services. Having done so, we set to work to repair the ravages of war and get going. Contrary to my anticipation, their absence of over four years in different and more strenuous activities had not distracted their attention as much as one might have expected. In fact, their experiences in having to meet ever-recurring emergencies seemed to have quickened their aptitude for coping with difficulties, and they plunged into problems with such vigour that by the end of 1946 we could begin to apply ourselves to the development of the business in times of peace.

From my notes on the Brewers' Society I have omitted a matter of importance to myself and the whole industry. After my second reluctant refusal of the chairmanship in 1930 I proposed emulating the Engineers and appointing a permanent professional Chairman; but as it was generally felt that Ministers would rather meet actual traders than salaried representatives, an appointed Director was preferred, and such appointment is now usual practice. Thus in 1934 Sir Edgar Sanders was chosen, a martinet but a man of real ability and a sincerity of purpose which raised the standing of our Society. To his sound judgement we owe the appointment of the much-respected S. A. Horwood, M.B.E., as Secretary and that of his own assistant, later his successor, Sir Robert Ewbank, C.S.I., C.I.E. In 1946 Sir Colville Wemyss succeeded Sir Robert.

15

My Marriage—Journey to France—Sir Norman Kipping—Chairmanship of N.T.D.A.—Presidency of Central Board—European Brewers' Conventions

The year 1946 was destined to bring me what turned out to be the happiest adventure of my life, which was my marriage. For a long time I had enjoyed the friendship of Madeleine de Lacy Wickham, a member of the well-known family of Wickham, the most noted member of which was William of Wykeham, Bishop of Winchester, the founder of Winchester College. She belonged to the Irish branch of the family; her great-grandfather, son of William Wickham, was one-time Chief Secretary of Ireland, having settled in that country after marrying Catherine Carr, heiress of the Burke property of Castleconnell. 'Madge' Wickham was a keen sportswoman of many interests for whom, in spite of the difference in our ages, I had long entertained an affectionate regard. She had taken an active part in various forms of social service during the war, some of which had involved problems on which she had sought my advice, and this had brought us together again.

The release of the younger members of the Board from the Forces (of W. H. Whitbread the present Chairman, and of J. E. Martineau and leading members of the staff) seemed to bring my long-delayed retirement into the picture; and feeling that I might now have leisure to enter into some of Madge's interests, I ventured to suggest the possibility of our marriage. To my gratifica-

31. My wife

32. *The Bull's Head*, Guildford

'. . . *a museum piece worth our while*'

33. Sir Albert Richardson at the opening of *The Bull's Head*

tion, she agreed and we were married very quietly on the 10th of October, 1946. In view of the difference in our ages and our interests (for I could hardly have foreseen how devotedly my wife would make my interests her own) I did not expect the alliance to bring me more than companionship and good fellowship; but I was to find that the years were to yield comfort and affection beyond anything I could have hoped for.

We decided to go to Monte Carlo, since in 1935 I had purchased a flat in Menton and we wished to see for ourselves how it had fared during the war. I had already heard from my agents that it had survived, though somewhat damaged by neglect and with some of its contents lost to pillagers. So we travelled by car, taking with us my chauffeur, Tull, who had been with me for several years and had now returned to us after demobilization.

The first night of our journey we spent in Paris at the Hotel Scribe, and there to our surprise we met after dinner a few old friends of mine: Sir Guy Locock, past Director, Sir Norman Kipping, Director, and D. L. Walker, C.B.E., Secretary of the Federation of British Industries who were there to meet some 'high ups' on Federation business. Next morning we were touched to discover a truly generous offering of flowers, addressed to my wife with all their best wishes. They themselves had had to return to England early that morning.

During our conversations of the evening before, Sir Norman reminded me of our first meeting. Sir Robert Ewbank had asked me to lunch with him at the East India Club to discuss certain concerns of the Brewers' Society of which I was Chairman and he Director. The Club being crowded, Ewbank was asked by a member unknown to us if he might share our table. We agreed, of course, and as we made conversation, one of us mentioned the Federation of British Industries, on the Council of which I had been since 1922; I was just then taking a livelier interest in its concerns, and referred to the fact that Sir Guy Locock had retired from its Directorship and that a new Director—someone I had not met so far, and of whom I knew nothing—had been appointed. At this point our table companion said: 'Perhaps I ought to tell you, to save us all from possible embarrassment, that my name is Norman Kipping and that I have just been appointed Director of the Federation.' This was yet another of those curious coincidences which seem almost impossible and yet crop up in every lifetime. (I have already written of the coincidences attending my visit to America in younger days.) This unusual introduction to the new Director was recalled by Sir Norman himself when he wrote to congratulate me on the seventieth anniversary of my entry into business.

We found our way to Menton, spending two nights on the way in considerable discomfort, since hotels had by no means recovered from the disorganization and hardships of the war. At Menton we were welcomed, with that spontaneous affection which the French have no objection to displaying, by my housekeeper Louise Valetta. We found our flat in better condition than I expected and only partially pillaged and damaged, though central heating, constant hot water and telephone were things of the past. But thanks to Louise's influence—she seemed to have a friend in every public-services department and every related industry—we succeeded in obtaining electric heating and hot water supply with incredible celerity. It was in fact Louise who took me to the Electricity Department at the Hotel de Ville and insisted on my signing a declaration that power was needed for cooking only. Later that day, I was shocked to find that the man connecting the supply was the man before whom I had signed the declaration. Still, when I told Louise how anxious this made me, she said: 'Soyez tranquille, c'est mon cousin, celui-la.'

This was an interesting fortnight for us, spent in renewing old friendships and sympathizing with those many to whom the war had brought bereavement; then we started on our way home hoping to find more comfortable accommodation than had been our lot on the way out. But the days had gone when one could plan one's journey with reasonable expectation that a stop might be made anywhere one chose with the certainty of finding every need met. Many of the hotels were still not functioning and others were carrying on under great difficulty. However, we arrived home safely and had a good trip in spite of the lack of luxury.

On our way back we spent a few days in Paris; we both know

the city well, but this was an opportunity for my wife to see the 'Treasure of Notre Dame', not always on view by any means. While she went to inspect the church plate I took a rest on one of the hard chairs just inside the great doors, put my hat on my knees, and sank into meditation. As usual the great Notre Dame de Paris was thronged with people, some at prayer, some gazing at sculpture and stained glass, others following a whispering guide: so I did not particularly notice the little boys and their mother who stood near me—not until two little boys, eyeing me nervously, had dropped a few coins into my hat and at once received from their mother one of those sibilant French scoldings which say so much in so short a time. However, I had no time to listen closely, for almost before the coins had had time to pitch, they were snatched by an indignant nun—who managed to indicate to me, also sibilantly, that I was occupying a chair reserved for nuns of her order, who sat there to collect 'pour les pauvres'.

(Someone who read these words mentioned to my wife that the incident is not surprising, since I must have looked, as I sat dozing there, like one of the benevolent and cheerful friars of Alphonse Daudet—especially like Father Gaucher, whose delicious elixir was a joy and embarrassment to his order.)

On my return, although I retired from my day-to-day activities, my colleagues wished me to remain on the Board in an advisory capacity, and to continue my work in the various trade organizations; so instead of my interesting myself in my wife's concerns, she devoted herself to mine, and from that time onward we did much together.

This same year, 1946, brought me the Chairmanship of the National Trade Defence Association, now much more appropriately termed National Trade Development Association, a change which I had myself proposed as far back as 1920, but which at that time had not proved acceptable. As I said earlier, the function of this body was to promote friendly understanding among all interested in the Licensed Trade, both wholesale and retail, and indeed others, such as the allied trades, who depended for part of their business on the industry.

By this time it had become customary for ladies to be associated with Trade functions, and during my Chairmanship, when I travelled to various parts of the country to attend meetings and discussions, I was always accompanied by my wife; and between us we formed friendships and contacts up and down the country which have continued to the present time. Perhaps the principal event (for me) of 1948 was my Presidency, at the invitation of Captain Dyer, of the Central Board (or, to give it its full title, The Licensed Victuallers' Central Protection Society of London), the representative organization of the Retail Trade in the metropolis and surrounding country. The annual dinner is one of the most important events of the year, as members of both Houses of Parliament and other distinguished people are always numbered among the guests. We were fortunate in having with us in 1948 Lord Woolton, who replied for the House of Lords and, for the first time in history, I was able to persuade the Home Secretary to reply for the Commons, the Home Office being the State Department concerned with Licensing. The Home Secretary on this momentous occasion was Mr. Chuter Ede. The Great Hall of the Connaught Rooms, in which this dinner is held, is truly 'great', but not great enough to seat all who would like to be present; therefore men only attend the actual dinner, but their ladies may, if they wish, come into the Gallery after the dinner and listen to the speeches. On this occasion, my wife arranged a dinner party for the wives of the leading personalities of the licensed trade present at the Connaught Rooms, and when she later brought her party to the Gallery, they were delighted when the Home Secretary and Lord Woolton made a point of meeting them and having a few words with each.

In 1948, Captain Dyer, as head of the Licensed Trade, and a member of the Catering Wages Committee, asked me if I would join with him, in my capacity as Chairman of the N.T.D.A., in inviting the members of the Catering Wages Committee to a farewell luncheon given for Lady Franks, who was leaving the Committee on the appointment of her husband, Sir Oliver Franks, P.C., G.C.M.G., as our Ambassador to America. The guest on my right at this luncheon was that great Labour Leader, Dame Florence Hancock, then President of the T.U.C., possibly the only woman ever to act in that capacity. We compared notes on our early experiences, and I described how I had started as a brewer as a mere boy, and by degrees learned all I could about every aspect of brewing. In return, she told me about her own first job. At twelve and a half she had been washer-up in a café; but her employers, who treated her well, sold the business to others who had far different ideas. On the second morning after their arrival, the mistress brought her two pounds of tea, the cheapest tea obtainable for the staff and the best for 'master and mistress'. Although only a child, she was indignant and told her mother, who promptly said: 'My girl, there is only one thing to do; you mix both packets of tea together, put half the mixture in one packet and half in the other'. This Florence did, and so all drank the same grade of tea. At the age of fourteen she went to a factory, and that was the end of her career as a domestic worker.

My services to the N.T.D.A. and in other directions fell short of what I had hoped. The internal trouble, first evident in 1923, which had from time to time temporarily hampered me, had become more obvious; by the end of 1948 I was advised by my old friend, Dr. Edward Gates, that an operation was necessary; so in December 1948 I was taken to the Middlesex Hospital, subjected to a series of tests and 'observations', and although my heart appeared to give some anxiety, that great authority David Evan Bedford, M.D., F.R.C.P., advised that it was a reasonable risk, and I had the operation under the wonderfully skilful hands of Mr. Eric W. Riches, F.R.C.S. It would be impossible to speak too highly either of his careful kindness or of the nurses and hospital generally. My wife tells me that judging by the number of students who filed past the door of the room in which she was waiting for the fateful news, I must have been a notable case, providing an instructive spectacle.

During the following weeks my wife came to see me in the morning, went home to lunch, and spent the rest of the day with me. I was told I was a good patient, since I never rang the bell, but I think that her presence accounts for this. Good conduct apart, I believe I was a bit of a surprise to those responsible for me, as it seems that the behaviour of my heart caused no anxiety.

In fact, when my wife was allowed to look in and see me for a moment as soon as I was conscious, she found me reading the evening newspaper!

At the next dinner of the Central Board which took place soon after my somewhat unexpected recovery and return to currency, I was deeply touched by the warmth of my reception when I rose to propose the toast of my successor, that great man Lord Iveagh, head of Guinness.

I should like here to pay a tribute to the memory of Captain Albert Dyer, Chairman of the London Central Board and also the National Consultative Council of the Retail Trade, justly regarded as the greatest leader the Licensed Victuallers have ever had. He was a man of striking personality. Controlling several large houses, he combined a detailed knowledge of his business with high qualities of diplomacy and citizenship, and had been Mayor of Romford and Chairman of the local Hospital. He possessed a wonderful gift for speaking bluntly without giving offence and, though a man of considerable wealth, never failed to consider the circumstances of the humblest member of his society, whose interests he would champion with force and ability. I had occasion to do much with him, and added my own to the respect he deservedly won from both brewers and retailers.

I must not omit some account of the European Brewing Convention, initiated in 1947 to bring together the technical and scientific workers in the brewing industry from the various European countries, a Convention in which my wife and I took an active interest. The first meeting was in Switzerland, the next in Holland, the next in Brighton, and this was the first we personally attended, Whitbread's having assumed responsibility for a large share of the entertainment and hospitality extended to our continental guests.

Colonel Whitbread was then Chairman of the Research Committee of the Institute of Brewing and was naturally much in the picture. Mrs. Whitbread was happily able to speak at the large dinner at the Hotel Metropole in German and French as well as English. The City Fathers of Brighton, who welcomed such gatherings, gave us a reception in the Pavilion; we pointed out to our friends from other lands that this edifice was regarded by most of us as a triumph of architectural absurdity, though full of interest for admirers of the Regency period décor and furniture.

The Deputy Mayor was present to represent the City Fathers, and I was entrusted with the task of thanking the Corporation for their hospitality and proposing the toast to them. This seemed to me a fine opportunity for trying to explain that the Convention was a meeting of scientists mainly, working for the improvement of the fermentation industries, and not merely a gathering of business men concentrating on their commercial interests, as some people thought.

In 1953, the Convention was held at Nice. My wife and I attended and took the opportunity of revisiting many of the friends we had made in the South of France when we were able to visit it more frequently.

The next Convention, in 1955, was at Baden-Baden. That year we again took our car and drove at leisurely rate, stopping for a night at various places both going and coming.

As can be imagined, the scientific papers at these Conventions are read in various languages, though English usually predominates. Naturally the discussion of technical progress is the principal objective, but there is much hospitality and plenty of opportunity for contacts and friendships among the intellectual luminaries of the industry—possibly of greater value than the official business itself.

My activities at Baden were somewhat interfered with by an attack of gout, and as I had forgotten to bring my usual prescription, I had to call in a leading Baden medical man. He was not at all interested in my missing prescription, and when I suggested another he replied that they no longer treated gout with medicine. He gave me instead an injection, and promised to come next day to repeat the operation at a not inconsiderable fee. His ministrations appeared to be startlingly effective and when he suggested he should come a third time, I told him, with an eye on our rapidly diminishing currency, that I really could not trouble him further. As I was adamant, he pressed me at least to ring him and report on my condition. When, quite sincerely, I showed reluctance to trouble him even to this extent he begged me to do so, giving as his reason that as this was a new treatment he was specially anxious to know its effects. This enlightening explanation I received with mixed feelings, glad to be rid of my discomfort but none too pleased to have been used as a guinea pig at considerable profit to the experimenter. As a matter of fact it was a wonderful remedy, but when I tried to obtain the same in England I was told that, although known, for some reason or another it was unobtainable in this country.

At the next Convention in 1957, to my great pleasure and delight the Danes entertained the Convention. I have twice already referred to my early visits to the breweries in Copenhagen and the Convention offered too good an opportunity to be missed for renewing my old friendships. My younger colleague, Charles Tidbury, a young recruit to the Whitbread Board, offered to drive us to Harwich and generally look after us during our visit; so we left London early on the morning of Wednesday, the 29th of May, lunched at his home near Colchester, and arrived at Harwich an hour before the boat left. At this vital moment, by a feat of diplomacy he contrived to arrange that his car should be the last loaded on board, so that when we arrived at Esjberg it was the first off; we passed the Customs with little delay and started on our hundred-and-seventy miles drive to Copenhagen; a much easier journey than I had thought it would be.

The roads were magnificent and Charles proved himself an expert driver, by no means embarrassed by having to drive on the right-hand side. Denmark, as is generally known, consists of a number of islands. On our journey we travelled first across Jutland then across a long bridge to the island of Funen; and then by ferry boat from Myborg to Konsor on the island of Zealand, arriving at Copenhagen at seven-thirty that evening in time for dinner.

On Saturday evening we had been invited to dine with Mr. and Mrs. N. M. Steenberg, the Managing Director of the great Tuborg Brewery, who with real Danish hospitality were entertaining a number of visitors attending the conference. It was a truly wonderful feat of hospitality as the guests arrived in three different stages. Some were already in Copenhagen, some came later by air, others by train, the last arrivals of all. Their lateness was due to the loss of a wheel from one of the carriages in which they were travelling. As I was the oldest member of the party, and indeed the Father of the Convention, it was my privilege to take Mrs. Steenberg in. I had been advised that it was the Danish custom for whoever sat by the hostess to render thanks on behalf of all the guests. So I was fully prepared to do what was expected of me, and had even learnt a few words of Danish with which to embellish my speech. Yet I did not know at which stage of the dinner I was supposed to deliver my few words, so I explained my difficulty to Mrs. Steenberg, who kindly said she would give me my cue. This she did, shortly after the last contingent of her party had arrived and were safely seated.

The official hosts of the convention were the Danish Brewers' Association, who offered us a great welcome and entertained us with the dignity and the friendliness which are well known to all who visit that delightful country. The programme began with an official reception for the members and their ladies at the Hotel Angleterre, the principal hotel of Copenhagen. This was followed by the reading of papers on scientific subjects each day at the Congress Hall in the Hotel Mercur with entertainments daily for such ladies as were not interested in the scientific meetings. A reception was given by the City Authorities in the magnificent City Hall, Raadhuspladsen, and finally a grand dinner and dance at the Restaurant 'Wivex' given by the Danish Brewers' Association, at which a party of no fewer than nine hundred were entertained, and at which my wife had a notable experience. The evening before, she had been begged by the President, Mr. Ph. Kreiss, to express thanks on behalf of the ladies for the entertainment they had received. As this dinner was the grand finale of the week, the first speeches we heard, and fine speeches they were, were given by two of the foremost scientific authorities; after which, when the Company was beginning to resume conversation, the Toastmaster called for silence for Lady Nevile. This came as a surprise to most of the diners, and I sensed a certain feeling of nervousness at the possible length of a speech in which any lady attempted to convey adequately the gratitude which they all felt for the hospitality received. However, my wife, too, was aware of this apprehension, and brought down the House by expressing the appreciation of the ladies in what I believe to be a record of brevity, her speech numbering about twenty-two words. So ended the Convention itself.

My wife carries with her another pleasant recollection of this visit. It was Derby week at home, and one of our group organized a sweepstake. We of course took tickets, and she was the fortunate one who drew the favourite, Crepello, which duly won. Since my wife drew her winnings in Danish currency, we were able to extend our stay by two or three days.

The next biennial conference is planned for Rome, in 1959: it remains to be seen whether we shall be able to attend, and add yet another to our happy memories of these extremely worthwhile occasions.

16

This must be my last chapter. I feel as I used to do as a small boy, when at the end of a party I knew it was time to go home but could not find the appropriate words or method of making my exit. I am in my eighty-fifth year, and completed seventy years of brewing on the 19th of January, 1958. If I were a cricketer I might well say it was time to 'draw stumps'.

I like to think I have played the game. Anyway, I have had a goodish innings, including periods of service in various Trade Organizations which they tell me constitute a record. I look back on a life full of pleasant, if sometimes hectic, memories among a multitude of good fellows. I could have made more money if I had used opportunities when they came my way through information gained in confidence, but I have, to a large extent, satisfied my early ambition to find a constructive career in the Trade.

I imagine few in responsible positions today appreciate the successive crises through which the Brewing Trade passed during the earlier years of my experience, especially in the London district, where hardly a single large concern was paying any dividend at all. There was even much doubt as to whether they actually had the right to continue the licences of their public houses. Confidence was somewhat restored by the Act of 1904, then came the fight against the notorious Licensing Bill of 1907. No sooner had that been defeated by public opposition than the 1908 Budget introduced its penal licence duties, to come into force in 1909. These, however, largely failed in their objective, for the Courts decided that the increased charge formed grounds for a reduction of assessments for local rates and Schedule A.

The First World War brought us unprecedented problems. A deplorable increase in drunkenness, and other difficulties, led to a demand for prohibition by the militant temperance party, who openly claimed that 'if we miss this opportunity, we may never get another'. Then came the prospect of the cessation of brewing when the German submarine menace became so acute as to threaten the supply of grain, followed by the proposal that the Trade should be nationalized; nationalization to be continued after the war as a Government monopoly. Those were indeed anxious times, but as often happens in human affairs the emergencies of the war ultimately resulted in a healthier climate in several spheres of public opinion.

The findings of the Committee appointed to study the dietary of the nation established the value of beer as an element thereof; I have already quoted Dr. Beavan's witty summary preferring the sound economy of brewing techniques to the faulty economy of the pig's internal arrangements.

Another point in our favour was the general admission that an adequate supply of beer was an essential factor among the many that made for contented workers. Moreover, it had been established that drunkenness was controllable, that the habits of the people who were our best customers were far more elastic than had previously been recognized, and that price was not the fundamental criterion it had always been alleged to be. In fact, the view I had expressed in 1908, that brewers could prosper more in England sober than in England drunken, had been shown to be sound. Perhaps more important than any of these considerations was the altered tone of political and public opinion resulting from the patriotic policy of the Trade in placing themselves at the disposition of the Government. All these favourable circumstances made possible the constructive policy of 1919.

As I see it, every modern civilization has needed the soothing effects of alcohol, and scientific and social opinion seems agreed that alcohol is best taken in diluted rather than in concentrated form. This is what beer supplies, and to my mind justifies

Professor Armstrong's conclusion that it is 'the only safe drink all the world over'. Perhaps if this were more universally accepted we should hear less of 'tranquillizers' and other drugs which appear to be causing anxiety amongst social observers today.

The social change has been equally remarkable. Drink is no longer quoted as the greatest evil, nor public houses described by temperance orators as 'citadels of Satan'. The constructive ideas of improvement, promoted by some of us in the early years of the century and adopted as the general policy of the Trade in 1919, have made great progress. The serving of refreshment as well as exciseable drinks is now more general. The calling of the licensed victualler is coming to be regarded as a skilled industry; my elementary, and in those days somewhat cautiously received, experiment in technical education is being rapidly extended throughout the country by the National Trade Development Association in conjunction with local education authorities. The theory in old days that 'anyone can keep a public house' is fading into the realm of forgotten fallacies. In truth there has been what amounts to a revolution, both in service rendered and in the prestige and respect with which the 'local' is regarded.

A Socialist Home Secretary, himself an abstainer, has stated that public houses as well as schools and churches are needed in new neighbourhoods and should be there when the inhabitants arrive. Much has been quoted to show how our better types of public houses were appreciated by American and Commonwealth forces when they were in our country in the second war. I remember that when I was once discussing the prospects of export trade with a friend, an American officer remarked: 'Excuse my butting in, sir, but let me tell you the best export you could make to my country would be some of your public houses. We have nothing like them at home. I find in your inns a welcome and friendliness we don't have in ours.' It may not be generally known that the advertisements of the British Travel Association include the British Inn as one of the attractions to entice visitors to Britain. The inn is recognized as a dollar earner.

Apart from its being part of the commercial fabric of our nation, the value of the 'local' lies in its contribution to the happiness and goodwill so essential today between man and man, indeed between nation and nation; but there is room for much development if the Licensed Trade is to fulfil its almost unlimited potential in this direction.

The pattern of the Trade has changed much during the last seventy years. In round figures, if I may repeat myself, there are fewer than 425 brewers for sale, as against 12,000 in 1888. We produce about twenty-five million bulk barrels as against the thirty million of those days. Beer is lighter and less alcoholic, the cheaper beers containing about three per cent, as against the five per cent of Victorian days and costing now 1s. 2d./1s. 4d. per pint, as against the 2d. of those days. But perhaps the most startling change is in the revenue we collect for the Exchequer—something more than two hundred and forty million from beer alone, instead of the modest nine million in the days when I first had to work out a duty charge.

While it is no longer usual for the ordinary householder to keep a cask in his cellar, a custom which was the mainstay of many small breweries, since beer in bottle distributed by off-licences has taken its place, the licensed Trade is faced with the growing competition of the club, which is in effect a co-operative public house. Although every retail trade has to face this competition, a licensed victualler is hampered by a multitude of financial burdens and restrictions from which the co-operative club is free. In most distributive industries it is found that a majority of the public prefer the independent trader and it is to be hoped that Parliament in its wisdom will give attention to this matter: not by way of restricting the freedom of well-conducted clubs, but in sympathetic consideration of the difficulties under which the public houses labour. Such consideration should result in alleviation of licensed victuallers' burdens, enabling them to have greater freedom to render the service to the community which modern conditions require, and which contribute so much to public contentment and morale.

Among the most vexing problems are the difficulties of redistribution in these days when, as a result of replanning, large sections of the population are moved from one district to another, with the result that there are too many houses in one district and too few in new neighbourhoods. Some legislation to reduce these difficulties and to encourage better service is much to be desired. It has been said that 'licensing legislation is political dynamite'; and a healthy public relations campaign is needed to overcome the cynical view that recommendations by commercial men are based solely on hopes of immediate profit and not on the need to serve the community—the only permanent basis of the prosperity of any industry.

I should like to touch briefly on the controversial matter of the 'Tied House'. At least three-quarters of the capital of the brewing industry is represented by the public houses in its ownership, and yet it seems that the very name of the owners is a disadvantage, since it encourages the general conviction that the sole purpose of the public house is to push the sales of the named brewers' commodity to the exclusion of other forms of service. It is this notion which has made the 'tied' house an object of prejudice.

Since there are a few instances of houses so run this prejudice cannot be said to be entirely unreasonable; but they are a minority and the benefits of the 'tied' house are great, and usually much appreciated by the public. The constructive policy of 1920 onward could never have been put into effect if ownership of the houses had remained 'free'. Long-term planning requires large capital resources, and the brewers had both the capital and the determination to use it wisely and beneficially. The theory that a tenant who is under contract to buy his beer from the owning brewer is supplied with something of indifferent quality is easily torn to shreds; the brewer knows that the capital value of a house depends on the business it can command, and business is not built up on the sale of second-rate foods and drinks. From the tenant's angle, the 'tied' house gives an opportunity for entry to the Trade to men of vision and enterprise but short of capital to give them a start.

* * *

There can be few groups of men more generous or more patriotic than brewers in times of national crisis, or more reluctant to let their light shine when no national need exists. They have indeed been kind to me and patient with what must often have appeared my strange ideas. I attribute these attractive qualities to the existence of the large number of family concerns which, during my most active years, formed the backbone of the Trade; and I believe the nation owes more than is generally recognized to those old family businesses which, with their tradition of loyalty and sense of citizenship, were not dissimilar from the squirearchy of the Victorian times. I regret the passing of so many family businesses into great concerns, with consequent loss of personal leadership and goodwill in their separate neighbourhoods. It seems to me that the remote, cold mathematical control of financial magnates tends to lessen the sense of individual responsibility and service, to over-emphasize the profit motive, and to underestimate the sense of craftsmanship and individual joy of achievement, so great a driving force in British industry.

But enough said. I have not made a great personal fortune, but I look back on a happy, rewarding and, I hope, constructive life. My last words must be to say how grateful I have been, and am, to that host of friends, great and small, past and present, whose kindness, encouragement and friendly criticism I gratefully acknowledge during my seventy years' service in the industry I have loved so much.

But I must add a postscript to thank you, my reader, for the compliment you have paid me in reading the first and, as my family circle will certainly hope, my last literary effort.

Index